Psychology, Psychotherapy, Psychoanalysis, and the Politics of Human Relationships

Psychology, Psychotherapy, Psychoanalysis, and the Politics of Human Relationships

LAURENCE SIMON

Westport, Connecticut
London

Library of Congress Cataloging-in-Publication Data

Simon, Laurence R., 1940–
    Psychology, psychotherapy, psychoanalysis, and the politics of human
relationships / by Laurence Simon.
        p. cm.
    Includes bibliographical references and index.
    ISBN 0-275-97471-5 (alk. paper)
        1. Psychotherapy—Political aspects.   2. Psychoanalysis—Political aspects.
    3. Psychology—Political aspects.   4. Political science.   5. Authority.   I. Title.
    RC480.5.S527   2003
    616.89'14—dc21   2002190858

British Library Cataloguing in Publication Data is available.

Library of Congress Catalog Card Number: 2002190858
ISBN: 0-275-97471-5

First published in 2003

Praeger Publishers, 88 Post Road West, Westport, CT 06881
An imprint of Greenwood Publishing Group, Inc.
www.praeger.com

Printed in the United States of America

The paper used in this book complies with the
Permanent Paper Standard issued by the National
Information Standards Organization (Z39.48-1984).

10   9   8   7   6   5   4   3   2   1

Contents

Introduction

The field of psychology, its main application, psychotherapy, and the self-proclaimed jewel in the crown of therapy, psychoanalysis, are all involved in major struggles between and within their respective enterprises. While the terms of these conflicts are restricted to language common to science and the fields themselves, this monograph explores the thesis that what is also involved are inevitably battles between forces representing democratic/humanistic forms of political expression and relationships and those which stand for authoritarian and totalitarian political structures. The struggle to define the proper human relationship to authority and the manner in which societies are to be structured is as old as civilization itself and finds expression at all levels of human interaction. An examination of psychology and its applications from the lens of political theory is an outgrowth of what has been termed the "postmodern revolution," an intellectual development in which various sciences, humanities, and liberal and fine arts became the object of intellectual and critical examination. Louis Sass (1992) has suggested that postmodernism is, in reality, the next logical step in modernity's maturity. I suggest that postmodernism (at its best) can be understood as science grown self-conscious (Simon 1998), allowing us to examine psychology or any field from the vantage point of any other. This book is an attempt to develop a critique that throws light on the relationships of psychology, its applications, and society.

One of the goals of this book is to demonstrate that in the conflict between democratic/humanistic and authoritarian practices the democratic are losing ground to the politics of authoritarianism. I suggest that I. Bernard Cohen (1985) is correct when he postulates that the rise of science both reflected and enhanced Western culture's move toward democratic forms of governance. It is my belief that psychology is the science with the greatest unrealized potential to be a powerful force for democratization of society. Moreover, the type of relationships prescribed by various psychological therapies, especially modern psychoanalysis and the therapies derived from it, are, at least in their theoretical ideal, the embodiment of democracy, fairness, and humanism. The failure of democracy and humanism in psychological thinking and in the practices of various forms of therapy not only reflects similar losses in the society at large, but also deprives society of one of its modern wellsprings of democratic theory, practice and justification.

One of the main assumptions of this volume is that democratic and authoritarian forms of political relationship (or what Karl Popper, 1966, refers to as "open and closed societies") are what help create different forms of individual and group psychology in those individuals who become adapted to life, with its morals and rules, in these diverse political structures. As the consciousness and modes of experience of individuals emerge in any social structure, there exists a need in people to maintain and enhance the type of structure that has helped them create the personal narratives that define reality, truth, and moral goodness. I posit a bidirectional relationship between the individual and society. The individual participates in and penetrates the fabric of society and society penetrates and shapes the consciousness of the individual. Psychologists, psychiatrists, and other psychotherapists not only shape the politics of society, but also are, in turn, shaped by these same politics. Psychology and psychotherapy are now very powerful institutions in our culture and, for much of the twentieth century, have been shaping the individual and collective psyches of our society. Science, psychology, and its applications have profound effects on the politics of our culture but simultaneously reflect the politics of the culture in which they are embedded and operate.

This book not only documents society's political struggles as reflected in psychology and psychotherapy but seeks to add its voice to those, who with varying levels of self-consciousness, attempt to enhance the democratic/humanistic trends in the field. The bias toward democracy contained in this volume is based on the conclusion that if the voices of political democracy are fully stilled in my field, it will represent the demise of all that is best in these enterprises and thus will be a tragedy for society. I hold that tragedy is self-evident whenever there is a reduction or loss of democratic political structures and the human freedoms of liberty, dignity, and quality of life that these structures guarantee.

I now sketch the specifics of the thesis developed in this monograph. I begin by describing just some of the vast number of conflicts raging within and between various factions concerned with the processes of psychotherapy. I limit my discussion to a small number of conflicts, in part because I find it impossible to do descriptive justice to the kind of fragmentation and internecine warfare that exists at all levels of psychology and within and between all forms of psychotherapy.

I begin with Lewis Aron (1999), who in a theoretical expansion of the subjective, intersubjective, and relational theory of psychoanalysis, speaks of the analyst's (and patient's) implicit relationship to the "psychoanalytic community." The analytic community, which includes the theories, practices, and social relationships that enfold and influence the analyst and patient (especially if the patient is an analytic student or otherwise informed or involved with psychoanalysis), functions as a Third in the dyadic interaction of analyst and patient. While Aron acknowledges that the analytic community is itself embedded and influenced by the dynamics created by aspects of the larger society (I call these aspects a "Fourth"), his article deals mostly with those aspects of the Third that represent the legendary, intensely conflicted, and diverse divisions within the analytic community itself. However, he writes of these extra-analytic influences: "We also encounter these complicated dynamics now, as psychoanalysis has been besieged by managed care and health reform, assailed by academics as a pseudoscience, and maligned by hostile media reports" (p. 9). I contend that the future of our democratic way of life is metaphorically represented in the struggles that Aron writes about as somehow concerning just the theories and therapeutic processes, both internal to, and surrounding, psychoanalysis.

I begin with the words "besieged by managed care and health reform." Psychoanalysis considers itself a form of psychotherapy or treatment that helps those who it refers to as "patients" deal with various forms of mental illness or disorders. The putative father of psychoanalysis was Sigmund Freud who was a physician and a neurologist before he came to deal with the mentally ill. Psychoanalysis is, therefore, based on its historical origins, logically placed among the medical arts and sciences, and is part of what is known as the mental health field. Most of the early pioneers in the psychoanalytic movement were physicians and the few nonphysicians allowed into the field were referred to as "lay analysts." I will delay for the moment discussing the conflicts between the medically trained and academically prepared therapists, but note that regardless of conflicts based on credentials all therapists consider themselves, their schools of thought, and their theories, to be part of the mental health field. *All demand to be known as experts in mental health and illness.*

Managed care now besieges psychoanalysis and all forms of psychotherapy, in part because of changes taking place within the whole of medicine that involves cost cutting and shifts in decision making from medical to business personnel. Psychoanalysis is a long, difficult, and very expensive therapeutic procedure as are most of the variants of treatment that have been derived from analysis. All long-term therapies are under economic attack and are in danger of being replaced by short-term, less costly interventions. However, cost is only part of the reason that managed care is a threat to psychotherapy.

The real threat to all forms of psychotherapy, and one of the critical battle lines, involves the contention of biologically oriented psychiatrists that mental illnesses are true brain disorders and should be treated primarily with drugs, euphemistically known as medicines, by appropriately trained medical psychiatrists. Psychotherapists are in a life-and-death struggle with the combined forces of biomedical psychiatry and the massive drug companies that daily develop new drugs to treat those suffering from mental illnesses. The drug companies have virtually unlimited wealth and access to the media with which to sell their wares and push their philosophy.

Since the psychosocial therapeutic interventions have been historically tied to the medical field, psychoanalysts and other types of psychotherapists can hardly withdraw from the battlefield whose terms and contours are firmly established by biological medicine and medically trained personnel. After decades of M.D.'s being routed by the troops of Ph.D.'s and M.S.W's, the M.D.'s are counterattacking and are close to tasting sweet victory. All that psychotherapists can do to defend themselves from these less costly and less time-consuming medical procedures is to argue that psychosocial therapies are as, or even more, effective than the biological therapies being advertised to the public in the popular media. But the psychotherapists are in no position to make such claims of superiority. This brings us to Aron's comment "assailed by academics as a pseudoscience." A growing number of books by academics such as Robyn Dawes (1994) and Donald Eisner (2000) cogently demonstrate that psychotherapy, regardless of therapist training or theoretical affiliation, has not only been unable to scientifically demonstrate its superiority over biomedical procedures but has been equally unable to demonstrate its effectiveness at all.

I return to the conflicts between the medically and nonmedically trained psychotherapists. After World War II, large numbers of psychologists, and still later even larger numbers of social workers, flooded into the expanding mental health fields and challenged the supremacy of the medically trained psychiatrists within psychoanalysis. More important, these newly minted therapists also challenged psychoanalysis as the dominant form of psychotherapy, inventing many other variants of therapeutic intervention that reflected trends within academic psychology. For example, psychologists defining themselves as behaviorists created a variety of psychological therapies based on techniques derived from classical and operant conditioning. These therapies tended to be much shorter in duration and drew cache from their advocate's contentions that they were better grounded in hard science than were psychoanalytic varieties of care. The followers of Abraham Maslow and Carl Rogers pioneered the form of counseling and psychotherapy based on existential and humanistic theories of behavior. The so-called third force in psychology entered into conflict with both the analysts and the behaviorists. It is currently impossible to accurately determine just how many varieties of psychotherapy now exist let alone document the specific and often ferocious conflicts between them.

Why does such fragmentation and conflict exist within and between the Third and the Fourth in the field of psychology and psychotherapy? More important, what do these divisions and the reasons for the conflict have to do with the politics of human relationships and what the psychiatrist R. D. Laing (1967) calls the "politics of experience"? The fragmentation and conflict at all levels of the therapeutic enterprise exists, in part, because of turf wars involving the money and prestige that comes from being recognized experts on problems important to society. But deeper issues are also involved in these battles and among these are those which relate to historical dichotomies concerning the nature of the sciences involved in these fields and the manner in which they construct and study their subject matter. This book concerns itself with these deeper scientific, historical, and philosophical issues, but for the moment will focus only on what might be called the "politics of science."

Stephen Toulmin (1992) suggests that as a result of the politics involved with the Thirty Years War, the study of human behavior developed along the scientific lines defined by René Descartes rather than those favored by Montaigne. Psychology tried to create itself after the efforts of Sir Isaac Newton rather than those of William Shakespeare. The scientific study of human beings ultimately favored the universal over the particular, the general over the local, the timeless over the timely, and the rational over the humanistic, and I would add the existential. As a result of various political decisions modern psychology has emerged defined as a natural science rather than as one of the humanities. Psychology is more generally concerned with the objective study of behavior rather than an understanding of the subjectivity and moral concerns of individual human beings. However, these conflicts begun in the Renaissance have not been resolved, and are directly responsible for the fragmentation and turf wars that concern this volume.

Referring to socially unwanted, hard-to-understand patterns of thinking, feeling, and behaving as illnesses reflects the political bias of the field to be part of the natural sciences. The war between the medically and academically trained therapists reflects confusion as to just who should best serve as representatives and stewards of a naturalistic, objective science. Indeed, if psychotherapy truly belonged to the medical field and belonged with the natural sciences there would not be academically trained, nonmedical personnel dominating the field. I would be unable to claim that psychotherapy is an application of psychology and not biology and medicine.

The successful attempts of biological psychiatry to reduce psychological events to neurological activity are also predicated, in part, on its practitioner's desire to scientifically legitimatize his/her field of expertise. Psychologists have struggled to be part of the medical field of mental health because of mainstream psychology's desire to be a part of legitimate, successful scientific approach to normal and abnormal behavior. Why else would have the budding field of "clinical" psychology modeled itself after psychiatry at the Boulder, Colorado, conference in 1947, which established the direction of psychology's relationship with the mental health field up to this day? The quarrels among psychologists themselves begins with debates as to which theorists or schools are the most scientific and possess the best scientific methodology to understand human behavior. The dramatic and destructive battles within psychoanalysis can also, in part, be traced to these same confusions and ambivalence.

It is my contention that the ambivalent and always unsuccessful attempts to maintain my field as a natural science has led to a failure to correctly define and study its subject matter and as a consequence has produced much that is destructive to human freedom and dignity. Two destructive forces have been unleashed by the field's insistence that it is a natural science. First, it has produced numerous (if competing) visions of humanity that conceive of us as either some form of robot or machine behaving at the mercy of forces external to us or as a primitive animal controlled by impulses or drives within. The reduction of all psychological phenomena to neurological events is the latest and one of the most dangerous of these visions to have resulted. All that might otherwise be defined as distinctly human—including conscious experience; the emotions; the capacity to think, reason, and create; and the human capacity to make choices—are ignored or seriously downplayed as important in both theory and practice.

The second destructive force flows from the first and involves my field's confused and damaging stance toward human ethics and morality. The human robots and puppets envisioned by modern science are incapable of responsible and moral behavior. Therefore, their destructive behaviors, directed against self and others, are either excused as being out of their control or recast as mental illnesses and disorders. I hold that Thomas Szasz (1974), who society may one day recognize as a hero of freedom and democracy, is quite correct when he states that mental illnesses are moral judgments stripped of all moral and ethical significance. To call someone mentally ill is to do no more than call him/her a bad moral name. *Mental illness is modernity's dishonest and confused name for sin.* The sum of this scientific activity is to not only reduce human beings to puppets or robots but cast them as evil, weak, and dangerous robots at that. Dangerous, out-of-control robots (or animals) require external control. Puppets require puppet masters. Freedom for such beings is not only unthinkable but represents a dangerous idea at best.

The scientific experts who make these moral judgments refuse to recognize that they are doing so and therefore are oblivious to the fact that they act as political and moral authorities in the lives of those they claim to help. Science, they claim does not make moral judgments, it is morally neutral. The natural and logical activity of these therapist–moral authorities must be the control of their patients, cast as dangerous puppets, by whatever means possible and through means devised by the best of modern science.

The great majority of professionals fail to recognize that their patients are dehumanized in these procedures and reduced to the level of things. Just as invisible is the professional's ascent to the role of a god in the life of the patient. Moreover, by maintaining the fiction of scientific neutrality the mental health experts need not concern themselves with the historical roots of their moral visions nor with questions concerning for whom they control their mentally ill charges. The experts in mental health need not realize that they might be controlling those in society who are the victims of those who are the most powerful and politically abusive and, therefore, these experts are playing the role of political operatives in the lives of their patients.

Thus we arrive at my thesis that psychology and virtually all forms of psychotherapy are dangerous to freedom and liberty, as we know them. The growing use of toxic psychotropic drugs, and other brain-disabling treatments, to control all manner of unwanted behavior in adults and children diagnosed as mentally ill and the increased use of forced treatment and hospitalization have led Szasz (1987, 2001) to refer to our society as a "therapeutic state" and as a "pharmacracy."

The combination of failing to treat people as experiential, psychological beings rather than as stimulus-response machines, helpless products of sociological events, animals driven by unconscious drives, or as the sum of twitching neurons, as well as the confusion of moral judgments with medical diagnoses have left the field of psychology and its applications not only intellectually and morally bankrupt but dangerous as well. Many psychological theories and schools of therapy exist more as orthodox secular religions and cults than as examples of open-minded, progressive sciences. Lacking real scientific evidence to support their major contentions and justify their ultimately destructive and immoral interventions into people's lives they revert to cults of charismatic personalities. They justify themselves on the strength of their faith in their founders; individuals invested with godlike qualities.

For all of the profound difficulties besetting psychology and psychotherapy there is much that is scientific, creative, and democratic about these enterprises. While never dominant, and seemingly heard as individuals, there are powerful voices that both criticize and provide alternatives to the reductionistic, illogical, and unscientific theories crowding my field. The growth of what might be called "human psychology" emphasizing human consciousness and phenomenological experience as central to an understanding of human behavior, is significant as are attempts to create new theories employing evolutionary psychology and social and cultural constructionism. There are many signs that psychology might move away from models based on the sciences of physics, chemistry, and pure biology. There are new ideas and theories that do not rely for their existence on the authority and personality of charismatic leaders. Similarly, many forms of psychotherapy and especially psychoanalysis are moving in very different directions than those criticized here. All of these promote ideas and practices that embody and promote democratic/ humanistic human relationships. What is clear, however, is that if psychotherapy is to survive in forms that are democratic rather than authoritarian, profound changes in current thinking and practices now dominating these fields must take place.

I have no real idea how the current struggle between political authoritarianism and democracy will turn out, either at the level of my changing, conflicted field or in the larger society to which the field of psychology and its applications belongs. I am describing my view of a historical process of which I am a part. I am a bit player on the stage of history, a history that has helped create who I am and which history I seek to influence in my role as player. I make the reader aware that I am fully conscious of having changed the style of my writing in this paragraph from one written in the supposedly more objective voice of the third person, a convention of modernistic, scientific writing, to one expressed in the first person. I have changed my style to introduce another aspect of this book and that is the direct influence of the postmodern revolution mentioned earlier. I also write as if it were Montaigne and not Descartes who influenced the course of psychology.

I write with the knowledge that I am embedded in the historical and social processes that I am trying to influence. *I write as a citizen of my society as much as I write from the perspective of any other role.* No matter how dispassionate and objective I try to be I am writing in my own voice, from my own historical time and within a given society and culture. Moreover, I am motivated by my own self-interests for money, prestige, influence, and a recognized place in society and history. I also write as a very frightened individual who fears for the future of his children and grandchildren as he reads of psychiatrists and pediatricians being permitted by confused, overworked parents to control the behavior of active two- and three-year-old babies with methylphenidates such as Ritalin (otherwise known to the world of the drug addict as "speed") and other equally toxic and noxious drugs.

This book is comprised of nine chapters. The first chapter will try to describe the political differences between closed and open societies and the types of personality organization in terms of the cognitive and affective styles of interpersonal functioning associated with each. The second chapter will trace historical development of religion and science in terms of the manner in which each functions according to either democratic or authoritarian political principles. The third chapter is comprised of an analysis of how mainstream psychology, as it appears in the typical introductory textbook, developed out of the traditions of religion and science and its relationship to visions of open and closed societies.

Chapter 4 explores the myth of mental illness and the growing dangers to our democracy by the mental health field, biopsychiatry in particular. Chapters 5 and 6 discuss the practice of psychosocial forms of therapy, psychoanalysis in particular, and the type of politics practiced both within these enterprises and on the citizens who seek help from them.

The final chapters advance and develop a view of treatment based on democratic and humanistic principles first sketched in *Psycho "therapy"* (Simon, 2000a). Chapter 7 is devoted to a treatise on madness and philosophical discussion of various problems bedeviling our field, including those involving conceptual splitting of mind and body, nature and nurture, subject and object, and cognition and emotion. Chapter 8 develops a theory of personality based on the politics of human relationships and Chapter 9 briefly describes *psycho "therapy,"* my term for a humanistic, democratic form of psychological "treatment" based on a human psychology, and its necessary relationship to citizenship.

CHAPTER 1

Politics and Psychology

INTRODUCTION

An examination of an average college curriculum reveals that students can take courses from a large number of disciplines organized into a variety of departments. The college in which I labor is organized no differently. I teach psychology, which along with anthropology and sociology comprise the Behavioral Sciences. History, political science, economics, and philosophy comprise the Department of Social Sciences. The largest department in my college is the Department of English, which teaches the language arts and literature. Chemistry and physics make up the Physical Sciences Department; while biology comprises another separate department.

Each discipline is composed of experts in the separate subject matters that comprise academic disciplines. Most professors have earned a doctor of philosophy, or an equivalent, in their subject of interest. The academic degrees earned by these scholars are the result of intense years of study in institutions built along similar lines to those now employing them. It is, therefore, not surprising that very few college professors question the fact that most of these separate and independent disciplines speak very different languages, generally develop their subject matter within the discipline, and rarely discuss or debate topics across discipline lines. I raise this issue and suggest that these arrangements are peculiar because except for the physical sciences all of these separate disciplines are concerned with the same subject matter: Human Beings in the variety of their activities and social interactions. I suggest that all of these subject areas belong to the human sciences and that when individuals study one they are implicitly studying all.

I am not arguing that there is not a certain advantage to studying various human activities separately given the range and complexity of human endeavors. However, I maintain that the degree to which the various disciplines tend to ignore one another creates an illusion that each can exist separately or make sense of their subject matter without reference to all the others. I suggest that the current system fragments its common human subject matter in such a way that much of what is important for us to understand about ourselves as human beings is lost or drowned in a Babel of competing voices, language systems, and methodologies.

I further hypothesize that the current state of affairs has evolved, in part, because of the need to organize our various areas of study as "sciences" that can ultimately compete with the "real" sciences such as physics and chemistry (and to a lesser degree, biology). This chapter is not directly concerned with the problems of the university but with psychology, the various forms of psychotherapy, and their relationship to politics. However, the fact that there are so many problems within my discipline as well as difficulties in relating my own discipline to politics does stem from the kind of overly abstract and reductionist thinking involving the myth of isolated subject areas referring to themselves as sciences.

PSYCHOLOGY AND POLITICS

I begin by discussing "politics" as it appears in a popular textbook used in a political science course at my college. Thomas E. Patterson (2001) defines politics as "the process of deciding society's goals." He adds that "politics is more than the pursuit of shared ideals; it is also about getting one's own way" (p. 13). The author discusses the inevitable conflicts that arise as different people try and live together in a common society and culture while simultaneously getting their own ways. The author discusses the need to resolve conflicts and create common goals through the creation of government. He defines government "the institutions, processes, and rules that are specifically designed to facilitate control of a particular area and its inhabitants" (p.14). The discussion of government immediately creates a need to discuss and define power ("the ability of persons or institutions to control policy") and authority ("the recognized right of an individual or institution to exercise power").

It is clear to anyone reading this text that the author is implicitly discussing the social organization of any given society and hence is discussing sociology in terms of power and stratification of society. It is also clear that many of the common goals and conflicts within a society relate to its economics and the distribution of its collective wealth. A textbook on politics will also describe various forms of government including those that are authoritarian dictatorships, oligarchies, democracies, and other variations of government based on the distributions of power, wealth, and the constitution of authority.

However, my concern here is with the psychology of the "persons" who are in conflict and in pursuit of common ideals and goals as they organize and maintain government, struggle to become authorities, and interact with one another in terms of power. I am interested in what it feels like to be powerful or powerless in a given political institution as well as gaining insight into the beliefs and desires of those who seek power and those who seek to avoid it. I am concerned with the psychological development of individuals whose basic experiences in life take place under tyrannical authority and who live in terror of those who govern them as compared to those whose development is shaped in democratic and humanistic settings that promote individual self-expression and creativity.

Indeed, I am interested in why so many human beings seem to accept life, or even choose to live in dictatorships or under tyrannical rule and why so many individuals seek to be tyrants. Of critical concern to me as a psychotherapist are questions concerning the relationship of various forms of interpersonal governance and various forms of intrapsychic or self-governance. Therapists work with some individuals who seem to lack any real self-control as they act out in destructive patterns of behavior, while others who seek therapeutic intervention are unable to allow themselves any pleasure as they endlessly and painfully tyrannize themselves.

An examination of the science of politics will describe the settings but rarely the specific, individual human experiences of those participating and interacting in these political systems. In general, if individuals are dealt with at all it will be in terms of descriptions of various politicians and what they did and said in their roles within a given political system. What are usually missing are the subjective experiences and specific motives of the various members of the political system.

Because the psychological is generally missing from the study of politics, it seems to me that the field lacks as adequate a description of factors that drive various political systems that it might otherwise have. There is little to describe the creation, maintenance, and decay of social and political systems in terms of the psychology of those individuals responsible for the processes of birth and death of political systems. Currently, causative explanations might include discussions of economic factors or historical figures and various historical events might be invoked. But a political system is made up of individuals and is ultimately driven by the beliefs and desires of those comprising the system. I suggest that the study of politics will become more of a legitimate science as it continues to be integrated with a psychology of those who create, maintain, direct, and challenge the day-to-day operations of political systems. For that type of personal information one would expect to turn to psychology. However, if the field of political science lacks an adequate integration with a psychology of the individual, a study of psychology is bound to disappoint those seeking to add a psychological dimension to their understanding of politics.

If students examine the basic textbooks concerned with the science of psychology, those used to introduce students new to the discipline, they will most probably discover that the discipline defines itself as either "the study of behavior" or as "the study of mind and behavior." (I delay a more detailed discussion concerning the tenuous notion that psychology is, or might ever be, a real science.) I suggest that an examination of the index or table of contents of any these texts, which represent the core assumptions and methodologies that define the field's mainstream, will fail to find meaningful discussions describing persons either in conflict or in cooperative pursuit of common goals.

The students will also neither find few descriptions of people struggling with authority figures, nor those involved with power, powerlessness, and the abuse of power. The student will search in vain for discussions about individuals involved in governing or being governed at any level of human social organization from that of individuals with themselves, within their family constellations and communities, or with the wide variety of governments as they operate in the real world of politics. Searching students will not find descriptions of persons capable of thinking politically, of creating policy, either common or individual. They will fail to discover discussions of how people think or feel when involved in the political processes of their lives and, perhaps most important, how it feels subjectively to be an authority, to be powerless, or to abuse or be abused by those with power. Not only will these topics be missing but also the very words denoting these issues will be hard to find in any of the textbooks that induct the next generation of scholars into the field of psychology.

If individuals seek information on the interface of politics and psychology, on how those in a political system penetrate and shape each other's subjective experience of life, they will have to turn elsewhere than the mainstream of either political science or the science of psychology. A study of history, which is often the study of past political systems, the authorities and forms of government of a given era, and the lives of those living in that era will fill in some of the information that concerns me.

Still more insights can be gained by studying the genre of social and political theory as represented by the works of Dana Cloud (1998), Russell Jacoby (1986), Karl Popper (1966), Nicholas Rose (1999), Thomas Sowell (1987, 1996) and a variety of others. Works such as these do represent an integration of politics, sociology, and psychology. As interdisciplinary studies they represent an advance over the more traditional mainstream approaches to these subjects. However, none of these works deal with the specific relationship of individual personality, both in its "normal" and "abnormal" manifestations and their relationship to various political interactions. Perhaps the best sources of insight into the "politics of experience" (Laing, 1967) and the experience of politics can be gleaned by reading biographies and historical fiction, but as useful as these sources are they are still incidental to the formal studies that interest me.

A BRIEF PSYCHOLOGY OF POLITICAL PERSONS

I suggest that human beings are inherently social creatures, born into human families, communities, and a host of larger societal entities and do not become fully human unless, in their development, they are socialized to live as part of these social institutions. Except for those working in mainstream psychology this statement is both trite and a cliche. I further suggest that all human relationships must share common goals and find ways of cooperating in meeting those goals which define continued existence and the types of human satisfactions that seem to make life meaningful and worth living. I assume that the conditions of human existence might be threatened by scarcity such that each individual might see the existence of other individuals as a threat to his own. In such circumstances conflict between individuals is inevitable.

But even in the absence of scarcity, I also assume that all human beings are different, one from another, in a host of ways that make conflict and the need for conflict resolution inevitable. Politics exists in all human relationships and at all levels of social organization making me agree with Philip Tetlock (1992) that conceiving of every human being as a politician is a highly useful and necessary metaphor. However I go further and declare *that the politics that inevitably exist in all human interactions can be understood to literally define the nature of those human relationships as well as the relationships of individuals with themselves.* (I agree however with Jack Martin and Jeff Sugarman, 1999, that no matter how dependent human consciousness is on its social–political origins it is not reducible to those origins.) Unlike the college curriculum that treats psychology and politics as *dualisms*, these two disciplines are in reality *dualities*, two manifestations of the same phenomena. (Any two of the human sciences can be treated as dualities, and exposing the concepts of one through the lens and insights of the other will do much to restore meaning to each discipline. This chapter basically concerns itself with the duality of politics and psychological experience.)

I outline the concepts of a political psychology whose fuller development will comprise the remainder of this chapter. These formulations are developments of ideas expressed earlier by me (Simon, 1981, 1986, 1998, 2000a). The social and political arrangements that will have so much to say about the psychology of the individuals within any social system are nonetheless comprised of individuals who are also the constructed product of millions of years of biological, as well as social, evolution. While any definition of a human being must reflect her/his social construction I assume that no human being is merely a mirror of her/his social experiences. I will not invoke or develop any notion of human nature in this volume but will insist on a view of the human being as possessing a variety of cognitive skills and affective processes that are the product of natural and sexual selection as well as social and cultural evolution. These cognitive and affective processes, in turn, define the human being's inherent consciousness, awareness, self-reflective and self-corrective, and emergent qualities. Evolution has made us creatures with subjectivity capable of reflecting and reporting on our subjective experiences. I agree with Steven Pinker (1997), as well as many others, that human beings have a biologically created nervous system that is an information processing system of enormous complexity. However, I also agree with Jerome Bruner (1992), A. Giorgi (1970, 1994), William Helme (1992), and others that at the psychological level of human conscious experience a person is a meaning-seeking and meaning-making being.

I have theorized that the legitimate study of psychology is the study of human consciousness that I have defined as "an individual's purposeful responses to meaningful events and situations" (Simon, 1998:61). Human consciousness is the product of all aspects of the human adaptive struggle and it is through human consciousness that the adaptive struggles of all individuals are expressed. It is in the adaptive, emergent qualities of human consciousness that we see an active being engaging the large variety of events that make up a life, in this case the political activities of the other conscious human beings that comprise any social community. I propose that the individuals involved in their political interactions are never passive objects of political forces (even though they can be treated as such and can be victimized by the political activities of others) but are active participants and conscious agents in all social activities.

Human consciousness must undergo a development between infancy and adulthood if people are to assume a political role in their social life. Robert Kegan (1982, 1994) and Jean Piaget (1950, 1952, 1954, 1959, 1973, 1975, 1981) are two among many who have charted the nature of development that allows a helpless infant become a full member of a social–political system (even if their particular work does not address the specific issue of politics in the development of human subjectivity). As development takes place, human consciousness becomes organized into a self, whose working definition is "the hereness in the thereness" (Chein, 1972: 197). The self is defined by its identity, which for the most part is a direct result of the politics of human relationships.

The self is expressed by means of a narrative. Human political inter-actions involve the telling of stories that define the self as hero or villain, ac-tive agent or passive victim, creative artist or spectator of life. Past, present, and future appear in human narratives as time is bound, history told, and future anticipated. C. Wright Mills (1957) writes, "We have come to know that every individual lives, from one generation to the next in some society; that he lives out a biography, and that he lives within some historical se-quence. By the fact of his living he contributes, however minutely, to the shaping of his society and to the course of history, even as he is made by so-ciety and by its historical push and pull" (p. 6). Some of the most impor-tant chapters of our biographical narrative tell the story of the self and others in political interactions.

Two activities define the conscious strivings of human beings as polit-ical agencies (even though the nature of these activities varies not only from individual to individual but also during the development of each individ-ual). Both of these activities are the result of human biological and social evolution and both are critical to our adaptive success and failure. These ac-tivities are expressed through the use of two additional metaphors and the narratives that contain them: the individual as "scientist" and the individual as "moral philosopher."

As scientists (Kelly, 1955), we attempt to describe, explain, predict, and control the situations and events, including the political actions, of those with whom we interact, that make up our lives. We are forever asking, What hap-pened? Why and how did it happen? Who did what and to whom? Has it hap-pened before and will it happen again? What is my role in all of this and what is it that is my interest to do now and in the future? There are literally an end-less number of questions that can, and must, be asked about the world in and around us as well as about those who comprise our social relationships. There are a correspondingly large number of means by which to try to answer these questions. Science is but one of the means of answering the questions that matter to us, both individually and collectively.

But human beings are constructed to ask more than scientific ques-tions as they seek to adapt as individuals and as groups. Each human being is a moral philosopher as well as a scientist. The adaptive efforts of individ-uals and groups either succeed or fail. In the political struggles of getting our own way, some individuals and groups win and some lose. Some take what others have including their most prized possessions and that might even include their lives. In the perception of some, political power is being used; in the evaluations of others, it is being abused. Michael Polanyi (1967) suggests that success and failure in human adaptation is necessarily critical.

I stand as well with the philosophers Martin Buber (1976) and Em-manuel Levinas (1969) who conclude that the human experience of one another is inherently different than any other type of experience. Levinas suggests that throwing away garbage is an inherently different experience than that of throwing away people. Because of the inherent difference in experience, throwing away people requires a different moral justification than that of putting out garbage. James Q. Wilson (1993) argues that the peculiar human evolutionary experience has left all human beings with a moral sense. Jerome Kagan (1984) points out that by the middle of the second year human beings are aware of standards: "They will point to broken objects, torn clothing, and missing buttons, revealing in voice and face a mood of concern" (p. 124). I assume that morality is both basic and inherent to our human form of evolved, adaptive consciousness.

In addition to the question Who did what to whom? we ask Who is responsible or to blame? As scientists we ask What is and how does it all work? As moral philosophers we simultaneously ask What ought to be and is it fair? Throughout this book I will argue, along with Levinas, that not only is the ground, or basis, of our morality to be found in the fact that we reason as scientists, but that we reason as scientists because we conclude that such reasoning is good and, therefore, morally right to do. As a result of our inherent moral sense, by the time we are still very young children, we do not act toward others unless and until we have concluded that it is morally and ethically right to do so. Based on this argument I hypothesize that the moment we find ourselves justifying any past, present, or possible future act it is because we have already concluded, on some conscious level, that it is wrong to commit that act. If we were not concerned about the morality of our actions, we would not spend the time and energy justifying them.

It is important to note that my belief that we are all moral in no way implies that people will agree as to what specific behaviors and forms of governance are moral. One person's morality is another person's evil. The abuse of power for some is the moral expression of authority for another. Adolf Hitler and his minions proudly left a vast written and film record of their moral crusade to rid the Fatherland and the world of the human "disease" of the Jews and other "inferior" groups infecting the body of their Third Reich. When I suggest that we are moral beings I mean nothing more (and nothing less) than the fact that all human beings will seek to make their actions appear to be moral and ethical in their eyes and in the eyes of others. Human beings spend much of their intellectual energy morally justifying their own and the actions of others.

The ground of our science and the questions concerning 'what is,' and the ground of our questions 'what ought or should be' are inherent one to the other and hence represent another duality that operates in a bidirectional nature. We ask how things work in order to achieve goals that are prejudged to be moral. Our moral goals represent that which is truthful, beautiful, and good. Of course, we cannot really know what is good until that which is good is described and delineated from that which is bad. In addition, we judge the means by which the good and beautiful are to be achieved. A description of what is and how it works is necessary to achieving our moral goals but human beings always seem to find it necessary to justify their efforts to realize their goals.

What determines the nature of good and evil, beauty and ugliness, truth and falsity? I believe these are to be derived from the psychology of human beings as they have evolved in the adaptive processes of natural, sexual, and social evolution as I have mentioned. Specifically, morality relates to experiences involving pleasure and pain on both a physical and psychological level. It is beyond the scope of this book to further develop this aspect of the discussion at the present juncture.

The bidirectionality of the moral and the scientific are nowhere more in evidence than in our social and political activities where governance, authority, and power are exercised. All governments and authority exist only insofar as they can maintain their legitimacy. The legitimacy of authority is based on judgments of the competency of authority to deal with 'what is' as well as notions of fairness and justice. When human beings seek to resolve conflict they debate 'what is' and 'what ought to be,' 'who did what to whom' and 'were the actions ethically and morally correct.' Power is used in all social–political systems to determine who did what and what is right and wrong. The basic ground of authority and its use of power are the capacity to define who and what is right and wrong.

The meaning of the world for each of us begins with the adaptive cognitive processes that allow us to ask 'what is' and 'what should be.' But the full meaning of the events that we experience does not occur until we feel them as affects. Affect, comprised of the biological drives, and more for my purposes here the emotions, comprise a second aspect of evolutionary human consciousness. We not only perceive, think, and apply logic to our world but also experience a variety of feelings about the situations and events that are the objects of our cognitive processes. The specific emotions we feel, which exist on a psychological and physical level, depend on the cognitive appraisals, construal, and interpretations of the actual situations and events that are the object of our cognitive processes. What we perceive and think determines the emotions we feel. The full meaning of situations and events is comprised of our cognitive and affective responses to those situations and events.

Both our scientific and moral appraisals arouse a variety of specific emotions. If we experience ourselves to be the objects of another's admiration we might feel pride. If we see ourselves as having created something of value we might feel joy. Jean-Paul Sartre (1964) suggests that when we perceive that we have not been at our most creative we feel existential nausea. If we experience love from another, we might respond with feelings of love for that person. If we receive a gift we might respond with gratitude. If we lose one we love we might feel loneliness, despair, and grief.

If we judge that we have been just with another we might feel pride and rectitude, but if we believe that we have wronged another or not lived up to our highest moral standards we may well experience guilt. If we experience that others are unjust with us we might respond with outrage and contempt for them. If we see ourselves through the eyes of others, as contemptible or disgusting, shame might well be the emotion that defines the full meaning of that social interaction or relationship. If we are physically threatened by others fear, terror, anger, and rage might define the meaning of the moment and its history.

Anxiety is an important emotion requiring a separate discussion. Anxiety results when we fail to achieve our scientific function, which exists as our primary mode of adaptation. Anxiety begins the moment we experience a failure in our attempts to describe, explain, predict, or control the world in and around us. Anxiety as a special form of dread begins when we are faced with situations experienced as ambiguous such as sounds in the night, the medical diagnosis that has not yet arrived, or the sudden awareness that we cannot locate ourselves in time and space. Anxiety might begin as we experience emotions or needs that threaten our definition of ourselves as moral beings or any event that threatens to unravel the narratives that we live by. Finally, anxiety emerges when we are confronted by statements from those we depend on that may or may not be truthful; for example, those political situations in which individual's words imply one thing and their tone or the consequences of their actions imply another.

Our adaptive responses toward the events of our lives, and this includes our political responses toward those with whom we share a social–political system, are determined by our cognitive–affective experiences of these events as expressed in our biographical narratives. What we react to in others are the expressions of their cognitive–affective experience of other individuals and ourselves interacting in a social–political system. We simultaneously react to our own and each other's expressions of each other's scientific and moral interpretations and the emotions aroused by those interpretations. To add still additional levels of complexity to this brew I make clear that the appraisals being made during any given social interaction are not only shaped by the current events taking place but reflect beliefs and attitudes created during past experiences. We not only act in the present based on past experiences but also utilize these experiences to predict future events and the behavior of those with whom we anticipate interacting.

When we utilize the past to guide the present and anticipate the future we might hypothesize or we might prophesize. We might interact with others based on personal scientific theories that permit current information to direct our behavior and subsequently alter our social and political theories. Or we might interact with others based on sacred stories that are impervious to new information and remain unchanged regardless of the meanings expressed and intended by those with whom we share a social–political system. Our prophecies might fulfill and reinforce themselves because they remain impervious to change. It makes a huge difference when individuals govern themselves and others with personal political beliefs that are open to the possibility of error and change than when they are sacred stories rooted in absolute notions of truth, perfection, and moral rectitude.

Another related factor that can affect the nature and course of political interactions involves the use of deception. Evolutionists point out that all animals use deception to advance their attempts at survival and procreation. All animals develop skills of deception detection as well. Human adaptation takes place as an interpersonal struggle involving politics: contests based on symbols, language, and metaphor. Human deception and deception detection are achieved through the manipulation of language and various symbols, making the good liar the more successful competitor.

Psychoanalysis has long taught us that human beings can defend against internal and external threat by manipulating and changing the cognitive and affective interpretations that define meaning for the individual. I suggest that "psychological defenses," here conceived of as adaptive devices, play a critical role in our political lives. They convince the deceiver that the deception is the truth, not only making detection more difficult but also reducing the moral problems inherent in lying to one's fellow human beings. Accepting a lie as the truth might also have the effect of reducing anxiety associated with interpreting a socially ambiguous situation. Any analysis of differing political system must include how that system has been shaped by the processes of deception and deception detection.

Another important construct affecting the course and type of political processes in which we find ourselves might be governance that reflects a separation of scientific descriptions and moral judgments as compared to governance and the use of power that reflects a fusion of the descriptive with the morally judgmental. It is my contention that all psychiatric judgments are, in reality, moral judgments stripped of their moral language. *I argue that this is just one example of the nearly universal process of using moral judgments of people as if they were explanatory descriptions of their behavior. The deceptive process of fusing moral judgment with scientific description simultaneously creates the illusion that we understand the behavior of our fellow beings while justifying the use of political power to control them.*

DESCRIPTIONS AND JUDGMENTS

A description is a statement as to an individual's experience of an object or event. Descriptions begin with the words "I see, hear, touch, smell, or taste" and add the objects of these inherently intentional perceptual acts: "birds, bells, a child's face, baking bread, or sour milk." Description might include statements as to the internal affective reactions to the things or events experienced perceptually: "happy, surprise, joy, pleasure, disgust." I suggest that there exist three aspects of human beings capable of description. We can describe physical appearance. We can also describe people's behavior or what they do, taking care to also describe that context in which they carry out their behavior. Finally, we can describe or accept a person's descriptions of their own subjective experience of their actions. All we can ever explain about the actions of any individuals will be based on the descriptions of what people do in any given situation in terms of their intentions as contained in a description of their subjective experience of the situation. There seems nothing more difficult or vexing for human beings to describe, explain, predict, and control (based on a genuine psychological understanding) than the behavior of their fellow human beings, especially in complex social and political contexts.

Judgments can be defined as opinions concerning the value or worth of something. Beautiful and ugly, good and bad are common judgments. Our judgments are based on the value and worth of the objects, situations, and events that in one way or another have been experienced and implicitly or explicitly described. When we judge the functioning of human behavior we are perforce making a moral judgment of that behavior. When we use such terms as *lazy, ambitious, intelligent, stupid, honest, dishonest, sane,* or *crazy,* or any of the other thousands of similar words that exist in our language (and all languages), we are inevitably judging behavior. We are judging either a single act or a pattern of behavior or statements of someone's experience that we have first observed and described. All such judgments are moral, or ethical, in nature.

Our judgments of a person's behavior and subjective experience are based on descriptions of behavior and experience and since only descriptions can provide us with an explanation of behavior, our moral judgments cannot explain the behavior. Moreover, if our judgments are of the behavior then they should exist grammatically as modifiers of the verbs defining behavior and hence as adverbs. Grammatically, only verbs can be used to denote behavior. Therefore, if Jim does not do his work I can make a moral judgment of Jim's actions and state, "Jim behaved lazily or in a lazy manner." It is clear that "lazy" judges Jim's behavior (or the lack thereof) and in no way can explain Jim's actions.

But the real world of human social–political activity we rarely make statements such as "Jim behaved lazily." Instead we change the adverb to an adjective and move the reference of the judgment from Jim's actions to Jim himself. We now state "Jim is lazy." And in one wonderful, unscientific, wholly illogical, and magical act the judgment "lazy" becomes an explanation for Jim's behavior. Jim did not do his work so he is lazy and Jim did not do his work because he is lazy. We now ignore that we have engaged in totally circular reasoning, that an adjective and not a verb now accounts for a behavior, and that a judgment can be the cause of human actions.

With one burst of creative self-deception we have removed the necessity to struggle and come up with a genuine scientific explanation of human behavior without having to gain access to the varieties of conscious experience wherein lies the motives of behavior. We have also removed any need to understand the social–political context that formed the content of the individuals' subjective experience as well as the history of these individuals as they lived through, interacted with, and influenced a variety of other social–political contexts, life situations, and events.

In addition, the scientific observers of the behavior of those within a social–political system need not be concerned with the effect of the act of observation on the behavior of the observed. The scientist moves from the status of participant–observer to that of observer. People are now motivated from factors within themselves as sociological, economical, political, historical, and biological factors all disappear from view and are rendered unnecessary for any explanations we develop. Not only has the difficult and anxiety-provoking job of scientific investigation been made wonderfully easy and less time-consuming but also with the same creative act we have justification for acting to reward good actions and punish and control the bad. Good and evil now explain good and evil.

The same intellectual trick of creating an explanation for behavior and the justification to influence it can be used with any of the thousands of moral terms in our vocabulary. If we cannot understand why one person learns more quickly than another we label one intellectually gifted and the other intellectually retarded. We now believe that we can not only explain the difference in their speed of learning but also justify teaching one in an enriched program while placing the other in a very different sort of classroom. If we meet someone on the street loudly proclaiming that he not only speaks to God, but that God also speaks to him, we call him crazy, psychotic, or schizophrenic. Not only do we believe that we understand the reason why "he hears voices," that is, he is schizophrenic, but we can justify locking him up in a prison, euphemistically called a "hospital," and force him to accept treatments that he also wishes not to undergo. Moreover, we can deceive ourselves into believing that our actions are not political but medical; that we are not acting as society's political agent against the wishes of the "patient" but acting in his true and better interests.

TWO POLITICAL VISIONS

Based on the previous section we can discern and begin to explain various models of human psychology related to different models of political organization. I will not seek to discover which is primary, the psychology of the individual or the structure of political systems. I will, instead, invoke the model of social structuration proposed by Anthony Giddens (1984) in which the individual and society are seen as dualities. The individual is conceived of as an agent and society as the set of interactions between conscious, knowing agents over time and across space. Society can be described as an abstraction independently of the individuals that comprise it only by losing sight of those individuals, who as agents or selves think, feel, make decisions, and seek to influence those with whom they interact. The individual can be described as separate from the society only by losing sight of the social–political relationships that define the social individual. To ask which is primary—society or individual—is to lose sight of and destroy the dual nature of their relationship. The very act of either Giddens or I writing a book is a political act originating within a society that neither of us can ever fully hope to transcend. Asking what comes first, individual or society, is to put one outside the relationship of the other. The psychology described above is a product of the political system in which I live and have developed, and as such I could have logically first discussed the type of political system capable of shaping my psychology.

However, once I create a notion of society as comprised of individual agents capable of scientific and moral appraisals I have a basis to create both a science and a moral philosophy of persons. We are all both scientists and moral philosophers and can hold each other responsible for what we know and what we do about our knowledge. I can hope that change is possible within such a system of beliefs and that one type of political system can evolve into another, one more scientific and more moral.

In the same way I can avoid the individualisms of mainstream psychology in which people are described as completely free from any of their social interactions. I can replace persons without contexts with a psychology of interacting individual persons, each possessing their own individuality. Simultaneously, I retain a concept of the individual as moral agent rather than find myself in the moral nihilism of Skinnerian behaviorists and various postmodern, social constructionists who describe the primacy of the social (or environmental) over the individual and the individual as merely the invention or epiphenomenon of a social system's "stimuli" or use of language.

When human beings enter into social relationships and evolve a system of governance, they will be concerned with questions of 'what is' and 'what ought to be.' They will be guided by what Sowell (1987) refers to as a "vision, a preanalytic cognitive act. It is our sense of how the world works" (p. 14). A vision is also about how the world should be. Michel Foucault (1977) develops a similar notion when he discusses the "discourses" which direct our attention and shape our actions, but which rarely become the focus of our attention. I suggest that these political visions or discourses are comprised of descriptions and judgments and of scientific theories and moral sacred stories and operate according to the psychological principles just outlined. A political vision might be understood to be the conceptual nexus of psychology and politics. The political visions, narratives, and forms of psychology that concern me are those associated with democratic and authoritarian/totalitarian forms of social–political relationships or what Popper refers to as open and closed societies. I will use Popper's terminology interchangeably with the more common political language. I begin with the psychology of democratic systems of government and the open society.

Sowell suggests that political visions may be "constrained" or "unconstrained." Both refer to an implied aspect of human nature, namely, Are human beings modifiable and perfectible or is the nature of humanity fixed and unchanging? Contained within these ideas are notions of human development and how such development is to be affected by social interaction. There is a second aspect to these visions that Sowell leaves implicit in his discussion and that has to do with humanity's moral nature. Are we basically good, evil, or morally neutral? Enlightenment philosophers argued over both of these issues as well as the kind of government required by various combinations of the moral and the developmental.

Jean-Jacques Rousseau envisioned humanity as noble savages whose innate goodness emerged with as little and as benign political influence as possible. Thomas Hobbes saw humanity as essentially fixed in its evil nature, requiring continuing despotic control. John Locke conceived of humanity as morally neutral and as a tabula rasa, or blank slate, that depends on society for the directions its nature would take. Locke clearly preferred an open, democratic political system and therefore insisted that humanity required such governing. It is beyond the scope of this discussion to pursue and develop these ideas but I will return to them in Chapter 3 when I discuss their reappearance in various popular personality theories. I now sketch a description of the open and closed society.

VISIONS OF THE DEMOCRATIC SOCIETY

In what follows I do not create an extensive definition of or engage in a full discussion of democracy from the perspective of political theory per se. It is beyond the scope of this book and of my own expertise to do justice to a discussion of democracy as an institutional system of governance with free and competitive elections. I approach democracy more as a quality of life with certain intrapersonal and interpersonal social and psychological experiences. My attempts are, after all, to create a psychology of individuals within certain social settings and not to attempt to redefine another legitimate area of inquiry.

I propose that the democratic vision is based on an accepted wide-spread use of a personal science of subjective psychology and conceives of the human being as capable of will, choice, and desire as well as reason. The underlying assumption is that all human beings are possessed of minds. In this paradigm human beings are aware of making choices and predicting the consequences of their actions making them *existential and teleological beings.* Indeed, such beings experience the act of choosing and taking responsibility for the consequences of their choices as the defining characteristic of being human. It is this characteristic that separates the human being from every other evolutionarily evolved animal and it is what makes science, moral philosophy, creativity, and politics necessary in the first place.

In this social–political system there is an appreciation by each member that thoughts and feelings, beliefs and desires motivate every member. All members see themselves and their fellows as conscious subjective beings comprised of a psychology similar to one's own. In this system each individual might openly and honestly express the needs and desires that guide the political goals which achievement represents as getting one's own way. Each individual might be guided in their search for policies geared for the creation of common societal goals by their awareness that all the others in the system are possessed of similar psychological needs as their own. And each individual in the system might be aware that the psychological consequences of need satisfaction and deprivation feel much the same for all members of the system.

In the system under consideration not only are individuals described in psychological terms comprised of their human subjective experience but the moral judgments that each might make of the other are kept separate from and articulated with the descriptions on which they are based. Individuals are seen as being motivated by psychological factors and not the judgments that might be made of these motives. Moreover, in this system the visions of those creating policy are theories that are incomplete, fallible, probabilistic, and never fully capable of describing, explaining, or predicting the behavior of those in the system.

Authority figures, just as all other individuals in a social system, suffer anxiety and stress as they experience the constant and terrible limitations on their abilities to predict and control and hence carry out the responsibilities associated with its prerogatives and powers. The legitimization of authority is maintained through descriptive evaluation by the members of the group of the leadership's ability to function according to its agreed upon functions and goals. In this arrangement leaders are selected by participating members. The selection process involves an evaluation of the merits of those who seek to lead. Merit is predicated on a display of an individual's ability to demonstrate the social and intellectual skills to define and achieve goals based on 'what is' as well as 'what should be.' In this system any and all members might aspire to political leadership.

When authority utilizes its power to achieve social–political goals it does so with an awareness of the effects of its actions on the subjective experience of the members affected by its decisions. An awareness of what it feels like to be powerless, to experience the outrage and terror of losing one's possessions, freedoms, and even life, dramatically affects the manner in which an empathic authority exercises power. An empathic awareness of the terror and finality of death tends to make life appear precious to all the members of the group and acts to direct the common goals sought by the members as well as affect the manner in which disputes and challenges to authority are managed.

When authority understands its human limitations it must depend on its members for help in achieving goals and resolving disputes. Therefore, the adaptive skills of all the members of the group become important to the group's success. The members of such a system tend to be seen as equals and interdependent, making it less likely that deceptions will be experienced as necessary to each member's attempt to reach their individual goals. When individuals share responsibility for their collective adaptations in the light of their shared human limitations then the creative efforts of all of the members are valued and supported. Individual differences and diversity are perceived as beneficial to the life of the group. The boundaries of group life are porous and new sources of talent and abilities are welcomed.

A shared perception of limitations requires a shared goal of continued growth in all aspects of the life of the group. In such a setting science, the arts and humanities, and other forms of creative expression are nurtured by the politics of the group. In this system the underlying visions and discourses that guide political activity might even be self-reflexive, allowing members to examine and change their underlying visions or discourses. In this system politics is based on the practicalities of everyday life and infused with wisdom slowly collected over long historical periods. Ideology remains in the background as political theory is concerned with the lives of real people in the flux of everyday life.

Finally, the relationships of all members of a democratic social organization, and this includes the interactions of those with political power, with those who lack power exist in what Buber (1976) refers to as an "I-Thou" relationship. An I-Thou relationship is an encounter between persons each possessed of selves and identities. It involves face-to-face encounters involving the telling of life narratives that each experiences as real, authentic, and truthful. When comprised of I-Thou relationships, the political actions of those in the system form what might be termed "genuine communities." In a community based on I-Thou relationships life is precious, suffering is empathetically shared, and the individual differences of its members respected as long as they do not hurt the differences of others.

What is the morality of the political vision of the open democratic society just described? What political goals would represent truth and

goodness and what moral rules of political behavior would be predominant? The political morals of an open, democratic system are based on
moral humanism that stresses the preciousness of human life to all members of the social system and seeks to guarantee individual freedoms and
rights as well as justice based on fairness to all citizens of the system. I reiterate my belief that the psychology described lends itself to the positive
valuation of individual freedoms for all and a justice system based on fairness for all. However, a psychology of I-Thou relationships seems to pre-
dominate, or at least have their best chance of existing, when the citizens
(the term for human beings participating in the political process) of a system demand that the politics of the system be democratic. It is important
to note in this regard that a statement of moral principles is not merely
justified by the descriptive outcomes it might produce (in this case a sur-
plus of I-Thou relationships) but is justified because they are conceived of
as morally right and good.

A democracy guarantees that each and every human being is worthy of
"life, liberty, and the pursuit of happiness" or some variant thereof. There is
an ongoing struggle to define freedom in political terms and usually includes
freedom of speech and communication as basic to the health and morality of
the system. I agree with Isaiah Berlin (1969) that the morality in an open society be based on negative freedom, an individual's right to choose from
among alternatives or options that is unimpeded by others. I agree with Im-
manuel Kant that human beings are never to be treated only as a means to an
end but also as ends in and of themselves.

In a democracy, disputes between citizens are to be adjudicated im-
partially and fairly without regard to a citizen's place or status in the political system. The laws of society, which are attempts to codify a society's
moral system, are agreed to by all participating citizens who then willingly
subordinate themselves to its rule. Individuals accused of violating the rights
and freedoms of others, or otherwise breaking the laws are judged innocent
until proven guilty. A jury of their peers must prove the accused guilty in a
fair, unbiased trial. If found guilty of a crime, punishment must not include
more than the already grave decision to remove a person's freedom. Punishment should never be "cruel and unusual" (as defined by humanistic moral
principles) and include torture and physical and psychological debasement.

I concur with John Rawls (1971) that justice in a political system be
based on fairness rather than on utilitarianism. Individuals must choose to
give up what is theirs for the good of the group, there can be no justification
for the group to force them to do so. In this regard I particularly agree with
Robert Nozick (1974) *that there must be exquisite care taken in justifying forcing
individuals to do things believed to be for their own good.* While there can be no
guarantee of the economic or social success of any individuals within a system, attempts must be made to ensure equal access for all members to suc-

ceed. Those representing authority must be treated equally under the law and as citizens accorded the same rights and fairness as any others.

Another significant aspect of a democratic system involves a respect for the privacy of the individual and those possessions important to individuals. While there can be endless debate as to the extent of personal privacy and property that is appropriate, moral, and legal in any given case, individuals can expect that such debates begin with the assumption that some degree of privacy is a basic human right. Privacy is essential to any discussion of psychology and politics, especially the individuals expectation to privacy within one's home and within one's own person and thoughts. Closely related to the issue of privacy is the issue of free speech. Again, while arguments concerning the limits of free speech are endless, in a democracy such debates take for granted that free speech is a given.

One final note concerning the morality of the open society: Individuals hope to improve themselves and create personal moral and ethical goals defined by an idealized self. Collectively, the citizens of an open society dream and work toward a vision of a more perfect society and hence share a utopian dream. Sowell refers to these visions as "unconstrained," that is, there is a shared faith in human perfectibility. However, both the individuals and the collective realize that they have not and never will realize neither their idealized selves nor their utopian society. Both remain goals guiding moral effort but remain always out of reach. I have not exhausted this topic by any means but I turn to the visions guiding the authoritarian/totalitarian or closed society.

VISIONS OF THE
AUTHORITARIAN/TOTALITARIAN SOCIETY

A closed society is one in which power flows from top to bottom of a vertical, rigidly stratified layering of people. *It is authoritarian to the degree that those who comprise the top layers demand behavioral obedience of those below; it is totalitarian when authority seeks control of the very consciousness of those below.* Such systems are created and maintained with a very different organization of science and morality. A closed system confuses psychological descriptions with moral labels as described earlier. As the moral collapses into the psychological, individuals are described with a series of terms that define them as inherently superior or inferior, one to another.

Those in authority are referred to as "Your Majesty," "Your Lordship," "Your Grace," or even "Master," while those at the bottom are nameless, faceless, and especially voiceless. The wealthier might be seen as superior to the poor, the educated superior to the uneducated, the physically strong superior to the less well endowed, and those physically attractive superior to those judged unattractive. Any biologism, including age or sex, might be used to define moral superiority and inferiority. Religion, ethnic grouping, or any other social categorization might be used to justify superiority of some over others.

Authority rules on the basis of its inherent superiority without need to demonstrate the skills and abilities of leadership. Those with ability do the necessary work of maintaining society but it is the authority at the top that it is credited with achieving necessary goals. As authority becomes ever more idealized it becomes ever more immune to criticism. When authority fails to achieve its responsibilities those lower in inherent value take responsibility for the failures. Those at the bottom of the hierarchy are often those who suffer the most by the social–political policies of the powerful, and it is the victims who are blamed for the ills of the social group. The more tyrannical and dictatorial the leadership, the more it is likely that scapegoats will be constructed by authority to hide their own inadequacies. In an authoritarian structure those at the top can do no wrong, while those at the bottom can do no right except to obey and laud authority.

As long as everyone in the closed society accepts the labels that define them and "remembers their respective places" violence remains tacit and latent. But if individuals forget their place, demand an accounting of their superiors, or request the same economic and political prerogatives, then violence is often the means of settling disputes. It is interesting that if two citizens from the same level of the hierarchy use violence to settle a grievance then a crime has been committed. When authority resolves conflict with the same violence, then "discipline" is being meted out that is "deserved by and good for" its recipient. The goal of discipline is restore "obedience" to authority by the less deserving and "selfish" individuals who have forgotten to "respect" their betters. In this system, however, respect is often confused with the fear or even terror induced by authority's use of discipline.

Little is fair in an authoritarian hierarchy according to the standards of a democratic/humanistic system. The superior beings above deserve more than their inferiors below who always seem to have "brought their misfortune on themselves." In a closed society, relationships between those of different statuses are often "I-It" rather than "I-Thou." Dialogue is replaced by monologue as authority speaks to rather than with its inferiors. The monologues of the self-anointed (Sowell, 1995) are usually moral lectures that constantly remind the inferiors of their duty to improve and emulate their superiors.

The moral lectures of the powerful remind those who must listen that obedience to the forces that control them is the highest of virtues. In this system only the powerful have a right to express or even possess individual differences. Those lower in the social hierarchy are all seen as interchangeable. The expression of individual differences, especially those which would be praised as creative in a democratic system, are seen as breaches of etiquette, expressions of sin or mental illness, or outright punishable offenses in the closed society.

The need for protection and virtue often call for a war against the evil scapegoats. The mobilization of society for war assures the need for a vertical social structure and justifies the leadership's needs for extraordinary means to maintain the social order, control society's economics, and repress political opposition. James Madison wrote, "Of all the enemies to public liberty, war is, perhaps, the most dreaded, because it comprises and develops the germ of every other. War is the parent of armies: from these proceed debts and taxes; and armies, debt and taxes are the known instruments for bringing the many under the domination of the few.... No nation could preserve its freedom in the midst of continual war" (quoted in Szasz, 2001:127). Our society's scapegoats are many but none more terrifying to our citizenry than the mentally ill. The wars against mental illness and drug addiction are the types of permanent warfare that Madison warns us against.

Both morality and science deteriorate rapidly in a political system based on deception. Confusing moral judgments with description is such a deception. Individual liberties and freedoms are denied those considered inferior. The justice system operated exclusively by those in power inevitably favors those higher in the hierarchy over those lower in the political system. Laws are promulgated by those in power and imposed by decree on those who are powerless. The punishment of those who are "rebellious" and disobedient is often severe. Torture and the death penalty are seen as necessary not only to punish wrongdoers but also to make examples of them to others contemplating rebellion. The use of terror as a political tool is widespread in the justice systems of closed societies.

Descriptive, subjective psychology can virtually cease to exist in closed societies where individuals are seen as motivated by their labels rather than their thoughts and feelings. Needs and desires, especially whose satisfaction involves others, can come to be defined as weakness or outright immorality. The needs of people are denied and cease to play an honest role in political decisions. The politicians believe that the citizens need them; the doctors feel the same about their patients and the teachers about their students. Even the master believes that he does not need his slaves but that they require his control to survive. Much of the political activity in the authoritarian/totalitarian society is directed toward crippling and making real the dependence of individuals lower in the social hierarchy on those above them. Unless people come to believe that they are helpless and dependent on those with political power they demand expression of their own needs and the political power to achieve them.

All of the human sciences suffer as well in a closed society. History is replaced by a historicism that describes the current social order as natural and necessary and as the product of forces that cannot either be altered or tampered with. The narrative stories that describe individual efforts of the past as well as the general history of the culture become sacred in nature with the society seen as all good and heroic and enemies as evil and wholly corrupt. It is the transformation of the narratives that people tell each other from stories that concern human beings to myths concerning gods and things that perhaps best defines the difference between the open and the closed society.

The closed society lives by what I call "god-thing" narratives; those concerned with gods and devils, puppets and their masters, and, increasingly in our own society, machines and their engineers and programmers. The end goal of all forms of historicism and discipline is to convince everyone in the political hierarchy that their way of life is both inevitable and morally right and that it is futile and wrong to even contemplate changing it. The narratives of the closed society seek to define the unchanging essence of people and history. Those lowest in the political hierarchy are seen as essentially evil and always in need of social control.

One important feature in the visions of the closed society involves a myth of rewards for obedience to authority. Authoritarian society functions similarly to organized crime engaged in a protection scam. They offer the promise of respite from the terrors of living, especially those which society and those in power have created. Those at the bottom of the social hierarchy are to be convinced that their rewards will be very great indeed if they live a life of faceless, voiceless obedience in the eyes of their superiors. They must see the world through the truths of their masters in order to be doubly rewarded. The first reward is to be preserved from the terror of discipline, the second by promises of pleasures doled out by their betters.

Both free speech and privacy suffer in a closed, authoritarian society. In a totalitarian system where obedience is even expected with regard to thinking and feeling, one finds, in one way or another, the equivalent of George Orwell's thought police. It is expected, and often concluded by the members of totalitarian society, that all individuals will police their own inner consciousness and intrapsychic dialogues. An important facet of totalitarian societies involves the endless surveillance and spying of citizens on each other and their reporting of their observations to authority concerning the disloyalties and crimes of their fellow citizens. It appears to me that in our society teachers and mental health professionals often play the role of authority's spies despite protestations that their goals are to help their charges.

The individuals comprising a closed society believe, either willingly or through coercion, that their political leaders are fully realized beings that have achieved an idealized status. They also believe, or at least publicly maintain, that their society is utopian and along with Dr. Pangloss they insist that they live in the best of all possible worlds. Social critics are not appreciated and those demanding change are cast as either cranks or sick people to be marginalized, or traitors to be dealt with much more harshly. In these societies the citizens keep each other under some form of constant surveillance to see to it that malcontents and other troublemakers do not infect the rest of society with their lies and unhappiness. The closed society is marked by an excess of *ideology* that is unconcerned for the practicalities of daily life and the needs of individuals.

ANARCHY

I close this chapter with a very brief and poorly documented discussion of anarchy, which might be considered a third form of political organization and a viable alternative to both democracy and totalitarianism. *Webster's College Dictionary* defines anarchy in the following way: (1) A state of society without government. (2) Political and social disorder due to the absence of government. (3) A theory that regards the absence of all direct or coercive government as a political ideal and that proposes the cooperative and voluntary association of individuals and groups as the principal mode of organized society. (4) Confusion; chaos; disorder.

It is clear from the literature of self-proclaimed anarchists that their political goals are motivated by two interlocking beliefs. The first is that they have found life under some authoritarian/totalitarian regime intolerable and the second is their faith that all governments sooner or later become authoritarian. In fact, for many anarchists the mere presence of a formal government, even one fairly elected, is proof of authoritarianism. While there has never been a true anarchy except perhaps in the relationships of small numbers of individuals the various anarchists take, on faith, that large numbers of individuals can continue to pursue their own personal goals and simultaneously coordinate their activities and prevent social chaos from developing.

What is missing from my limited reading of the anarchist literature is a blueprint for how such a society might be developed and maintained. I invoke no notion of human nature in my argument against the realistic possibility of a working anarchy. (I reject arguments for or against any type of government based on appeals to human nature for reasons already discussed and for those yet to be developed.)

My first objection to the possibility of a sustained anarchy involves sheer problems in how the activities of large numbers of individuals can be coordinated even if the participants share common goals and a willingness to cooperate by delaying gratification of individual desires for the common good. Consider the predicament of a large number of automobiles traveling from four directions into a busy intersection without traffic lights, stop signs, or a traffic officer. It is impossible for the various drivers to signal their intentions from one to another under these circumstances especially when the speeds of the cars vary and might be considerable. Under such conditions there will be chaos and disrupted patterns of traffic. It would appear that some form of governance is required to simply coordinate activities when conflicts inevitably arise.

My second objection to the possibility of a successful anarchy relates to the problem of children and others either not equal or unwilling to share in the responsibility of organizing and maintaining a social group. It appears to me that the socialization of children involves some degree of governance by parents, teachers, and other adults responsible for their scientific and moral development. My clinical work with children has shown me that children living in an anarchy are, by definition, neglected and abused and represent some of the most difficult personalities with whom to engage. Such children know that they are missing vital love, discipline, and direction in their lives and often seek out gangs and religious cults of extreme authoritarian natures as compensation. In fact, history shows us that the outcome of social anarchy is often compensatory totalitarianism.

Similarly, unless a society lives under the rule of law, those transgressing against society must be brought to justice by the rules established by differing individuals. The twentieth century has seen several attempts to establish economic communes in which there would be equality without enforced governance. Experiments in Russia and China among other nation–states have produced some of the most destructive and vicious dictatorships the world has yet seen. The mass starvation and murder of those refusing to live in these systems were ultimately the products of highly closed and hierarchical cultures and carried out at the dictates and whims of individual politicians and often involved perversions of law and justice. In the end, the personalities to be observed were those of authoritarian systems, not anarchy.

A FINAL WORD

My discussion of the adaptive psychological model and the two political visions were sketchy at best but totally failed to discuss either the actual functioning of such societies or what might be termed the "politics of the individual." For a psychotherapist, teacher, parent, or anyone concerned with individual human consciousness and its development, it is the intrapsychic consequences of life lived in families, schools, hospitals, churches, communities, and countries that are either open or closed, democratic or authoritarian/totalitarian that must be of paramount concern. It will be those individual differences and what might be done about them that will be the main focus of the rest of this book.

However, one final observation is in order. Throughout this chapter I have discussed dualities. The individual and society and the study of politics and psychology (as well as any two disciplines comprising the human sciences) are but two that will precede others that will include discussions of the mind and the body as well as nature and nurture. However, the visions comprising closed and open societies are not dualities but true dualisms even if any given society can be a mixture of both. Life in open and closed political systems is not merely incompatible but in the end incommensurate. The two systems cannot exist in harmony and must oppose each other in principle. They are visions that swear to the destruction of the other and can live in harmony only when a closed society deceives itself into believing it is democratic.

CHAPTER 2

Politics, Religion, and Science

INTRODUCTION

In this chapter I explore the bidirectional relationship of religion and science with democratic/humanistic and authoritarian/totalitarian political systems. I believe that such an analysis is necessary if we are to understand the historical development of our society, in general, and of psychiatry and the struggles between the proponents of open and closed political systems within it, in particular. At the same time I continue to develop the psychologies of those living in closed and open political systems. Religion and science are ubiquitous aspects of virtually all cultures, particularly our own. My thesis is that both organized religion and science can function according to either the visions of the closed or open societies and that the frequent historical conflicts between science and religion occur when either one or both operate in an authoritarian mode. I reiterate that social institutions such as organized religion and science are to be conceived of as dualities with the society that they help configure and which in turn enfolds and shapes their own existence.

My discussion will not pit science against religion but will take a stand against both science and religion when they fail to support democratic and humanistic political processes embracing instead authoritarianism and totalitarianism. In this chapter I will develop the notion that much politically destructive activity in the world has, and is, being perpetrated in the name of both religion and science. I contend that in our current age our democratic institutions are perhaps as much in danger from what calls itself science than religion. I suggest that there are inherent differences between science and religion as social institutions and while I find it important to develop these differences my analysis concerns itself more with open and closed political systems than with religion and science. I admit a bias toward a scientific view of the world, after all this is a book of and for science, but only for a science that is inherently democratic and morally humanistic in its operation.

THE DEVELOPMENT OF COGNITION

In Chapter 1 I introduced the ideas of political visions as sets of usually unexamined notions or discourses that guide political activity. I examined differences in these visions or belief systems as to whether they generated democratic/humanistic or authoritarian/totalitarian forms of political activity. I suggested further that political action and its underlying visions are aspects of human adaptation. I further hypothesized that among other differences that might exist between varying political systems in an open system beliefs and descriptions are kept separate from moral judgments and in a closed system the moral and the descriptive are fused together. I now state that these and other differences in political visions can be understood to involve differences in the styles of cognitive evaluation employed by different individuals.

In my earlier discussion of human adaptation I briefly mentioned, but did not develop, the idea that as human beings struggle with the processes of adaptation their cognitive skill develops and changes in a variety of ways. One reason for cognitive differences to exist between individuals involved in interpersonal political processes involves the development of their cognitive processes. The interpersonal politics of children will differ greatly from those of adults not only because of differences in the number and nature of their previous experiences but because the reasoning process of children are inherently different than those of adults. I believe that one of the unexamined aspects of various visions or discourses involves the style of reasoning utilized by the various individuals participating in the political process. For my analysis of religion and science as political systems to proceed I must further unpack some ideas related to cognitive development. (I believe this discussion is relevant in attempts to understand all political systems.)

The thumbnail sketch provided here is based particularly on the work of Robert Kegan (1982, 1994) and Jean Piaget (1950, 1952, 1954, 1959, 1973, 1975). The reader interested in developing a working familiarity with the wide range of Piaget's oeuvre can begin with the work of Jean Flavell (1968). Piaget suggests that each human being constructs the meaning of the world as they engage in the process of adapting to that world. As persons develop, their continued interaction with the objects, situations, and events that make up their lives changes the nature of the interpretations of those events and the skills with which they deal with them. Satisfying needs and solving problems produces change in the intellectual and cognitive modes that define an individual's definition of reality. Piaget suggested that individuals construct and reconstruct the meaning of their world a potential four times across a lifetime. Infancy is marked by sensorimotor cognition, early childhood by preoperational thought, while later childhood and adulthood are defined by the achievement of concrete and formal operations, respectively.

Without discussing the differences in the four stages of cognitive development outlined by Piaget we can elucidate various interrelated trends in intellectual development across the stages. Among the developmental trends that can be traced as individuals move from less to more mature we can discern the following: A movement from more to less egocentric; from greater to lesser embeddedness in the time and space; from living in a fluid, ever-changing world to one comprised of stable, predictable objects and events; and from cognitions that are literal to those that are abstract. (My use of the expression "from less to more mature" is admittedly both a moral judgment and reflects the bias of my political beliefs.)

The younger the developing person, the more egocentric the individual. Egocentrism is defined as the inability of a person to take the viewpoint of another. Infants demonstrate an extreme form of egocentrism before they develop object permanence defined as the ability to recognize that objects continue to exist even when the infants are not in perceptual contact with them. At the mature end of development individuals recognize that the very large universe of which they are an infinitely tiny piece will go on very nicely when they have died and ceased to exist.

There are a number of psychological phenomena related to egocentrism and cognitively less developed individuals that change with development. The less mature the individual, the more they are psychologically embedded in the environment and hence are unable to separate their thoughts, emotions, and motives from the objects and events external to them. The inability to make this separation also involves interpersonal relationships. I assume as do a number of psychoanalytic theorists such as Jessica Benjamin (1998) and Steven Mitchell (2000) that the human being begins life as part of an interpersonal matrix of feelings and must learn to experience a separation between self and others. Socially, egocentric children recognize only their own needs, often confusing them with the needs and emotional demands made by others.

The more mature the individual, the better able the individual to understand their own thoughts and feelings as separate from the thoughts and feelings of others. Equally important, especially for the politics that define human relationships, with maturation individuals become capable of empathic identification of the needs of others.

For the very young the inanimate world is perceived as animated and filled with human (or animal) feelings, thoughts, and motives. Trees moving in a breeze, the back and forth of the tides, and the movements of heavenly bodies are all invested with the qualities of biological and psychological beings. Similarly, all natural events are experienced by those dominated by preoperational thought as having a teleological purpose and of being capable of seeking to satisfy human needs and moral purposes. Moreover, nature appears capable of acknowledging the presence and needs of humanity and of making moral judgments concerning human political activity.

With continued development children become capable of object constancy, which involves comprehending that the mass of an object is unrelated to its shape. Still later the child learns to represent the object world internally and begins to develop imaginary processes. With representation the child can develop operations, defined by Piaget as mental acts with reversibility. The ability of individuals to reverse themselves cognitively involves a number of related activities. They can make mental comparisons between what is and what was and therefore can begin to conceive of what will be. The same comparisons can involve the moral and therefore 'what should be' as well. Reversibility also allows the developing individuals to overcome the tendency to center on a very limited number of aspects of a visual field and by decentering perception include many more qualities of objects when making comparisons and building stable categories of objects and events.

As the external world is represented symbolically the mental operations of the individuals become more complex and powerful. The development of formal operations permits individuals to think about themselves and others as stable entities. They learn to question and correct their own psychological processes, including their emotional reactions to the world. The individual becomes better able to separate the experiences of fantasy and reality and become aware that their inner imaginative fantasies are not the same as perceptual experiences of the external or real world. They come to own the psychology of their childhood rather than being that psychology.

Individuals show improved ability to utilize information about the past to make predictions concerning the future. Moreover individuals can form stable categories (concepts) not only about themselves but also about others and even the relationship between themselves, others, and even society itself. Individuals can now understand the differences between the animate and living objects and those which are inanimate and without life processes. They can now divest the object world of their emotions and motives and understand that the natural world is neither alive nor endowed with teleological aspirations.

Still another related characteristic of developing cognition involves the move from the literal to the abstract. Infants can deal only with the actual objects that comprise their world through direct sensory contact with them.

Later they will be able to symbolically represent their world but only through the use of images of those actual objects. Still later, words and numbers will be used to represent whole categories of objects and activities and, finally, individuals learn to imaginatively transform their symbols from what is to what might be. It is the power to move imaginatively from one time and place to another, to move from worlds known to those which are as yet unknown, and to be able to transform the landscapes, horizons, and events that make up one's world, which defines mature creative artistic and scientific activity.

The less mature the thought processes, the more individuals live in the moment without awareness of past or future. The construction of a stable and constant time line in which there is a historical past and probabilistic future is one of the important achievements of maturing cognitive development allowing individuals to live in more than a moment conceived of as forever. Equally important is the development of operations that permit individuals to seriate concepts, whether descriptive or moral, and thereby understand subtle differences between ideas rather than see more as the most, less as the least, good as the best, and bad as the worst. *A politics based on perceptions that individuals are the best or worst for all time is a politics of the closed society and one difficult to move to a politics of an open society.*

I contend that the development of democratic political structures paralleled the widespread development of individuals capable of mature cognitive activity in a Piagetian sense. In Western society the Enlightenment and the scientific revolution were defined by a movement within the general population from cognitive activity describable as preoperational to those understood to be formally operational. What philosophers, scientists, and even a growing number of artists referred to as "reason" involved the developing hegemony of the use of formal operations. Individuals who still utilized preoperational logic in a majority of their adaptive struggles were increasingly referred to as "irrational" and as "mentally ill." I will return to these themes later and at that time discuss my theoretical beliefs as to why individuals might not develop cognitively along those lines demanded by their culture and the cultural biases and prejudices that these beliefs represent.

RELIGION

I believe that science and religion exist for exactly the same adaptive reasons. Both originated as attempts to describe, explain, predict, and control the events and situations that confront human beings as they live their lives. Both exist because they are perceived to be necessary to lengthening and improving human existence. While the goals of the two enterprises are the same, their underlying assumptions and means of inquiry tend to be radically different. Science, and by that term I refer to the modern Western version of science, emerged historically from religion via philosophy whose history can be seen as one moving from the religious to the secular. While it is beyond the expectations of this book to create a genuine history of either science or religion some historical discussion is required. (For a brief history of religion, see Karen Armstrong, 1994.)

My position is that the majority of our historical forbears lived in a world in which perception and thought conformed to what Piaget described as "preoperational." It was a world in which the inanimate was perceived as animate and possessed of human qualities and motives. Our ancestors lived in a world of magic in which thoughts were real and the physical and psychological were interchangeable. Nature endlessly transformed itself with each natural event motivated by its own will conceived in human terms. Our forbears experienced the present as fused with both the past and the future making the now into forever. For the most part thinking was literal and the past and the future fused into the present. Moral judgments separated the good from the bad, the good seen as perfectly good and the bad as eternally and thoroughly bad.

Religion began when human beings first realized how fragile and helpless they were in the face of nature's fury and how short-lived they were even under the most supportive of conditions. Driven by a need to deal with the terror of suffering and death and an awareness of the inherent injustice of life as individuals competed with one another for the means of continued existence, humanity began to negotiate with the forces of nature made in the image of themselves. They created gods partly in their own image. But these gods were free of those human qualities judged to be shortcomings in the struggle for survival and justice. *The gods were omniscient, omnipotent, omnipresent, and morally perfect.* They were seen as the fountain of explanation as to how things worked and as the source of justice and morality in all human affairs. In this matrix of beliefs, politics involved dealing with nonhuman and superhuman authority figures. The political goal of each individual and each collective involved getting the gods on one's side.

Erich Fromm (1950) suggests that throughout human history religions came into existence in protest against earlier religions that had become authoritarian, oppressive, and especially corrupt. Those who spoke with, to, or for the gods often seemed to have little problem justifying their use of political power in creating adaptive advantages over their fellow citizens. Newer religions were defined by democratic and humanistic practices until they too grew oppressive and demonstrated politics reflective of closed societies. Why does this evolution take place? I will not attempt an answer at this juncture and even when I do I will not provide a very satisfying explanation as to why most organized religions become authoritarian and totalitarian and generate closed societies.

If we examine the progression of development through the Judeo-Christian religions we see a constant professing of humanistic and democratic ideals: "All men are brothers" and "Do unto others as you would have others do unto you," as well as the Ten Commandments demand for the epitome of politics reflective of the open society. The Jewish struggle for universal justice was followed by Jesus Christ's entreaties for universal love, forgiveness, redemption, and especially freedom of conscience and faith. Yet in the end political practices flew in the face of the expressed ideals.

Established religion seems to become hierarchical over time as the clergy charged with the interpretation of scripture become convinced that they speak for God(s) and are inherently more knowledgeable and morally perfect than those they lead. For example, Seth Farber (1998) describes the evolution of the visions of Christianity from one based on a vision of love and freedom to one in which humanity is guilty of original and ineradicable sin making freedom impossible. By the fourth century A.D. Augustine was preaching that "original sin was as universal and inevitable as life itself," and "The infant is bad: though little, he is already a great sinner" (quoted in Farber, 1998:52). In the centuries that followed, the notion of inherent human depravity grew, reaching its peak between 1400 and 1700 with Luther and Calvin. Calvin is quoted as saying, "Infants bring their own damnation with them from their mother's wombs; the moment they are born their natures are odious and abominable to God" (quoted in Farber, 1998:74).

Can such sinful, depraved creatures be trusted with freedom and the responsibility for their own lives? Obviously not! The clergy must, in fact, be responsible for saving ordinary people from themselves. The church was required to become totalitarian and see to it that all impure thoughts and feelings were controlled and destroyed. Farber (1998) points out that as the secular political state grew more powerful the church forged alliances with the kings and emperors and added secular authority to the lists of the holy and those anointed by God to lead. Can there be any more powerful justification for maintaining a hierarchical society than one in which the leaders speak for an authority all- knowing, all-powerful, and all righteous? Based on a literal god-thing narrative a society allows the whim of tyrants to become the word of God(s).

It is important to note that it takes most or all of the citizens of a society to create and maintain an authoritarian, closed society. Those who speak as if they were gods or anointed by gods must be accepted as having the powers and moral purity that they claim to possess by those seeking the protection and justice of superhuman figures. As in all closed societies, once authority takes power it tends to become increasingly hostile to those who resist and challenge their authority. Those in power increasingly and extravagantly paint themselves as wise and perfectly moral, while those lowest in the social hierarchy are defined as ever more abject and inadequate. Since human beings can never have the powers or moral purity of god(s) and those individuals treated as things are never as inadequate or evil as they are painted, any discussion that suggests otherwise is deadly to those in power. Any expression of genuine humanity is a threat to the justification of a society based on authoritarian/totalitarian politics.

In any religious grouping there are always those whose prayers are for peace and the strength to be kind and understanding toward their fellow human beings. In every such grouping individuals have their lives given meaning by religion and discover the strength to achieve noble and important moral goals. Culture thrives as individual differences are permitted to express themselves both creatively and artistically. There are always those who practice the Golden Rule that idealistically underpins most, if not all, of the great religions of the world.

But at the same time there are those whose prayers are for victory and domination over those considered sinful and evil. These individuals seek to solidify power by creating enemies even when no real enemies present themselves. Often the declared enemies of those in power, and hence of gods, are any individuals who seek to displace, criticize, or even question the authority of those who rule as gods with godlike qualities. The history of religion seems to have been written by those seeking to rule through a god-thing narrative rather than those, usually isolated and powerless individuals, seeking democratic/humanistic forms of religious politics.

Between the fourth and fifteenth centuries A.D., Western Europe fit the definition of an authoritarian, closed society. Except for art approved of by the church individual self-expression was treated as heresy. Scapegoats abounded both within and without Europe. The crusades were attempts to wrest control of the Near East from the "barbarian and heretical" Islamic community. (It is interesting to note that in our modern era theocratic Muslim governments speak of those in the West as "The Great Satan" and demand jihad, or holy war, on those who centuries before persecuted them, a belief that of this writing threatens to embroil the whole planet in a cultural world war.) The Jews of Europe began to experience increased religious hostility and intolerance, culminating in the expulsion of the Jews from Spain and the institution of the Inquisition. Anyone challenging the truth of religious doctrine could be tortured and put to death in order to save them from themselves. In the search for scapegoats and the endless need to silence heresy, endless wars wracked the face of Europe.

Perhaps no one has brought the differences between the visions of democratic/humanistic and authoritarian/totalitarian forms of religion more clearly to light as well as make real the themes I have been developing than Dostoyevsky (1995) in *The Brothers Karamazov*. In a chapter entitled "The Grand Inquisitor" the author describes the reappearance of Jesus Christ in Seville on a day in the sixteenth century when over one hundred heretics are burned to death for the benefit of the king and his entourage and the education of the assembled masses. The Grand Inquisitor watches as Christ performs miracles convincing the crowd that he is indeed the Messiah and has Him arrested. In the monologue of the Inquisitor to a silent Jesus we are able to clearly see all of the intellectual and moral justifications of the visions of a closed society.

The Inquisitor is a righteous man, completely convinced of the correctness of his beliefs. He sees himself as selfless and perfectly moral. While others with whom he is aligned might seek personal adaptive advantage through their political control over the masses of people at the lower levels of the social hierarchy, the Inquisitor is motivated by a surfeit of morality. He knows what is good for the people he leads even more than Jesus who speaks the word of God. The Inquisitor has placed himself above the God he is sworn to serve. He speaks for the masses of humanity. He refers to the masses, terrified of their church and the Inquisitor, as his "flock." The common use in religion of referring to people as sheep and the church as their shepherd makes clear not only a severe social hierarchy but justifies the church's use of power to control the faithful.

The Inquisitor berates Jesus for his faith that humanity can go without bread for the sake of reaching higher moral goals. He scorns Him for his belief that they can live with the guilt engendered by knowing good from evil, and most important, that they can live as individuals who, in choosing freedom, take responsibility for their own lives. The Inquisitor demands that Jesus accept his essentialist view that people are "weak, base, and vile" and that what they really want is *miracle, mystery! and authority*" (p. 266; emphasis in original). They seek the safety of a mob in which individuality does not exist and which moves according to the dictates of a powerful authority. Those in the mob fear real understanding, especially of God, and seek instead miracles that will lift the pain of life from their shoulders. They seek explanations that shroud the truth of their lives in mystery; in effect real science and genuinely creative art is their enemy and hence define heresy. The Inquisitor makes clear that the war against heresy must continue until the entire world is under the domination of the true church.

With these attitudes the Grand Inquisitor foreshadows George Orwell's (1949) horrific vision of the world of "1984" in which the slogans of the state are WAR IS PEACE, FREEDOM IS SLAVERY, and IGNORANCE IS STRENGTH. Armed with the power of the state the Inquisitor invokes the slogan "It is God's will" to explain and justify not only all natural events but also every political action taken by those in power. He invokes a religious historicism that defines as both inevitable and morally perfect every decision he and those at the top of the political hierarchy make to invoke terror in the masses, keep them ignorant and impoverished, and create for them the very purpose of their existence. Moreover, the Inquisitor sees the course of human history in teleological terms. It is a course created by God and directed to the moral perfection of all humanity.

Like all dictators and tyrants, the Inquisitor believes he understands human nature completely (and invokes the scientistic concept of human nature as part of his historicism) without any insight into the effects his politics have on the people and society in which he rules. The Inquisitor cannot begin to question his belief that human beings are inherently afraid of political freedom. He cannot imagine that his flock does not freely accept the tortures and abuses of the church. In short, he will not entertain the possibility that their behavior is a function of the political processes he controls rather than of their "human nature." The Inquisitor is the ultimate expert on 'what is' and 'what should be.'

What is the goal of the Inquisitor in terms of the psychology of his flock? Clearly, he demands behavioral obedience to the moral dictates of the church, especially of the vile and lowly commoners and serfs at the bottom of the social structure. However, the Inquisitor demands obedience in their beliefs as well. The flock must see the world through the eyes of its church. The 'what is' and 'what ought to be' expressed through the dogma of the church must be perfectly mirrored in the minds of the flock. How was this to be achieved? The church in the first millenium A.D. pioneered a method of mind control through a combination of techniques involving the confession of sin and the induction and relief of terror.

The Roman Catholic Church's rise in power (culminating in the Inquisition whose tyranny and corruption can be said to have contributed to the Protestant Reformation) involved convincing the public that their sinfulness was as great for bad thought as it was for bad behavior. God not only watched what you did but what you thought and felt as well. God punished evil thinking and feeling as well as evildoing. From early childhood the populace was told increasingly lurid and horrific tales of punishments that were to be meted out for sinful thoughts, emotions, and desires of the flesh. These horrific punishments would take place in hell and the torture would go on forever. Hell was described in detail as a place of fire, and of endless pain and suffering. If a person died in sin, eternal suffering was their lot. But if their souls and minds were pure and free of sin then eternity was spent in heaven, a glorious place of peace, plenty, and eternal life.

The specific mechanism of thought purification was the confessional in which a priest heard confession, not as a man but as the true agent of God. The confessing individual engaged in an endless ritual of self-examination in which impure thoughts were confessed and forgiven in the confessional. If individuals did not confess and repent of their sins then it might be assumed that a demon, the devil, or some other evil force had taken control of their soul. To save the souls of heretics, witches, and other fallen individuals, torture would have to be applied until a confession was forthcoming.

The burning of heretics was done as a test of the effectiveness of the torture and other exorcisms of the evil forces controlling an individual. If the person burned they were innocent and free of evil. Individuals who confessed prior to burning would be strangled to death so as to spare them the horrors of the fire. Those failing to confess were burned alive. The Inquisition had a 100 percent success rate in saving souls!

The demand for confession of sin had an important political function beyond assuring control of the thought processes of errant individuals. Unless individuals accepted the church's definition of sin and the reality of possession by evil spirits the church lost its moral justification to maintain the confessional and the political machinations representing the Inquisition. The Grand Inquisitor, like any other human being, must be able to justify his claims to perfect knowledge and perfect morality. He must enlist the full cooperation of those he controls in this effort. Otherwise his flock becomes his victims rather than his beneficiaries. This same mechanism operates in the mental health industry's demand that patients accept their status as mentally ill or disordered.

It must be noted that in the long history of religious authoritarianism, women were generally placed lower in the moral hierarchy than men. God has generally been given a male persona. It was Eve who was punished for her seduction of Adam in eating of the fruit of the tree of good and evil. The Hebrew covenant with God was made with Abraham and not with his wife Sarah. The covenant was sealed with the ritual circumcision, forever preventing women from achieving parity with men in the eyes of God. God had a son and no daughters. Most of those tortured and burned during the Inquisition were women. There has never been a female allowed to play the role of Inquisitor, or even a humble priest. I will return to this theme several times, but especially when I discuss the role of feminism in the modern struggles to democratize psychoanalysis.

I do not mean to imply in this discussion that in my opinion human beings do not behave wrongfully and that society does not have the right to not only punish wrongdoing but to seek ways to prevent its occurrence. The use of religious dogma and authority to achieve a moral society either by creating a political system that is frankly religious or a secular system guided by religious principles can certainly be justifiable in both moral and descriptive terms. Similarly, a system that encourages individuals to confess wrongdoing to alleviate guilt, seek forgiveness from others wronged, and restore damaged relationships makes sense for both individuals and groups.

Patrick Glynn (1994) has argued that confession and forgiveness be considered important categories in any political process. My argument has to do with the creation of a theocracy that crushes the inherent humanity, individuality, and freedoms of most of its citizens in the name of religion. The notion that thoughts are evil, observed by supernatural forces, and must regularly be monitored and confessed destroys any notion of real privacy and creativity. My commitment to a liberal democracy based on humanistic principles compels me to condemn in principle any totalitarian system, even one justifying itself in the name of god(s) and religion.

SCIENCE

The various modern formal scientific enterprises arose in Europe as an integral part of a wide number of societal changes that might be termed "revolutionary." I attempt no accurate historical discussion of these changes but suggest that they include the Protestant Reformation already mentioned, the Age of Reason, and the Enlightenment, with its huge increase of secular philosophers, artists, writers, and painters. I. Bernard Cohen (1985) argues that the scientific revolution was part of a vast explosion of ideas and new knowledge that was synonymous with new definitions of what human beings were and how they should be governed. I concentrate on the rise of science and its various interactions with the political landscape.

At the heart of the scientific revolution was a growing belief that knowledge was the result of following particular attitudes and methods of inquiry rather than as the product of revelation by authority, particularly divine authority. The newly emerging mode of thought was comprised of several interrelated aspects, all of which had profound political consequences. First, there was an immediate change in the power of the church to define truth and, hence, a shift in political power from the religious to the secular. The God(s) and the Grand Inquisitor would ultimately lose the power to define 'what is' and with it not only much of their credibility but the power to reward or punish with the promise of heaven and hell. Second, the ability to learn shifted from the inherent characteristics of the individual to various methods that anyone could learn. It became widely believed, and to a degree actually practiced, that ordinary individuals could master an understanding of their world and become the intellectual equal of any other individual.

The third aspect of the scientific revolution involved a growing hegemony of formal operations and with it an unavoidable increase in self-awareness. "Science," wrote George Herbert Mead, "was evolution grown self-conscious" (quoted in Mahoney, 1991:118). With the rise of science individuals split their attention, focusing not only on 'what is' but 'how is it to be known?' Questions were not only asked about the objects of knowledge but also about the means employed by the knower to know. The scientific revolution simultaneously became a psychological revolution with profound intellectual, moral, and political consequences.

By shifting attention to the modes of inquiry used to understand the world, human beings created and began to formalize a new political and moral discourse, one between individuals and themselves. Individuals asking What are the rules of science to be? inevitably also ask What *should* the rules of science be? What is the most effective way for me to think? evolves into What *should* my thinking be like, how *should* my relationship to myself take shape, and how *should* I relate to both the physical and the social world? The changes in moral–political relationships motivated by such questions are too vast to be considered in any but the cursory way that follows. But it is worth noting that no human relationship went unquestioned and all rules governing power were subject to change and disruption.

The use of formal operations drastically reduced the view that the natural world was animated by humanlike motivations and was replaced by the idea that nature could be understood to be a passive mechanism with moving parts and processes capable of being dissected and analyzed. Religious dogma that defined eternal, absolute truth was replaced by theory (sophisticated educated guesses), that were to be tested by observation, experimentation, and a variety of other techniques. *One of the hallmarks of all forms of science involves rejecting any and all explanations of causality based on any notion of the supernatural. All explanations have to be based on purely naturalistic phenomena.* Indeed the religious beliefs in the supernatural were often derided as superstition. Sigmund Freud even went so far as to call religious belief "neurosis," a form of mental illness. Karl Marx referred to religion as the "opiate of the masses."

Science at its best forced its practitioners to live with endless doubt and the notion that all theories were eventually to be found wanting and would be replaced as newer information invalidated even the most loved theoretical formulations. Scientists accepted as routine that both the methods and the results of their efforts would be published in journals and both would be open to the critique of colleagues and any other interested parties. Philosophers such as Karl Popper (1961) and Richard Rorty (1991) make clear that open dialogue between peers became the accepted moral of practicing science. Science at its best not only flourishes in but also creates an inherently democratic atmosphere.

Science increasingly became defined by methods of inquiry that were empirical in nature. The empirical attitude demands that the object of scientific interest come under direct observation of the scientific practitioner. The validity of a scientific claim was based on the shared observations of particular phenomena, rather than on the moral status of the claimant. Armchair philosophy and speculation gave way to increasingly sophisticated means of defining and observing the subject matter that could become the object of scientific study. The use of laboratory experiments in which the effects of one variable on another could be isolated and controlled was developed. Rigorous experimentation was added to the growing use of naturalistic observation, surveys, and a host of other techniques to study any and all aspects of the physical and social world with which human beings interacted. The large and the small, the near and the distant, the inner and the outer all became objects of human curiosity and critical evaluation.

One of the developing hallmarks of scientific thought, and one of its most complex and ambiguous, was the demand for objectivity. Objectivity has had a variety of definitions, some of which enhanced democratic thinking. Bertrand Russell (1948) has argued that the prime function and power of science was its objectivity or ability to prevent individuals from seeing the world in terms of their wishes and desires. The shift to an empirical attitude and the requirement that scientific thought be based on reason (logic defined by formal operations) created an implicit (and sometimes explicit) rule that either a theory or explanatory law avoid any reliance on the supernatural. God(s), angels, evil spirits, miracles, and any other and all appeals to supernatural dualisms were to be rejected and replaced with purely naturalistic explanations. As mentioned, the supernatural was now to be considered merely the product of human wish fulfillment and nothing more. If human beings were to maintain a social hierarchy based on moral values the supernatural could no longer be invoked to justify it.

Moreover, if causes were naturalistic and impersonal their effects had no moral significance. The job of science was description, explanation, prediction, and control *but not judgment*! The scientist was an individual who must remain impartial and nonjudgmental concerning the objects and phenomena to which he attended. It is clear to me that this aspect of objectivity involves maintaining a separation between description and morality. It does not mean being morally uncritical about one's work or its consequences, a potentially dangerous situation.

Another hallmark of science involved the increased use of technology to study the natural world. The use of the telescope and the microscope profoundly changed human understanding of the world that humanity inhabited. Technology used to master and tame nature became synonymous with scientific activity. For the first time in human history scientifically generated technology freed huge masses of human beings from stoop labor and permitted human beings to ascend to the very pinnacle of the food chain. Humanity could have lunch without being lunch. For the first time in human history great masses of ordinary people had the leisure time to read, study, and develop artistic, spiritual, athletic, scientific, or any other interests. With the development of the scientific and psychological revolutions, individuals became the objects of their own interests and the improvement of the self became the overarching concern of millions.

The combination of scientific inquiry and technological evolution transformed agriculture, transportation, communications, medicine, and every other human institution and endeavor. Science and technology became synonymous with the idea of human progress. People were living longer and, in the opinion of many, much better and richer lives. Science's most spectacular success was defined by a new ability to define and control infectious disease. By the end of the eighteenth century secular universities became the recognized source of knowledge and human expertise. The goal of a formal, secular, and scientifically based education became the basis for defining the educated person. Even fields such as politics, the organization of society, and the relationship of the individuals to themselves and society became defined as "the social sciences" and became open to critical inquiry. The Grand Inquisitor found himself being increasingly removed from the center of political power and replaced by secular experts now known as "scientists" and "engineers." Openness of information, debate among and between peers, naturalistic theorizing, and objectivity increasingly defined both the statistical and the moral norm of human relationships.

Both the content of the new arts and sciences as well as the expansion of voices demanding to be heard led to the rise of moral humanism, in which humanity and not gods became the standard of right and wrong. Historians greatly increased their descriptions of the role of the "common" people in the accounts of those who shaped society and history. Art focused on ordinary individuals as well as the more politically and economically powerful, and its themes included the secular and profane as well as the religious. Any individuals following the emerging rules of scientific inquiry and their own curiosity could become experts on what is. An explosion of literacy and inexpensive and easily available written material allowed any individual to become an expert on what should be. The American and then the French Revolutions grew out of the intellectual and social ferment of the fifteenth, sixteenth, and seventeenth centuries and with them the emergence of popularly based democratic forms of government.

By the end of the nineteenth century the philosopher Friedrich Nietzsche declared God to be dead and the poet Stephen Crane would write:

> A man said to the universe:
> "Sir, I exist!"
> "However," replied the universe,
> "The fact has not created in me
> A sense of obligation."

In short, much of the power to say 'what is' passed to secular intellectuals and with that power the ability to justify 'what should be.'

However profound the changes in attitude that define the rise of science, the revolution these changes represent remain embedded in their historical roots. These changes not only created conflict with the predominant social and religious modes of understanding the nature and function of the natural and social world but set standards of behavior that did not sit well with many of those referring to themselves as scientists. As a result there was still not only conflict over how to define the boundary between science and nonscience, but also great difficulty as well in living up to any of the accepted tenets of what constituted good science. The scientific revolution remained incomplete and in many ways became the basis of newer and even more authoritarian/totalitarian politics.

Scientists are no more or less human than any other individuals with whom they struggle to adapt. They are no less afraid of death and can be intimidated by those in power no less easily than their fellow citizens. Moreover, they are as easily seduced by the rewards they receive by joining with and using their skills to increase the political power of grateful authorities. They are no less desirous of being certain of their knowledge, especially in the face of questions and problems that do not yield up their answers easily. As human beings, scientists wish to defeat death and others defined as enemies and have the same needs to protect their children and other loved ones from the ravages of uncontrolled nature, famine, war, disease, pestilence, and whatever other "horsemen of the apocalypse" might create suffering. *Therefore, scientists too, have found ways to create god-thing narratives to guide their lives and define their politics.*

From the beginning of science's rise to power, scientists revealed both intrapersonal and interpersonal conflict about the lives they would have to live if they carried out the moral and ethical dictates of being a scientist. Dava Sobel (2000) documents these conflicts in the life of Galileo, one of the first true pioneers of the new science. She makes clear that however excited Galileo was in exploring the heavens with a telescope and carrying out empirical studies on the motion of bodies here on Earth, he was forever fearful of being declared a heretic by the church and being brought before the Inquisition. Moreover, Galileo was also a man of deep faith who saw no conflict between studying the motion of bodies and the astronomical placement of the planets and the existence of a divine and all-powerful creator. For him "the bible was a book about how one goes to heaven—not how heaven goes" (Sobel, 2000:67).

It is clear from this that Galileo could differentiate between the metaphorical, supernatural heaven involved in morality and the literal, naturalistic heaven that makes up the physical world. But Galileo did run afoul of the Inquisition when Pope Urban VIII found himself in political difficulties and felt he could ill afford to look weak in the eyes of his many followers whose preoperational view of heaven did not permit the luxury of Galileo's dichotomy. In the end Galileo was found guilty of heresy and recanted his "error" in upholding Copernicus's view of a heliocentric universe in which the Earth moved around the Sun. (Copernicus, himself, had died as the soldiers of the Inquisition were on their way to arrest him.) Galileo feared the political wrath of the church as well as the loss of his metaphorical heaven.

The same conflicts involving his position to church and God beset René Descartes as they did Galileo. Descartes is often cited as one of the founders of modern science. Ian Hacking (1995) reveals that Descartes conceived of the human body and the rest of the natural world as belonging to one plane of existence and the human soul as belonging to another and higher plane. The soul was able to manipulate the body and interact with the physical world by means of the pineal gland to which it was attached. Mental activity had its source in the soul and it was the separation and elevation of the soul over the physical world that provided the basis and justification of his notion of scientific objectivity.

In this scenario objectivity is not achieved by controlling wish-fulfilling desires, separating description from judgment, or by the free discussion of different points of view but by the inherent superiority of mind over matter. With Descartes's failure to avoid a supernatural dualism, in this instance, between the scientist and the object world, the seeds of a new version of an old hierarchy were sown. While Descartes's "soul" would eventually be attacked as mere superstition, scientists retained the notion that they stood on a platform from which they and they alone were privileged to see Truth. They did this by investing the so-called scientific method with mythical qualities and powers it could never have. By employing these methods the observing scientist believed that he had a perfectly transparent window through which to observe reality and make truth statements. The scientist, with his new status and power in society, thereby became the secular mirror image of the Grand Inquisitor as the source of perfect and incontrovertible wisdom.

Thomas Kuhn (1970) created a furor when he described the commitment of scientists to maintain their theories even in the face of damning anomalous evidence. He suggests that normal science rarely is defined by open-minded scientists following Popper's (1961) first rule of science to discard theories that either cannot be tested or are confronted with objective evidence that run counter to the theories' predictions. Instead, Kuhn argues, scientists tend to discount or ignore evidence that runs against their theories or else tinker with the theory to incorporate the newly observed evidence. Scientific revolutions occur when scientists grow old, retire, and die, or when pushed out by younger scientists. It is closed mindedness, pride, and wish fulfillment that generally mark the normal processes of science.

One of the consequences of an authoritarian political process within a given field of science often involves defining science with a particular method of study. The rigid use of a particular method can stultify science, especially if it is inappropriate in relation to its subject matter. I will return to this theme in Chapter 3 where I suggest that mainstream psychology defined itself as a science based on the use of methodologies that worked perfectly well in physics and chemistry but violated the basic subject matter of psychology, namely, human consciousness and the subjective self. In fact, psychology's reliance on what is referred to as "*the* scientific method" did not even allow human subjectivity to be studied from an empirical point of view. I raise this issue at this juncture to make clear that my personal use of the word *science* refers to a set of attitudes discussed previously and not merely to a particular set of methods.

The study of early science reveals a constant battle between contradictory forces within science creating and supporting both open and closed political systems. R. D. Laing (1982) writes of Sir Francis Bacon, who is credited with establishing many of the methodological procedures of the physical sciences, "We are beyond the still very human lack of gallantry of the Renaissance Francis Bacon. For him 'nature is a lady.' She is 'not to be left free and at large.' We must constrain and vex her. Then 'when by art and the hand of man she is forced out of her natural state and squeezed and moulded she may tell us what we want to know'" (p. 21). Susan Griffin (1995), quoting this same passage, differs from Laing's conclusion that the scientist is depicted as nature's torturer and casts her interpretation from a feminist perspective. Passages such as these reveal science to be nature's rapist. The mostly male scientists who think in these terms can do nothing but harm to nature and women who are seen as inferior beings to men.

Not only was the evolving notion of objectivity invested with an inherent moralistic dualism but for many scientists objectivity also meant divesting science from any and all human emotions and perspectives. The godlike scientist reported his observations in the third person, avoiding any words that reflected personal opinion or emotion. Scientists were supposedly cognitive entities without interests, curiosity, or excitement about their subject matter. Moreover, it is emotion that connects us to the object world and ourselves. A lack of affect also defines a psychological state in which there can be no sympathy, empathy, guilt, shame, or any other emotion that guides and defines moral judgment. To simply say something is morally or ethically wrong in no way commits an individual to a moral or ethical course of action. Moral commitment requires psychological connection and psychological connection requires emotion.

Laing (1982) points out that this version of objectivity turned all the objects of scientific interest into objects without subjectivity including the scientists themselves. More important, he writes, "It is ironical that scientists cannot see the way they see with their way of seeing" (p. 21). Without such self-reflection, scientists, or any other human beings, cannot institute self-correction and fall prey to the same lack of insight that made the Grand Inquisitor and most dictators so politically dangerous to those they are sworn to lead and protect.

Scientists were also pretending to themselves to be without social context, personal histories, political entanglements, ambitions, or day-to-day jobs and lives that had to be lived. Once scientists lose their awareness of personal context they also lose awareness of who pays their salaries and for whom they work. C. Wright Mills (1959) describes how so many scientists and other intellectuals work in large, bureaucratic organizations without ever asking themselves either about the politics and social policies of these organizations or the ultimate effect the organizations have on the millions they serve.

As long as the subject matter of scientific study involved objects such as falling balls, spinning planets, interacting chemicals, or even biological organs, the net effect of objectivity violated only the subjectivity of the scientist. When the objects of scientific scrutiny involved human beings (and even in certain cases animals) the inherent subjectivity of individuals is completely ignored. When people are turned into objects or things their inherent humanity is denied. As a result of this posture the scientific enterprise has been, for much of its history, either the source or the accompaniment of human terror and horror. I document only a few of the dehumanizing roles played by modern science since its rise in popularity and power.

Playing god with human beings turned truly deadly as scientists joined the political processes involved with war and the defense of nations. Not only are scientists often afraid of the charge of treason if they do not produce weapons of mass destruction for their governments but they are as motivated by the fervor of patriotism as any other group of citizens. Jacob Bronowski (1963) gives voice to the role played by so-called objective scientists when he writes, "Science has created evil by amplifying the tools of war while scientists have taken no moral stance on their use or production. Scientists did not create or maintain war but they have changed it. They have engaged in acting the mysterious stranger, the powerful voice without emotion, the expert, the god" (p.142).

Scientists have also allowed their theories to be perverted and twisted for other political purposes. Carl Degler (1991) describes how, during the rise of capitalism, European intellectuals twisted Darwin's theory of evolution into a justification of brutal oppression of people for economic purposes and the maintenance of class hierarchies. Darwin, himself, avoided pursuing the full implications of his own theory that humanity is just another evolutionary accident that developed through the processes of natural selection and neither represents a teleological goal of God or of nature nor has an inherent purpose for its existence. But other scientists, speaking in the universal voice of truth, blinked and declared that mankind was the true end product of nature's labors and the poor were inferior to the rich because of evolutionary processes. (Protestantism had taught that God predetermined who the morally strong and weak were to be before birth and that economic success and failure in business was merely making God's will manifest. Now poor tortured and raped Mother Nature replaced or added to God's will to justify unjust economic and political activities.)

The use of evolution to promote the idea that humanity represents nature's intended goal is but one example of science presenting itself as an inevitable moral necessity. Brian Vandenberg (1993) writes that "our understanding of history shifted from the sacred to the secular, from a concern about salvation to a veneration of progress. Science, it is argued, not only represents the high point of human evolutionary progress but its theories and applications are inherently progressive. How many of our citizens today challenge the notion that technology represents progress and exemplifies the moral best in humanity?" (p. 192). How often does a new medical treatment get reported by the media as a "medical miracle"? Is there any significant awareness that the saving of our immortal souls by religion has been replaced by a doctrine of scientific progress that claims it will cure all the ills of our minds and bodies? I suggest that this authoritarian doctrine makes science a most dangerous political force.

It is simply beyond the scope of this discussion, whose goal is to establish the context of psychiatry as a totalitarian system and a pseudoscience, to do justice to the destructive role played by science and scientists in the recent history of human politics. The participation of well-respected and well-recognized scientists were involved in the creation of the scientistic concept of race as well as maintaining so many of the sexist myths used to justify controlling the lives of women. Eugenics, the science to improve the genetic quality of the human race, has had and still involves the enthusiastic participation of many scientists.

One of the most troubling authoritarian uses of science can be found in the twentieth-century theories involving eugenics and the use of science to improve the human race by preventing inferior human beings from procreating. Robert Whitaker (2002) provides a detailed and horrifying summary of how entrenched this supposedly scientific set of ideas became in Western science and in biology and medicine in particular. The full flowering of eugenics can be found in Hitler's death camps but the horrendous treatment of the mentally ill in Europe and the United States can be understood in terms of the eugenicist's perception of the mentally ill as morally inferior due to inferior germ plasm.

Scientists have been at the forefront of the intolerable totalitarian and dehumanizing economic and political policies that have marked the twentieth century and turned much of its history into that of a charnel house. The Holocaust, with the systematic slaughter of 13 million human beings, of which 6 million were Jews, was a marvel of scientific thinking and technological precision. We know that Stalin employed the scientific community to torture and "rehabilitate" those who rejected his version of the perfect worker's state in ways well described by George Orwell in *1984*.

But for the purposes of understanding psychiatry I close this chapter by briefly turning to the problems created when medical practitioners speak in the objective voice of the godlike scientist, serve large bureaucratic governmental agencies or profit-making corporations, and refuse to ask whose political and economic needs they might be serving. Medicine is the link between the biological, social, and psychological sciences. Physicians are the emissaries from the world of science to that of everyday life and have achieved a level of respect and power once possessed by the clerics of the major religions. How medicine treats those it serves and the role it plays in the politics of human affairs matters greatly.

Merely a century ago the physician's main role involved reducing the suffering of patients while holding to the Hippocratic oath to first do no harm. Since then the role of the physician, and medicine in general, has greatly expanded to include the cure and prevention of disease as well as the general extension of the life span. It has not been empirically established just how much modern medicine has prolonged or improved our lives but the general consensus in our society is that we depend for our very lives on the medical profession. Every aspect of human growth and development is enfolded in a variety of medical rituals. People may well pray to God when they become ill but their prayers are usually uttered on the way to the doctor's office or hospital. A sick person or the frightened parent of an ill child often invests the doctor with the powers of life and death and might demand of the physician more than he knows or can realistically deliver.

T. M. Luhrmann (2000) describes the training of medical residents in large teaching hospitals in terms very similar to my own experiences while I worked in psychiatric clinics and provided seminars for medical residents. The young doctors work long hours under difficult conditions providing services to often desperately ill and frightened people. They are fully aware that errors in judgment can carry lethal consequences. Their supervision is fully authoritarian and seems to follow a logic that the best way to help doctors learn to avoid mistakes is to induce fear, fatigue, and intense humiliation if an error is discovered. A hospital is a model of a hierarchical society in which senior doctors stand at the apex, the medical nurses far beneath them, followed by the orderlies and the maintenance staff. Given the authoritarian circumstances and so much to gain and lose it is no wonder that the young residents adopt the stance of the great, godlike scientist and seek to find a place as high in the authoritarian political structure as possible. (I am convinced that the training of doctors does not really help reduce mistakes that are often unavoidable but rather teaches them to better hide errors or displace responsibility for them. In fact, while I cannot prove it, it is my contention that the current authoritarian system increases the number of mistakes actually made by preventing the kind of learning that takes place whenever open discussion and contrary evidence can be brought into open view.)

Lurhmann (2000) points out that in these circumstances the patient easily becomes the other. She writes, "They (the residents) quickly learn detachment. . . . As they memorize the hyperdetails of bodily processes, they similarly turn the emotional horror of disease into a scientific entity. . . . This is a model of disease in which the body is unmindful, in which human intention and personality disappear from the body like figures from a photograph bleached by the sun. . . . The narrative of a person becomes the case study of a body" (pp. 86–89). I submit that while this might be experienced as adaptively necessary for the doctor it ultimately opens the door for all manner of bad medicine and political horror.

I offer the following as examples of what happens when physicians turn a blind eye to their politics and see their patients as objects or things without subjectivity. We can study the role played by medicine during the Holocaust in Nazi Europe. The Jews and other political prisoners were cast as a disease of the Fatherland and medical doctors were enlisted to cure the disease. Each concentration camp was run by a physician, the most notorious being Dr. Mengele at Auschwitz. (See Robert Lifton, 2000, for a more complete history of Nazism and medicine during the Hitler era.) It would appear that few dictatorships have had many problems recruiting medical personnel to further their political aims.

My primary interest is the role of medicine in our own society, supposedly a democracy in which doctors would be less likely to experience coercion in order to harm patients for political purposes. However, even in America we have reason to be on guard to prevent human experiments and illegal treatments that reflect physicians and other scientists from treating human beings as mere objects and not as people. Jane Jules and Howard Jones (1992) describe the administration of syphilis to unsuspecting black prisoners in a Tuskegee, Alabama, prison. These individuals were never treated, as the doctors involved merely wanted to see the long-term effects of untreated syphilis. Allen Hornblum (1999) also describes human experiments at the Holmesburg prison (Philadelphia, PA) without the knowledge or consent of the subjects.

Ruth Fader (1976) and Eileen Welsome (1999) both describe in horrific detail the thousands of medical experiments using radioactive substances done all over the United States on unsuspecting, uninformed people in all age groups during the Cold War. For example, doctors working on government-sponsored studies interested in seeing the effects of various types of radiation on human subjects put plutonium in the cereal of orphaned children and followed their medical histories to document the results.

In recent times serious charges have been leveled at physicians experimenting on often uninformed subjects with procedures and drugs with which the physicians have proprietary and other financial interests. (For example, see the article by Duff Wilson and David Heath, 2001, exposing illegal and unethical experiments on cancer patients at the prestigious Fred Hutchinson Cancer Center.) Editorials in *Lancet* and the *Journal of the American Medical Association* have described how medicine is compromising its integrity and effectiveness under the economic influence of big drug company money. Thomas Szasz (2001) refers to the United States as a growing pharmacracy as huge, powerful, and extremely wealthy multinational corporations enlist large segments of the medical community, the research facilities of major universities, and even the most prestigious of scientific medical publications to break with legitimate research protocols in order to sell their drugs.

My own fears for the nightmare role being played by science is best realized by Aldous Huxley's dystopic visions in *Brave New World* in which scientists literally re-create humanity to serve the purposes of the state. Huxley's work is, of course, a sequel to Mary Shelley's *Frankenstein* but one in which the creativity of objective science is writ large and all-embracing. What makes me personally frightened is that I agree with Anthony Burgess who in *1985* suggests that humanity will be seduced by science into giving up its freedom rather than losing its soul merely because of the application of force. I argue that it is medicine and its offshoots of psychiatry and psychotherapy that are at the cutting edge of this seduction.

In Orwell's *1984*, as O'Brien tortures Winston Smith into accepting Big Brother, and if necessary believing that $2 + 2 = 5$, he confidently describes the power of the state over the individual once it has the cooperation of science:

Did I not tell you just now that we are different from the persecutors of the past? We are not content with negative obedience, nor even with the most abject submission. When you surrender to us it must be of your own free will. We make him (the heretic) one of us before we kill him. In the old days the heretic walked to the stake still a heretic, proclaiming his heresy, even exulting in it. The commandment of the old despotisms was "Thou shalt not." The command of the totalitarians was "Thou shalt." Our command is "*Thou Art.*" (1949:258–259; emphasis in the original)

Griffin (1995) concurs with Orwell when she writes,

Whether Marxist or capitalist cold war nuclear technology, Fascist eugenics or Western genetic engineering, the continuing movement in the twentieth century to unify the world and nature according to one scientific idea has all the characteristics of a Greek tragedy . . . the prefix "scientific" for the modern system and "unscientific" for the traditional knowledge has less to do with knowledge and more to do with power. Underneath the obvious lust for social and political control that the use of knowledge evinces dwells an unexamined wish, the dream-like desire for the power to define reality. (p. 135)

In Chapter 4 I will argue that modern psychiatry exists basically for the purpose of defining modern humanity's sense of reality and moral sensibility.

CHAPTER 3

Psychology

INTRODUCTION

Sigmund Freud is considered the father of psychoanalysis and therefore can be considered part of the paternity of many of the myriad number of talk treatments for mental illnesses or disorders that now compete for the attention of vast numbers of our society's citizenry. Freud was originally trained as a physician and research neurologist. He later became involved with the treatment of mental illness at a time when it was believed that all such syndromes or patterns of behavior were the result of some biological abnormality. Unlike the view of modern biopsychiatry that claims that mental illnesses involve some form of brain disease, at the end of the nineteenth century other biological systems often accounted for aberrant behavior.

One of Freud's teachers was the noted French physician Charcot. Many of Charcot's patients were women considered to be suffering from "hysteria" a syndrome arising from problems in the uterus and ovaries. (Women have been and still are disproportionately diagnosed as mentally ill relative to their numbers in our society and compared to the number of men diagnosed.) While Charcot used hypnosis to demonstrate the psychological nature of hysteria, its treatment often involved a hysterectomy and/or ovarectomy. Psychoanalysis came into existence both as a theory of behavior and a method of treatment when Freud published papers suggesting that the symptoms of hysteria were the result of *repressed memories* of sexual trauma suffered in childhood.

Since mental illnesses involved the repression of memories and fixations of sexual desire, and these phenomena are psychological in nature,

Freud contended that his theory and therapeutic interventions were more psychological than biological. As a result Freud demanded that nonmedical personnel be accepted for psychoanalytic training as "lay-analysts" and given all of the privileges of medically trained therapists. When Freud visited Clark University, in Worcester, Massachusetts, in 1909 he entreated those in America to respect his wishes and not try to make psychoanalysis into a medical specialty. Having said that, Freud still used medical terminology to describe his therapeutic procedures (therapy is essentially a medical term) and never fully created a psychological theory. My purpose here is not to recount the manner in which Freud's wishes were ignored by American psychiatry but to elucidate some of the reasons why psychotherapy is contributing more to the processes of closed, authoritarian political systems than to democratic and open systems.

I contend that Freud's failure to fully develop psychoanalysis as a genuine psychology capable of promoting democratic/humanistic politics shares the same roots that have left the field of psychology unable to achieve these same goals. I understand psychotherapy to be a social, moral, and political encounter between two or more conscious persons in which one of the participants, the therapist, tries to help the other participant change the manner in which he/she understands and reacts to the world around and in him/her. It is my contention that psychotherapy provides an environment in which people can learn to better deal with their own psychological processes, change the political arrangements that define their social relationships, and attempt to live more moral and, especially, creative lives.

While I will develop these ideas more fully later, I make clear that my view of the therapeutic process requires a great deal of psychological understanding on the part of the therapist, insight that must also be articulated with biology, sociology, and the other human sciences as outlined in Chapter 1. I repeat, and further develop, my charge, articulated earlier, that psychology has utterly failed to develop such insights with the result that virtually all forms of psychotherapy developed along lines dominated by psychiatry, a pseudoscience that is neither medicine nor education and is not based in psychology, biology, or sociology. I will develop my thesis concerning psychiatry in the next chapter but in this one I will discuss psychology's contribution to the general and political crisis in psychotherapy.

My discussion of psychology's failures regarding psychotherapy will, of necessity, be sketchy and will not cover every aspect of the field. I will try to explicate the politics shaping psychology and the politics implicitly and explicitly practiced by psychology, both in the activities of psychologists and in the theoretical formulations created by various schools of psychology. I will concentrate on what I call "mainstream psychology," humanistic and existential psychology (the so-called third force in psychology) and, of course, psychoanalysis (psychology's second force). A fuller discussion of the latter requires a separate chapter since, in many ways, the history and development of psychoanalysis is the history and development of psychotherapy.

MAINSTREAM PSYCHOLOGY
AND ITS VISIONS OF HUMANITY

Martin Buber (1972) writes,

Rabbi Bunam Von Pryzysucha, one of the last great teachers of Hasidism, is said to have addressed his pupils thus: "I wanted to write a book called *Adam,* which would be about the whole man. But then I decided not to write it." . . . In these naïve sounding words of a genuine sage the whole story of human thought about man is expressed. From time immemorial man has known that he is the subject most deserving of his own study, but he has also fought shy of treating this subject as a whole, that is, in accordance with its total character. Sometimes he takes a run at it, but the difficulty of this concern with his own being overpowers and exhausts him, and in silent resignation he withdraws—either to consider all things in heaven and earth save man, or to divide man into departments which can be treated singly, in a less problematic, less powerful and less binding way. (p.118)

I contend that Buber is overly optimistic and generous if he applies his analysis of the emotions of those who try to understand humankind to most psychologists as they have functioned during the twentieth century. Psychology has gone forward with great confidence in creating one image of humanity after another that degrades and undermines its human subject matter. For the purposes of this book I contend that these images of humankind reflect visions that are the direct result of authoritarian, closed political systems as they are of creatures incapable of creating and engaging the political process.

Sigmund Koch (1999) one of psychology's strongest and acerbic critics, writes,

Throughout this century (and before) psychology has been under gracious dissemination—whether in school, bar, office, or bedroom; whether by book, magazine, electronic propagation, or word of mouth—to a voracious consumership. People everywhere have been given, gratis, revolutionary reconceptions of the nature of man—reams, truckloads of them—all based on cogent and valid *scientific* evidence. They have been analogized, even hypostasized, as cockroaches, dogs, monkeys, and especially rats; as telephone exchanges, computers, or colligations of billions of the latter; as configured systems of protons, electrons, neutrons, and neutrinos, or as epiphenomena of direct current distributions in electrolytes, or as a code-bearing macromolecules [*sic*]; as products of insufficient prophylaxis, or of neurobiotaxis, homeostatics, conditioning, reinforcement contingencies, cognitive maps, cell assemblies, TOTE hierarchies, or computer programming lists; as empty intersection areas between S's and R's, topologically differentiated Jordan curves, collections of exponential functions, or schematic sowbugs; as cybernetic mechanisms, information-processing entities, or finite automata; as utilities optimizers, game strategists, pleasure-principle protagonists; as mutual voyeurs, ego titillators, or mastubators; as collections of traits, attitudes, dispositions, instincts, or factors; as reactors, agents, achievers, self-realizers, autonomy maximizers; as id-ego-superego structures, orgone recepticles, plastic-phallus copulators, vibrator cohabitators, as elements of group mind, filings in social force fields, cooperating or competing or reinforcement bartering *socii*. (p. 294)

Why has psychology cast humanity in such ways but, more important, what are the effects of such theorizing, especially as they relate to psychotherapy and its politics? I have already laid the groundwork to understand, at least in part, psychology's dilemma when it comes to defining its subject matter and adopting its methods of study and application. Throughout the last century psychologists have defined their science as one that competes with physics, chemistry, and biology (the natural sciences) with the greatest status and apparent success. I have traced the rise of these sciences as they replaced, at least in part, religion as society's fountainhead of knowledge. Science replaced religion because of its ability to explain and control a variety of infectious diseases and, perhaps more important, by developing technologies that made life easier for the masses of humanity and exponentially increased the power of politicians to make war and control human behavior.

I have also suggested that while science at its best fosters equality between individuals as it emerged from the shadow of organized religion it tended to adopt ideas that, like those of religion, functioned according to highly authoritarian, god-thing narratives. René Descartes assumed that the human mind–soul was of a higher plane than the subjects of its inquiry. This privileged point of observation provided human beings with a window of ultimate truth about the phenomena studied. While science ultimately rejected Descartes's soul–mind it still retained faith in its superiority to glean the truth of the world by creating a myth surrounding its methods of study. By adopting extreme standards of objectivity and empiricism, science concluded that it had created a place on high from which it could observe and study the world as if it were on another plane of existence.

Not only have the methods chosen by psychologists tended to conceptualize human beings in terms of technology and machines (as well as lower life forms often conceived of as automata) but mainstream psychology has insisted that its methods be measured by the most extreme standards and definition of objectivity. It is the godlike superiority built into psychology's definition and methods of science that in one way or another leads to the recreation of the field's subject matter from human to nonhuman and unleashes a wide variety of destructive political activity.

I turn to the current textbook used by my college department for introductory psychology to develop my argument and help the reader grasp the full consequences of psychology's imitation of the physical and natural sciences with its consequent intellectual, moral, and political impoverishment. Dennis Coon's (2000) opus is well written, full of light and humorous touches, and reveals a grasp of the field of psychology as it currently exists. It is also, in its content, the virtual clone of many other texts in the field, covering all of the same topics in almost the same order with the same lack of criticism of itself, the field, or any of the positions taken within it. An examination of popular texts by Douglas A. Bernstein and Peggy W. Nash (1999) or Charles G. Morris and Albert A. Maisto (1999) confirms my basic contention.

Further, I make clear in what follows that I mean no personal disparagement about Coon as an individual human being. I refer to him as a prototype of those who write books whose purpose is the indoctrination of the next generation of psychologists and educated citizens of our society.

I begin with Coon's (2000) definition of psychology: "The word *psychology* comes from the roots *psyche*, which means "mind" and *logos*, meaning "knowledge or study." However, the "mind" is notoriously difficult to observe. That is why psychology *is defined as the scientific study of human and animal behavior*." Coon goes on to define behavior as "anything you do," and suggests that psychology is a science because it is empirical, "*Information is gained from direct observation and measurement*" (p. 2; emphasis in original).

There is much to explicate in Coon's handling of psychology's definition. (I reiterate that an examination of virtually any introductory text reveals a similar definition of psychology.) It is full of implicit meanings that are not addressed and cannot be unless examined from a historical perspective based in philosophy and politics rather than science. Coon has compacted and conflated a whole set of historical and conceptual problems into several very short paragraphs. The problems begin, and warning flags should go up, when Coon fails to define what he means by "mind." Instead, Coon demands that if we study "mind" scientifically it requires our being "empirical." If we are to be empirical we must be able to not only directly observe the mind but be able to *measure* it as well. We now have an interesting conceptual conundrum to unravel. That which is not defined must nevertheless be measurable. It must be measurable if it is to be scientific. Therefore, the phenomenon that concerns us cannot be defined in any way that will render its study unscientific.

The demands of being scientific may well be the reason that mind is so difficult to observe, indeed, these demands may be the reason why *mind* cannot be defined by Coon in the first place. In fact, I believe that is the case. The psychology presented to students by the mainstream is driven by a need to be scientific in a manner that competes with the more successful sciences of physics and chemistry. Rather than struggle to define *mind* and then choose appropriate methods for its study psychologists have chosen a method and insisted that the subject matter conform to the method.

The very idea that the mind exists as some sort of object that can be observed and measured dates back to the problems created by Descartes with his idea that a human being could be understood to be a ghost in a machine. While I will eventually address what Antonio Damasio (1994) refers to as "Descartes' error," it is Coon's need to maintain psychology's dogmatic insistence that it is a natural science that concerns me here. Not only does Coon define the mind as a noun he assumes that it must be publicly observed and measured. The mind is "notoriously difficult to observe" and, hence, to measure explains the decision to instead observe behavior. However, Coon never explains the relationship of mind to behavior. Moreover, and perhaps more important, Coon, as with the majority of mainstream psychologists, seems totally nonplussed by his failure to adequately define the subject matter of his field of interest. Indeed, he seems to be totally unaware of the problems being created by this illogical and unscientific decision. Why is Coon so confident in the decision to observe and measure behavior and so blind to the logical, philosophical, and conceptual problems created by his dealing with "mind" in the way he does? The answer lies in Coon's faith in the methodology psychology has adopted to study behavior.

Immediately after his very brief and, in my opinion, disastrous definition of psychology, Coon follows the pattern of most other mainstream psychologists and provides a lengthy description of the methods used to empirically study behavior. He is blind to his failure to deal effectively with his subject matter because he believes that it is the right methodology that establishes psychology as a legitimate science. He demonstrates the faith of most mainstream academic psychologists that the proper methods of study will open a window or a perfect mirror (Rorty, 1979) that will permit a clear and accurate view of the subject under consideration. *His position assumes that his act of observation in no way creates or influences the phenomena under study but instead reveals it as it is, in its very essence.* Every introductory text lovingly and clearly describes the methods of scientific psychology. The methods section comprises the bulk of the introductory chapter; a bulk better used to grapple with the difficult philosophical task of figuring out what mind is as well as why, too, there is a need to measure it.

Coon further makes clear that the height of psychology's success as an empirical science is in its use of the controlled experiment. The people to be studied are removed from their normal surroundings and placed in a laboratory where it is easier to isolate and observe the variables under consideration. The variable in whose effects we are interested is referred to as the "independent variable." The outcome variable, the one representing the behavior affected by the independent variable, is known as the "dependent variable." All other variables that might affect the dependent variable are to be controlled so that they can be discounted as a source of variation in the measurements made of the dependent variable.

The belief in the power of a well-controlled laboratory experiment made to yield appropriate amounts of statistical data is so great that all Ph.D. candidates in psychology must carry out and defend such an experiment as the final hurdle to gaining their degree. I argue that psychologists have come to believe that they will be able to understand the *essence* of their subjects through these procedures and as such this essentialism represents psychology at its most closed and authoritarian.

Coon does not say so (I am not sure just how conscious he is, or any mainstream psychologists are, concerning the philosophy that does under-lie their work) but the variables used in a psychological experiment deemed scientific (this type of experiment is part of what made physics and chem-istry so successful) must conform to certain standards and patterns of lin-guistic usage. Psychology's imitation of the "hard" physical sciences is guided by the philosophy of science known as "logical positivism" (Carnap, 1966) and the work of R. W. Bridgman (1927) and his concept of "opera-tionism," an extreme form of empiricism. By following the tenets of logical positivism and operationism, especially in a laboratory experiment, the typ-ical mainstream psychologist believes the essential truth about humanity will be revealed. (Koch, 1992, points out that psychology's Bridgman bears little resemblance to Bridgman's Bridgman. He reveals that Bridgman never intended that his work as a physicist be applied so arbitrarily to the field of psychology. Moreover, Bridgman expressed bitter disappointment that be-cause of psychology's inaccurate adaptation of his ideas, psychology could shed little light on the work of any actual scientific work, which Bridgman understood to be private and wholly subjective.)

Briefly, logical positivism states that for a concept to be scientifically meaningful it has to be described in perfectly transparent and objective lan-guage. Every aspect of language used in a scientific statement has to refer to things that could be publicly and mutually observed, measurable, and verifi-able. The researcher must avoid being influenced by any of his/her own subjec-tive experiences, personal opinions, desires, wants, likes or dislikes. If the researcher is successful in his/her attempts at objectivity then the language he/she uses while writing up his research will be devoid of anything that reflects those psychological states of mind. Logical positivists (as well as other aca-demics) often equate language with mind, another dubious assumption at best.

Operationism is similar to logical positivism in demanding that every concept be defined by the very operations used to measure it. For example, if we are interested in the effects of hunger on how much people eat the sci-entific psychologist would define his independent variable as the "number of hours the subject was food deprived." We cannot say that the subject ex-perienced hunger and desired to eat. The dependent variable would be some measurable amount of food ingested during an allowable phase of "eating behavior." This then would define scientifically meaningful variables whose precise interactions could be charted through the use of the experiment.

The consequences of employing the "scientific" model of psychology are widespread and disastrous, both to the field itself and to any of the applications derived from the model. The disaster can be traced to several interlocking flaws in Coon's assumptions concerning experiments based on logical positivism. The first is that these methods do not provide a transparent window on the true nature of the subject under study; and the second is that the laboratory is not the neutral environment Coon would have us believe. Coon ignores, as do most other authors of modern textbooks of basic psychology, the cogent and ever-expanding list of works critiquing logical positivism and psychology's reliance on methods conforming to logical positivist definitions of science (Bickhard, 2001; Grace, 2001; Leahy, 1980). For example, Kurt Danziger (1994, 1997) contends that the methods used in psychology define or construct the subject in a certain manner rather than illuminate the real subject as is. I suggest that the laboratory experiments, so admired by mainstream psychology, transform human beings into something quite different and far less human than if observed as they experience life as they live it in real-world settings. Psychology's transformation of living human beings engaged in the pursuit of a wide variety of adaptive personal and social goals as well as endless political–moral activity into subhuman automata reflects psychology's unreflective, unacknowledged, authoritarian political stance.

I suggest that Coon is dismissing in the subjects of psychology, but not in himself, most of what he and I would refer to as our "subjective experience of self and others" (as well as any vestige of what might be called "common sense"). He simultaneously dismisses the world in which we live and struggle to make meaningful both scientifically and morally. I will not attempt to define *mind* at this time as I am just as intimidated as Buber's rabbi to do so. However, while I cannot define *mind* I think I know it when I see it. Let me quote further from Coon's book to make my point and begin to explicate just what Coon has been forced to leave out of the psychology of people as he holds true to his methodology.

In the preface to his volume Coon is introduced to us both in a brief biography and in his own words. Next to a picture of a happily smiling, casually dressed man in his thirties we read, "My first psychology course was taught by a woman whose intellect, warmth, and wisdom had a lot to do with my decision to major in psychology. In the years that followed, I was inspired and challenged by other gifted teachers. Their voices, as well as my own, can be heard throughout this book" (p. vi). The brief biography that follows tells the reader that Dennis Coon is married, and that he likes hiking, photography, painting, and both playing and building musical instruments. This multitalented, passionate, and clearly creative human being has also written a "best selling trade book entitled *Choices*." The biography ends by stating that Coon is glad to have relocated his life to the Arizona desert where he now lives because it has provided him the opportunity to teach scorpions to tap dance.

Coon refers to himself with the word *I* and his possessions and life with *my* and *mine*. He has already told us that behavior is anything "you" do. Who or what are the "I" and "you" of which he speaks? Must not these have something to do with the "mind" so casually dismissed from Coon's definition of psychology? Is not the "I" causally related to the behavior psychology is to study? Coon knows he exists as a self, which he observes to be an agent capable of teaching scorpions to tap dance, and writing books on making choices. He has chosen to get married and engage in a lifetime of activities that he enjoys and which enrich and ennoble his life.

Coon tells us in Chapter 1 that he is a scientist who learns by observing and measuring human behavior, building and testing theories and guiding his activities by adhering to an ethical code that ensures that his work will better humankind. In fact, I have little doubt that if asked Coon would tell me that he seeks to live a life of moral purpose as he knows that only such a life is worth living. He also might reveal that his career is more than a means of earning his living, it represents part of his efforts to make his life as meaningful and rich as possible.

Coon also experiences himself as an object of other self-agents. He has been the recipient of the efforts of wise teachers and many loving individuals. He knows that he is capable of love and hate, loyalty and betrayal, honesty and deception, and even of a delicious use of irony in relation to the book *Choices*. Nowhere in Coon's discussions of scientific psychology are there any individuals capable of making choices. Is it not clear to Coon that he is a storyteller and organizes his life as an ongoing narrative in which he struggles to be a hero and avoid being a villain? He clearly struggles to be an artist in and of his own life. He has dreams and fantasies some of which he shares and others that he tries to hide even from himself. Does Coon vote and engage the political process? Does he seek to expand the choices of his students and does he not find democracy and humanism precious?

None of what is precious to Coon is observable to others, in any way measurable or exists during an experiment in a university laboratory. Once we enter the chapters describing the results of various experiments done to illuminate various psychological processes humanity disappears. Coon assumes the voice of the disembodied, disinterested observer, reporting on the field from a privileged position on high. The human beings being studied become "subjects" and lose their humanity. Look in the index of any psychology textbook for the words *love, hate, wisdom, folly, loyalty, betrayal, irony, hope,* and *despair* or any words related to real life. They do not appear. (Actually Coon's book contains one of the only discussions of love I have come across in an introductory text. Of course, he defines love as follows: "Romantic love is marked by high levels of interpersonal attraction and emotional arousal" and then discussed in terms of a love scale that is able to measure the "attitude" [p. 556].) Look, also in vain, for persons who are agents and objects of the intentions of other self-agents. Except for clever subheadings such as "Id came to me in a dream" (p. 385) which appears in a discussion on Freudian theory, Coon himself disappears except as the disembodied voice of a neutral reporter lacking any critical opinion of the psychology that comprises his book.

Moreover, Coon's position renders the entire field of psychology as useless in relation to politics. Stephen Frosh (1999) writes, "Without a theory of subjectivity, of how the individual's experience becomes organized, there can be no complete approach to politics" (p. 15). I would add that a full understanding of political interaction requires psychology to come to grips with how intersubjective experience develops and becomes organized as well.

What we find in a psychology text are "organisms" (living beings without the selves necessary to achieve the status of persons). We meet subjects whose behaviors in experimental studies are solely a function of the independent variable. We are introduced to disembodied psychological processes such as perception, memory, and thinking as defined by the operations of their measurement and the whole host of metaphors assembled for us by Koch. Richard Rorty (1991) makes clear that metaphors are often used to create new scientific insights. The use of mechanical metaphors such as a computer to add insights into human behavior is extremely helpful in understanding our cognitive processes. But, Rorty adds, when metaphors become literal and concrete and when they are confused with the actual reality of the objects or processes that they stand for then these same metaphors can cause knowledge to stagnate and prevent new insights from gaining the light of day. Psychology's inferiority complex in relation to the physical sciences has led psychology to utilize methods and concepts that concretized otherwise useful metaphors and prevented, rather than enhanced, our understanding of the human condition. We find, too, a field of study riven with conflict, fragmented into tiny, wholly illogical, and incommensurate pieces.

The bulk of Coon's and the typical text are concerned with an examination of a variety of human processes. The human being is taken apart, divided into its component processes, and analyzed much as a chemical compound might be when separated into the molecules that comprise it. Each separate process is discussed in its own chapter. Typical of its kind, Coon has well-written chapters entitled "Sensation and Reality," "Perceiving the World," "States of Consciousness," "Conditioning and Learning," "Memory," "Cognition, Intelligence, and Creativity," and "Motivation and Emotion." The human being once dissected loses sight of how all of these processes relate one to another as they function according to a fully functioning human being in-volved in real-life situations. Each chapter presents a variety of laboratory studies focused on the particular psychological process. It is clear that psy-chology believes it can thus make universally true statements about human behavior in this manner. For example, Chapter 2 deals with the biological human and outlines the structure and function of the nervous system from the level of the individual neuron to the brain itself. The chapter remains bio-logical in nature never attempting to discuss the nervous system in terms of its complex bidirectional relationship to conscious experience.

Typical of mainstream psychology the reader is left to wonder at just what the relationship of mind and body might be and the manner in which they are the same and yet different. Most important, these chapters never inform the students that science has yet to scratch the surface of the really important questions concerning mind and body. While a burgeoning set of facts are emerging about the neurological functioning of the brain, in gen-eral, virtually nothing is known about normal individual differences in brain function and how these contribute to differences in human adaptive func-tioning. The relationship of neurological functioning and consciousness is not discussed; indeed, consciousness and its various states are analyzed in a separate and later chapter that makes no reference to the brain and its role in the genesis of consciousness.

While Coon learns about the world through his activities as a scientist, the rest of us learn in a very different manner. For example, the chapter on learning is almost exclusively based on B. F. Skinner's concepts of classical and operant conditioning. The studies reported have largely to do with the behavior of rats and pigeons performing tasks in a "Skinner box," a labora-tory device that permits detailed measurements of both the stimuli that sup-posedly control behavior and the responses that are either "elicited" or "emitted" by the organism being studied. George Kelly (1955) demands that we conceive of all human beings as scientists who attempt to describe, ex-plain, predict, and control the world in which they live. I argue that the social and political experiments carried out by all of humanity are always guided by ethical and moral considerations of one sort or another.

We are infinitely more complex than rats and pigeons even if we share the same evolutionary roots. None of this is true according to Skinner, whose work stood astride academic psychology like a colossus for much of the twentieth century. People emit behavior like a bulb emits light while psy-chologists seek the truths of human behavior. The juxtaposition of Coon who learns like a scientist and the rest of humanity that learns to associate simple stimuli with one another reveals the political–moral hierarchy made inherent and invisible by psychology's methodology.

Daniel Robinson (2001) writes, "And behaviorism, with its nifty demonstrations and arresting circus tricks, can stand as a theory of human nature only insofar as that nature has allowed itself to be traduced into a species of avaricious machinery" (p. 423). Skinner's theory was certainly the most influential attempt to re-create psychology in the image of the physical sciences but it certainly was not alone. (Robinson's comments can be extended to all of the theories that employed the animal and mechanical images used to represent human beings.)

Skinner's fortune has been eclipsed of late by the cognitive sciences that now dominate mainstream psychology's discussions of thinking. Coon writes,

Thinking takes many forms, including daydreaming, problem solving, and reasoning (to name but a few). Stated more formally, thinking, or *cognition*, *refers to mentally processing information*. Studying thinking is similar to figuring out how a computer works by asking, "I wonder what would happen if I did this?" But in *cognitive psychology* (*the study of human information processing*) the "computer" is the brain, and thinking is the "programming" we seek to understand. (p. 336; emphases in original)

Not only do I find these sentences incomprehensible but they also suggest that human beings can be understood through comparison to a machine that they themselves have invented. We have been demoted from the level of rat to that of the machines that many Americans now worship as if they were gods. My students used to rebuff my attempts to raise their level of academic work by telling me that I could not hold them responsible because they had been conditioned, now they tell me they have been programmed.

I could continue to describe the remainder of the chapters seeking to describe the universal processes that make up a human being. Instead I state that these analyses result in a hodgepodge of topics designed to confuse already confused students, most of whom take psychology to increase their understanding of themselves and their own lives. In the chapter concerned with emotion the student is taught that we learn because we are "curious." A perplexed student asks me, "What gives, Professor? How can all of those ideas be true and which is it? Are we conditioned, programmed, or do we learn because we are curious?"

An adequate and honest answer to my student is not easy and no small matter. I must explain that psychology has defined itself as the study of observable behaviors with the behaviors described free from any subjective contaminants. These behaviors are not purposive, nor do they reflect the intentionality inherent to human behaviors. Moreover, they are described as if they take place in the supposed vacuum of a laboratory rather than in some physical–social environment in which the human subject struggles to survive and flourish. The topics covered in the text are limited to those amenable to the methods approved of by psychologists. They must be limited to patterns of behavior that can be measured by pencil and paper tests or the direct observation of the researcher. The topic selection does not grow out of discussions that attempt to define important social and personal issues of real people living real lives. Brent Slife and Richard Williams (1997) write, "Psychology, however was born of a determination to apply the positivistic science to human beings. Only those questions that could be cast in ways amenable to scientific study were to be taken up by the discipline" (p. 119).

I must explain to my students that Coon is forced into the position of observing people only from a third person perspective. In his stance as scientist he must omit not only the possible reality of an ontological self as political agent and object, but also the perspective of the individuals now under scrutiny. Alan Watts (1972) illuminates the consequences of Coon's decision with the following paraphrased conversation. Person A: "You walked past my window this morning." Person B. "No I didn't, I went to the store this morning." I submit that ignoring the first-person perspective to avoid the difficulties in observing mind makes even minimal comprehension of the person being observed next to impossible. Moreover, it allows all human differences to be expressed as numbers on a continuum making it impossible to understand within subject differences over time. In fact, there is an underlying assumption in all of this that time does not matter and that the snapshot taken at the moment of testing and experiment creates a timeless and universally true picture of the essential human being.

I help my students understand that the insistence that as psychologists they must study human beings in laboratory settings in order to have valid results is both a myth and a decision reflective of authoritarian politics compounding all of the problems already elucidated as deriving from positivistic thinking. The experiment reduces human behavior to an automatic response to whatever independent variable is under consideration. The personal experience of the experimental subject is not factored into the results and is usually controlled for by either lying to the subject as to the purposes of the study or simply omitting them from the instructions given the subjects as they engage in the experimental task. This whole procedure is of dubious moral value but suggests that the results of these studies involve individuals who are either left guessing as to the reasons they are working on the tasks confronting them or are deceived as to the true purposes. This hardly makes of the experiment and the laboratory either typical or value-neutral procedures and situations they are supposed to be. (It has long been pointed out that most academic studies use a captive group of students one of whose requirements for introductory psychology courses is to be subjects in their professor's research protocols. This makes college freshman the most studied group of individuals in the world—and they are hardly representative of the general population.)

Michael Billig (1994) exposes the myth of the experiment's scientific neutrality as well as its violation of its subject matter with the following self-explanatory narrative:

"Oh my God, what am I doing here?" Vanessa was thinking as she passed yet another name-plated door along the corridor. Please report to Dr. Snitting's Room, Second Floor, Department of Psychology, two o'clock, the letter had said. Well it had now passed two. And it wasn't her fault if Dr. Snitting had the most out-of-the-way office imaginable. . . .

Vanessa glanced at her watch and knocked.

Scuffling inside. Then nothing. She knocked again. The door opened slightly. A beard, spectacles and frown popped round: "Yes?"

"I've come for the experiment."

"Oh, sorry, oh, two already?" The door opened fully. "Please. Dr. Snitting."

Thus, the short bald man introduced himself. He wiped his mouth on his right hand, which he held out to Vanessa. . . . Wiping his mouth again, he bent over some computer paper: "Vanessa Jones, is it? Welcome."

Vanessa noticed a half-eaten sandwich on the desk.

"Sorry," he said again. "Please, come this way."

Vanessa followed him through a door at the back of his office into a tiny, windowless, cluttered room. "Would you sit down please?" Vanessa did as she was told.

What the hell am I doing here? She was asking herself.

She was alone with a stranger in a room, hardly bigger than a broom cupboard, at the back of the most forsaken room in the whole department. And Dr. Snitting was now standing right behind her, whispering: "This experiment involves judging patterns. I would like you to watch the screen. Soon I will turn out the lights and. . . ."

As Snitting spoke, Vanessa found herself thinking of his interrupted lunch. Oh God, it must have been an egg sandwich. (pp. 307–308)

The narrative suddenly brings a human being into focus, similar to the biography that tells us about Coon as a human being. It simultaneously explodes the myths surrounding mainstream psychology and especially that of the laboratory as a place where neutral, superior observations can be made. Dr. Snitting thinks he is observing and measuring learning as a universal process but in fact he is observing learning in a frightened young woman who is confused as to what is expected of her. Snitting is unaware of his subject's fuller humanity and his effect on her as a person. Moreover, Dr. Snitting seems unaware of the politics of the situation and his position of power as a professor over his student.

He seems unconcerned that she is a woman who might very well feel different about the situation than if she were male (even though Snitting probably has equal numbers of males and females in his study and believes that this controls for the effects of sex and gender). His subject might have felt differently about being in the same experiment twenty years ago, an era when politics had not been influenced by feminism. Thus Snitting is unaware that his study is subject to the laws of history and reflects the local time and place in which the experiment is unfolding as a social and political event rather than some timeless, universal process. Dr. Snitting is unaware that he is constructing his subject perhaps even more than learning about her. As Snitting observes and measures his subject, his subject is observing and measuring him; as a social being he does not measure up very well in her esteem.

I suggest that interpreting the results of psychology's laboratory experiments is always ambiguous at best. The studies that make up mainstream psychology are rarely replicated once completed and published. They become another line on a resume that helps the researcher attain academic tenure as well as add to his/her prestige. They exist, therefore, in part, as political, as well as scientific, documents. Even if the typical study were to be replicated in another laboratory, the results would not be published if they were not positive in nature. The peculiar politics of psychology states that negative results are not to be accepted for publication in mainstream psychology journals. Because these studies must conform to the demands of positivism and operationism they mostly concern themselves with the trivial rather than anything important. Once published they are soon forgotten and have little effect on developing a meaningful body of scientific literature. In short, most of what comprises mainstream psychology is trivial except to the careers of those doing the research. This would not be a problem except that psychology ignores most of what is important to people who seek in it some wisdom for their lives as well as rendering the field blind to the destructive politics inherent in its assumptions and, as I will soon relate, its political alliances.

PSYCHOLOGY BEYOND THE MAINSTREAM

Students reading Coon's (or any other) introductory text will become acquainted with more than research based on the logic of positivism. They will also encounter a variety of theories that attempt to describe the whole person rather than isolated psychological processes that result from laboratory experiments based on logical positivistic assumptions. There are several such theories, which I refer to as "grand theories," that have made their way into the consciousness of psychologists and as such must appear in most, if not all, psychology textbooks. The adaptive theory of Jean Piaget, discussed earlier, is central to chapters dealing with child psychology and/or human growth and development. Coon includes a discussion of aspects of Erik Eriksen's ideas in the developmental chapters although his work can just as likely be found tied to a sketch of Freud's psychoanalysis in the chapter dealing with personality.

Chapters on personality open with a definition of personality reflective of the mainstream, "Personality is a person's unique and relatively stable behavior patterns" (p. 454). The definition is usually followed by mainstream psychology's attempt to explain these stable, observable, and fully measurable patterns of behavior with the concept of traits followed by a behaviorist view

of behavior based on Skinnerian notions of operant and respondent conditioning. However, much of what is nonmainstream in psychology appears
within the chapter on human personality including psychoanalysis (often limited to the Freudian model) and the work of Abraham Maslow (1968) and
Carl Rogers (1961) both of whose theories represent psychology's third force,
humanism and existentialism.

I turn now to a brief discussion of a general critique of all the grand
theories that appear in the introductory textbooks of psychology followed by
a brief description of Humanism in the light of the critique. The grand theories differ from mainstream psychology in that they are concerned with the
whole person rather than specific functions of persons. But these theories are
still a product of thinking that derives from the type of science that implicitly
behaves as if it represents a god's-eye view of its subject matter.

Whereas an experiment seeks to describe the essence of thinking,
memory, learning, or some other psychological function, the grand theories
seek to describe the essence of the whole person. In an experiment, individual psychological functions are divorced from the persons who perform
them and examined independently of the actual environments in which
they actually function. In a grand theory, specific psychological functions
are rarely discussed but the whole person is described as an abstraction independently of the actual social–moral–political environment in which
individual lives are lived out.

Like the self-images of the scientists who create these psychological
theories or master narratives, the subjects or characters that inhabit them
exist as integumented monads with clear boundaries, living and developing
largely independently of their environments. The subjects and their environments coexist as dualisms rather than as dualities in which the individuals
that comprise their social environments interpenetrate one another. Actual
politics are, therefore, not topics relevant to these theories and only appear
within them as conflicts between the individual and a vague generalized society, or in the case of psychoanalysis, problems within the family most often
a function of an inadequate mother figure. Politics exists only in the most
simplistic and implied fashion.

The specific type of political interaction required by any grand theory
depends on the view of human nature contained in the theory. Development
of the individual in a grand theory, and this is particularly true in Piaget, Humanism, and Freudianism, is pushed by some notion of the essential nature
of the beings described in the theory. (In the case of behaviorism the nature
of the subject is a Lockian blank slate, and development of the individual is
pulled by the environment.) Descriptions of the human nature are both
fused with moral implications and contain some teleological goal toward
which nature seeks to achieve.

Piaget's theory is concerned with the cognitive and intellectual development of the individual and the individual is pushed toward the achievement of formal operations, clearly the type of thinking reflected in the scientific enterprise and Western culture's definition of *reason* and *rationality*. Piaget's view of history reflected his belief that the individual's cognitive development paralleled historical development of Western culture's cognitive development, which in turn reflected the teleological movement of evolution in producing formal operations. Similar to so many of the grand scientific theories these developments are seen as morally necessary and representing progress.

I will delay a discussion of Freud's rather Hobbesian view of human nature and concentrate on the Rousseauian view of human nature contained within the work of Maslow. Maslow's theory involves a "hierarchy of needs." These universal needs are conceived of as a pyramid; the physiological and security needs at the base being those we share with the rest of the animal kingdom. Love and belongingness sit atop security and represent the first of those needs that begin not only to be peculiarly human but *transcendent* as well. (Newer research on our hominid ancestors suggests that similar needs may exist in those groups as well.) Still higher in the pyramid are the penultimate and ultimate goal of humanity, esteem needs and the need for self-actualization.

While I think it important that Maslow and other humanist/existentialist psychologists recognize and highlight those aspects of human functioning that most define the human being, I think it equally important to examine their failure to make explicit its political, social, and moral implications. It is these implicit political assumptions that not only render the theory useless to the development of an explicit theory capable of explaining and differentiating between closed and open societies but make it, in many ways, hostile to democratic societies as well. Maslow's theory, like many of those developed mid-twentieth century, reflects two embedded, interdependent political myths or narratives. The first is that of the cowboys and the pioneers of the American West: rugged individuals overcoming all difficulties through perseverance, fortitude, and courage. The second is a virtual worship of individuality and personal freedom developed against the backdrop of totalitarian Nazism and Communism, two systems committed to the crushing of the individual. The problem is that a genuine democracy requires interdependent people with individuality, not disconnected beings representative of political individualism. The isolated human beings described in Maslow's theory with its virtual lack of social theory represent an implied collective more like anarchy than democracy. The many suspect assumptions in his theory can also lead one to view his ideas as antidemocratic and quite totalitarian. I examine these assumptions.

Maslow makes clear that human development, in general, and the search for actualization, in particular, is not only peculiarly human but is "instinctoid," the human version of an instinct. If we do not achieve our innate and essential human potential it is because of hostile, nonnurturing environmental conditions preventing the satisfaction of the lower needs. Those who overcome adversity often display personal courage, a virtue to be much valued, admired, and emulated by others facing difficulties. Therefore, need satisfaction abetted by superior moral qualities appears to be the main mechanism of psychological growth.

The relationship of need satisfaction and moral courage is an ambiguous one in Maslow's work. Is courage the result of need satisfaction or does it inhere to some essential difference between individuals? To claim the former is to suggest that society should provide all of its citizens with the wherewithal of need satisfaction and with it the opportunity to achieve their individual and collective human potential. To claim the latter is to create a hierarchy of persons reflective of a god-thing narrative and one belonging to a closed rather than an open society. I argue that in the end both assumptions prevail and together provide a blueprint for an authoritarian society.

Maslow advances an extremely weak theory of human development that implies that the well fed may be more courageous than those left hungry. He never develops a social theory of need satisfaction that makes clear that the hungry and well fed might also differ in the presence or absence of loving parents, economic poverty or wealth, and/or educational opportunities. There is no mention of the type of politics that supports or inhibits intellectual growth and self-expression or that intellect is an important attribute in human functioning. He leaves free the idea that need satisfaction must be balanced with self-control and the capacity to endure deprivation or that the escape from deprivation is a powerful stimulant to the development of many useful and necessary skills. In the end gluttony is seen as a key developmental principle.

In the end Maslow focuses on individuals and differentiates among them, as do many humanist theories, with the concept of courage. However, courage is not a descriptive term, it represents a virtue and therefore belongs to the realm of the moral. We are, therefore, confronted not with descriptions of individual differences but with a moral hierarchy, a layering of individuals with varying moral worth. The rugged individuals with courage ultimately prevail over those inferior beings without similar virtues and go on to actualize themselves. As actualized beings they are creative, resourceful, infinitely insightful, and capable of transcending virtually any hardships while transforming the worlds inside and around them.

I submit that the essentialism that pervades Maslow's theory as well as the confounding of the descriptive and the moral ultimately make his work one of supermen and their inferiors rather than of individuals of varying abilities who possess equal moral worth and value. The combination of an elite and a population requiring constant satisfaction of every need is a model for a new type of dictatorship. It is one based more on the visions of Aldous Huxley's *Brave New World* than George Orwell's *1984*. In fact, I argue in the next chapters that the mental health field as the leading edge of a welfare-consumer society has moved quite close to the realization of what Thomas Szasz (2001) calls a "pharmacracy." I close this chapter with a brief discussion of Coon's presentation of the topics of abnormal psychology and psychotherapy.

Every introductory text has at least two chapters devoted to psychology's involvement in the mental health field. The first comprises a discussion of abnormal psychology or, as it might be referred to, psychopathology or mental illness. The second chapter introduces students to the myriad psychotherapies claiming to cure or otherwise ameliorate the various pathologies described in the earlier chapter. It is in these two chapters that we see the tragedy of psychology's failure to develop an appropriate image of humanity and methods to help understand the human condition at least as it is revealed and shaped in its social, moral, and political contexts. What we discover in these chapters is psychology's intellectual and moral capitulation to medical psychiatry. I argue that psychiatry and its pathetic imitator, clinical psychology, is science and especially medicine's largely successful attempt to wrest morality out of the weakened grip of religion and substituting a religion of its own peculiar making for traditional religion. After some brief closing remarks I develop this thesis and moral indictment in the following chapter.

IS PSYCHOLOGY A SCIENCE?

In a now famous paper, Gregory Miller (1969) urges psychologists to give psychology away. In an equally famous retort, Sigmund Koch (1999) suggests that psychologists should take it back. Were psychology a science, I doubt there would be a need for Koch's critique, his ultimate conclusion that the best we can hope for for psychology is its fragmentation into separate, largely incommensurate psychological studies, or for this chapter. I strongly argue that psychology can still be a science if it thoroughly reevaluates its reason for being.

Psychology must begin with a proper definition of its subject matter and then go on to develop appropriate methods of study. Perhaps more important, the field might have to recognize that it must give up, at least temporarily, its grandiose goal of discovering the essence of the universal human being. Most important, we must remind ourselves as professionals that our attempts to study humanity is always an attempt at understanding ourselves and therefore we must ultimately begin with a moral analysis of our relationship with our subject matter. We must treat our subjects as we demand to be treated both conceptually and ethically.

Robinson (2000) writes of science in general, "Progress in science is won by the application of an informed imagination to a problem of genuine consequence; not by the habitual application of some set of formulaic mode of inquiry to a set of quasi-problems chosen chiefly because of their compatibility with the adopted method" (p. 41). He writes of psychology in particular, "In an attempt to 'ape' the developed sciences, psychology as a discipline has regularly lost sight of its own identifying mission, its raison d'être. The mission of such a field is to enrich our understanding of the causes or conditions surrounding the more significant factors of individual and social life" (p. 42).

I suggest that the focus of our work be the conscious experience of those seeking to adapt to specific situations and events as they occur in actual time and space. I urge us to see our subjects as persons possessed of selves of varying developments that make them both active agents and subjects of the actions of others. The goal of our science might be that suggested by Gregory Bateson (1979) *which is to try to simply understand the pattern of things.*

What are the patterns of human consciousness and how do these account for the moral–political activities of human agencies at both the individual and collective levels? How can we understand the development and organization of selves that account for actions taken at a given moment in local time and place, both in terms of the history of those selves and the forces acting on those individuals at the moment actions were taken? How can we understand development in terms of the bioevolutionary factors that precede the development of all human beings, the specific cultural, political, linguistic, economic, and interpersonal events that enfold and shape all human beings? How, too, might we even begin to inquire as to the emergent qualities of human psychic experience that might contribute to human individuality and also not be reducible to the other factors that shaped that consciousness?

Where might we begin? What significant social problem might occupy our field as we search for methods to reveal their underlying patterns? I suggest we begin with the events of September 11, 2001, when two hijacked airliners were purposely crashed into the World Trade Center in New York City by a group of young men intent on killing themselves as well as their intended victims as part of a well-planned politically and religiously motivated exercise.

How can we understand the consciousness of those who perpetrated this action without labeling them as "fanatics" or "lunatics" and using those moral judgments as explanations for their behavior? How can we understand the myriad reactions of those individuals directly and indirectly involved in the fires and collapse of the towers without referring to them as either "heroes" or as "mentally ill" (post-traumatic stress disorder and the like) and using those moral labels as explanations of behavior? Can we begin to do this and hold in mind that no matter how objective we might be we can never fully transcend the events that enfold and shape us all, both subjects and their observers?

If we can even begin to use our imaginations to create hypotheses and develop appropriate methods to shed some light on these events and on so many others of the political atrocities that have taken the lives of hundreds of millions of human beings in the last one hundred years we might have a science to be reckoned with. We might begin to develop a body of psychological knowledge that R. D. Laing referred to as the "science of science." I turn to this task in Chapter 7 where I present my own contribution to the work of a number of psychologists attempting to develop a human psychology.

CHAPTER 4

Psychotherapy I: Psychiatry and the Myths of Mental Illness

INTRODUCTION

The previous chapters allow me to turn to a discussion of psychotherapy and its relationship to politics. However, there can be no understanding of modern psychotherapy without an understanding of its debt to and dependence on psychiatry. I restate my contention that psychiatry is the evolved product of modern science that is also the heir of religiously based morality. I will demonstrate that the underlying visions of psychiatry fuse description and explanation with moral judgment, corrupting both the science and the morality as practiced. The result of this corruption is that psychiatry today is a powerful force against democracy and our society's continuance as an open society. In the following discussion I use the word *psychiatry* to include not only that profession but that of clinical psychology and social work as well as any other field that relates itself to psychiatry.

I make as clear as I can that many of the individuals practicing as psychiatrists and psychotherapists of many stripes are often quite successful in establishing relationships with their patients that are humanistic, democratic, and reflective of an open society. However, these successful therapeutic efforts are achieved in spite of, rather than because of, the underlying ideology of psychiatry. These therapists find ways of ignoring or subverting the basic political thrust of their field and do so with varying levels of awareness. I explicate the authoritarian ideology of psychiatry.

I begin with several sentences from the preface to Edward Shorter's (1997) congratulatory and apologetic history of psychiatry:

Today, it is clear that when people experience a major mental illness, genetics and brain biology have as much to do with their problems as do stress and their early-childhood experiences. If there is one intellectual reality at the end of the twentieth century, it is that the biological approach to psychiatry—treating mental illness as a genetically influenced disorder of brain chemistry—has been a smashing success. *Psychiatry is, to be sure, the ultimate rulemaker of acceptable behavior through its ability to specify what counts as "crazy."* Yet there is such a thing as mental illness. It has a reality independent of conventions of gender and class, and this reality can be mapped, understood, and treated in a systematic and scientific way. Just as one would not insist that Parkinsonism or multiple sclerosis are socially constructed, one may no longer argue that schizophrenia and depression are social constructs lacking a basis in flesh and blood. (pp. vii–viii; emphasis added)

I suggest that the following myths are contained in the previous sentences and I shall deconstruct each in turn:

1. Mental illnesses are actual "things" and have a corporeal reality beyond their existence as social constructions. The concept of mental illness or disorder invokes a myth and a destructive and dangerous myth at that.
2. There is clear and compelling evidence to support the notion that the so-called mental illnesses have a genetic and/or a biological basis. There is no such clear and compelling evidence beyond the wish fulfillments of those who declare the case to be closed and those who have money and influence enough to influence a gullible, uneducated media and public that such evidence exists.
3. Parkinson's disease, multiple sclerosis, and the range of mental illnesses are not social constructions. While it is true that Parkinson's and multiple sclerosis are true medical diseases in that they fit the definition of such as outlined in the next section they are still socially constructed. At another time in history these afflictions might have been explained as manifestations of demonic possession. The existence of the neurological damage present in Parkinson's disorder is not in question but how it is named, categorized, and managed is certainly socially constructed. While mental illnesses lack any medical evidence to support their existence as true medical problems, they, too, are clearly social constructions. Without psychiatry they would be named, categorized, and managed quite differently than they are. It is one goal of this book to achieve a redefinition of the patterns of thought, affect, and overt behavior to other than medical conditions.
4. Psychiatry is both a science and a smashing success. Shorter's (1997) unexamined but true statement concerning psychiatry's current role as our society's chief moral arbiter begins to give lie to the notions that it is anything but a scientism and authoritarian pseudoreligion that harms far more than it helps. Not only does psychiatry damage large numbers of individuals but it is also in the process of undermining what little democracy still exists in Western society and in America specifically.

THE MYTH OF MENTAL ILLNESS OR DISORDER

I begin with the standard psychiatric argument *against* the acceptance that psychiatry and all of its applications and spin-offs are based on a myth, a lie, and the inappropriate use of metaphor. Paul R. McHugh (1992) attacks Thomas Szasz's proposition that the term *schizophrenia* is socially constructed and does not represent a true medical condition. He writes, "The only reply to such commentary is to know the patients for what they are in schizophrenia—people disabled by delusions, hallucinations, and disruptions of thinking capacities and to reject an approach that would trivialize their impairments and deny them their frequent need for hospital care" (p. 499).

In short, neither McHugh, Shorter, nor the majority of mental health professionals who echo this argument have even an inkling as to the logical deconstruction of the concept of mental illness. My own experience with a large number of clinicians tells me that most do not believe that a counter-argument exists nor have many read the large and robust literature that refutes psychiatry's basic premises and empirical evidence in their support. One need only look into virtually any standard academic textbook on the subject to find that counterarguments to the notion of mental illness are rarely, if at all, presented, and that students have no opportunity to debate these vital issues. I, along with a number of others critical of institutional psychiatry and psychology, have long concluded that these fields exist more along the lines of authoritarian religions than robust sciences.

The argument against the idea of a literal mental illness is first and foremost logical and definitional in nature and only secondarily empirical. None of the psychiatric critics suggest that the observable patterns of thinking, emotional expression, or overt behaviors that end up as diagnoses do not exist. I know of no professional involved with those labeled as "mentally ill" that has ever suggested that the individuals who think, feel, and behave in ways that earn them a psychiatric diagnosis such as schizophrenia do not suffer nor need some type of help. Our disagreement is with psychiatry's interpretation and the meanings it creates when it claims that these patterns of human experience are medical in nature.

PSYCHIATRY VERSUS GENUINE MEDICINE

Szasz (2001) presents a history of the development of the concept of medical disease. By the late nineteenth century the field of medicine agreed that its province was defined by observable problems in the cellular functioning of the body's biological organs. The subjective experience of the symptoms and discomforts of these organic difficulties, the experience of being ill, were what brought the patient to the physician whose job it was to diagnose and treat the underlying biological infestation, structural abnormality, physiological dysfunction, or other pathology creating the patient's difficulties.

Medicine became successful because it applied the scientific method and demonstrated that various pathogens, toxins, cancer, and so forth could account for the patient's complaints. Medicine concerned itself with harmful deviations in the anatomy or physiology of the body, its organs, tissues, and cells. The use of technology to examine blood, bones, and various internal organs made the diagnosis of disease easier and more accurate while the patient still lived. The true benchmark of diagnosis, however, remained the post-mortem autopsy. It was through the thorough scientific examination of the dead body that medicine could best provide physical evidence of biological disease processes. *A medical diagnosis is a judgment that some biological process has deviated from an established standard and that this biological deviation, stated in purely descriptive terms, is harmful to the person or organism so affected.*

The process of deriving a psychiatric diagnosis is of a totally different order than making a medical diagnosis. The psychiatric diagnosis begins with patterns of behavior, thoughts, or feelings that someone, either the patient, a relative, other acquaintance, or societal authority, finds strange, offensive, or otherwise unacceptable. It is *something a person does* that brings them to psychiatric attention while it is *something that someone has* that leads them to search for medical help. *The psychiatric diagnoses, based as they are on behavior of one sort or another, represents by definition a moral rather than a medical judgment. Judgments of what people do, think, feel, or say can be nothing other than moral in nature.*

I agree with Theodore Sarbin and James Mancuso (1980) that the concept of mental illness is invoked when people are confronted with unwanted behaviors. Those individuals might include family, friends, school officials, or any societal observers including the individual doing the behaving. I add to their notion that mental illness is invoked when behaviors are not only unwanted but their motives are also not understood by those observing the behaviors. When behavior is unwanted but motives are comprehensible to the observers, the behaviors are usually judged morally or placed in the category of criminality. When individuals are upset by their own behaviors, it is usually because their own motives are not clear to themselves.

Even when psychiatry claims that mental disorders are true brain diseases the diagnosis is made based on the observation or the reports of various forms of human activity. It is clear that if any particular pattern of behavior were to be shown to be a function of a brain disease then it would be a true medical disorder and the afflicted individual would be treated by a neurologist, a real medical doctor. *There would still be no true mental illnesses or disorders.* The whole catalog of mental illnesses would still represent a host of moral rather than medical judgments masquerading as medical terminology and stripped of their overt moral meaning.

One of the many illogical inconsistencies in psychiatry is the fact that diagnoses of brain diseases based on patterns of behavior, thought, and feeling are treated by psychiatrists, while brain diseases confirmed by laboratory findings are tended to by neurologists. Shorter (1977) ends his history by suggesting that the number of psychiatrists in training keeps falling, while the number of neurologists keeps rising. He wonders if psychiatry might eventually be absorbed by neurology.

I demonstrate my contention that mental illnesses and disorders are moral judgments rather than medical illnesses by analyzing both some particular diagnoses and the so-called medical book containing the whole range of psychiatric disturbances. I begin by discussing the bible of psychiatry the *Diagnostic and Statistical Manual of Mental Disorders* (4th ed.), known in the profession as *DSM-IV*. I refer to this document as the "big book of bad names" and suggest that it is more political in nature than medical or scientific.

Paula J. Caplan (1996), Stuart Kirk and Herbert Kutchins (1992), Herbert Kutchins and Stuart Kirk (1997), and others have described the actual processes by which the diagnoses of mental disorders are created. Standing committees of psychiatrists constantly review existing diagnostic categories and remain alert for the possible creation of new ones. It is one of the remarkable facts of our time that the number of recognized mental illnesses has risen from perhaps thirty to several hundreds between the publication of *DSM-I* and *DSM-IV*. Were the general public suffering afflictions of new medical diseases to the same degree it would represent the most catastrophic public health emergency in human history. New diseases such as AIDS do appear, new medical diseases are discovered, and established diseases increase and decrease in the number of cases diagnosed. But psychiatric diseases are invented and old ones deconstructed; the rate of both processes seems to be based in politics and economics, not science and discovery.

What is the process of inventing and removing diagnostic categories? When a pattern of behavior (unwanted and not easily understood) emerges in society that might be the basis for a new diagnosis, research is done to see its prevalence in the general population. If sufficiently prevalent to warrant psychiatric attention, the committee concerned with the age or demographic group most "afflicted" creates wording that names the new disease and defines its principle symptoms. The committee then votes to accept the new category and bring it to the larger membership of the American Psychiatric Association. If accepted by the parent body, a new mental illness is introduced to the public along with recommendations for its inclusion in the latest edition of the *DSM*. Caplan (1996) describes the backbiting, lying, deal making, and power politics involved in this process.

Diagnoses are removed in a similar process; they are voted out of existence. When I was a student I was taught that both oral sex between consent-
ing heterosexual adults and homosexuality were grave mental disorders. In
fact, most, if not all, of the sexual diagnoses found in the psychiatric lexicon
were based on the work *Psychopathica Sexualis* written by the nineteenth-century psychiatrist Richard von Krafft-Ebing. Shorter (1997) suggests that this
work is "a kind of schoolboy's masturbatory compendium" and makes clear
that Krafft-Ebing was very much a product of the Victorian morality of his
time.

With the sexual revolution of the 1960s and 1970s cunnilingus and
fellatio became foreplay. Instead of being labeled "mentally ill" for engaging in oral sex people found themselves deficient for refraining from such
activities. Homosexuality came out of the closet and the Gay community,
as the collective of homosexuals came to be known, decided that its behavior was neither sinful nor mental illness. I have little doubt that the removal
of homosexuality from the *DSM* was as much a product of those gays
within the psychiatric community than it was political pressure from without. Can anyone imagine similar political processes taking place with real
illnesses? Could cancer or diabetes be voted in or out of the International
Classification of Diseases?

I focus briefly on three mental disorders supposedly afflicting children:
312.8 Conduct Disorder, 313.81 Oppositional Defiant Disorder, and 314.01
Attention-Deficit/Hyperactivity Disorder [ADHD]. If my readers conclude
that these disorders are not true medical diseases but are instead sets of moral
judgments with clear political aims then it must raise doubts about every
diagnosis in *DSM-IV*. I quote from the section entitled "Diagnostic Features":

The essential feature of Conduct Disorder is a repetitive pattern of behavior in
which the basic rights of others or major age-appropriate societal norms or rules are
violated. These behaviors fall into four main groupings: aggressive conduct that
causes or threatens physical harm to others or animals, nonaggressive conduct that
causes property loss or damage, deceitfulness or theft, and serious violations of rules.

The essential feature of Oppositional Defiant Disorder is a recurrent pattern
of negativistic, defiant, disobedient, and hostile behavior toward authority figures
that persists for at least six months and is characterized by the frequent occurrence
of at least four of the following behaviors: Losing temper, arguing with adults, actively defying or refusing to comply with the requests or rules of adults, deliberately
doing things that annoy other people, blaming others for his or her own mistakes or
misbehavior, being touchy or easily annoyed by others, being angry and resentful or
spiteful and vindictive.

The essential feature of Attention-Deficit/Hyperactivity Disorder is a persistent pattern of inattention and or hyperactivity-impulsivity that is more frequent and
severe than is typically observed in individuals at a comparable level of development.
(pp. 78–93)

Even a cursory examination of these three diagnostic categories must lead to the conclusion that they represent a moral code for children's behavior based on adult perceptions. Can words such as *defiant* and *disobedient* be anything other than moral in nature? Can these categories be anything but a wide net that morally accuses and finds guilty virtually any child that misbehaves at home, in school, or in the larger community? Is it logically possible to disagree with Sarbin and Mancuso (1980) who would have us see psychiatric diagnoses as anything but a set of moral verdicts of what they refer to as "unwanted behaviors"? Can it be logically argued that there is anything in the training of medical doctors or research psychologists (the Ph.D. is essentially a research degree) that makes them any more expert in moral philosophy than any other citizen in our society?

THE CORRUPTION OF SCIENCE, MORALITY, AND DEMOCRACY BY PSYCHIATRIC IDEOLOGY

A closer examination of these so-called mental diseases further reveals their existence to be nothing but metaphors that are treated literally. I first list several of the symptoms of each mental disorder as they appear in *DSM-IV*. I make no attempt to reproduce the entire list of symptoms comprising each mental illness and will for my purposes simply mix symptoms from each category:

1. Often bullies, threatens, or intimidates others;
2. Often lies to obtain goods or favors or to avoid obligations (i.e., "cons" others);
3. Often does not follow through on instructions and fails to finish schoolwork, chores, or duties in the workplace;
4. Often fidgets with hands or feet or squirms in seat.
5. Often argues with adults;
6. Often actively defies or refuses to comply with adult's requests or rules.

I produce this list to illuminate several assumptions inherent in the notion of mental illness. First, the behaviors in question while clearly infractions of some set of moral rules established by adults are here seen as symptoms or products of the illness. Therefore they are not the products of thinking, feeling, conscious beings possessed of selves of varying maturity who are acting and reacting to the physical and social environment in which they find themselves. Like so many of god-thing scientific narratives already discussed the problematic behaviors listed in the *DSM* are of "things" rather than of people. These behaviors take place in other-than-real environments, particularly settings defined by political interactions.

While it is clear that these children are being judged and found guilty for their actions they are simultaneously not held responsible for them. *All of the behaviors in the* DSM *are simply the results of illnesses and it is unreasonable to hold an illness responsible for its symptoms.*

It must be clear that in the psychiatric formulation there are no individuals seeking, and if necessary struggling, to adapt to a succession of situations comprised of myriad events. There are no persons possessed of selves that are worthy of respect and dignity, or that can be held responsible for their actions. As a result not only is there no subject matter available for scientific–psychological analysis, there are no individuals to be held morally accountable for their actions. We cannot ask how the environment affects the individual nor inquire how the individual affects the environment, socially or physically. We are left with an illusion that a moral label is a medical disease and that the observed offending patterns of behavior, thought, and affect are simply the product of the disease. We have succeeded in completely corrupting our efforts as scientists and moral philosophers and as long as we uncritically accept any DSM as a scientific document we are completely unaware of our failures in both endeavors.

Robinson (1997) advances the argument made here when he writes,

One need not declare allegiance to *all* that the medical sociologists have been saying in recent years—one need not be uncritical of the influential writings of Michel Foucault (e.g., Foucault, 1975)—to accept the general proposition that *psychological* disorders tend to be contextually defined. Indeed, as history painfully makes clear, the defining contexts have often been so transparently political as to render the alleged disorders nothing less than badges of merit. (p. 675; emphasis in original)

Each and every description of a symptom begins with the word *often*. How often is often? Unlike medical judgments that are based on clear descriptions of some palpable phenomena that can be precisely measured and defined, psychiatric symptoms are expressed in vague, subjective terms. The boundaries of any category of mental disease or disorder are extremely elastic and capable of covering as many children as convention or economic and political need requires. When I describe these "diseases" to my students their first response is usually that these three disorders as described in *DSM-IV* can be made to include every child alive today. Indeed, childhood itself has been turned into a disorder. A perusal of *DSM-IV* leaves its visitors convinced that each and every person on the planet suffers from a multiplicity of mental illnesses.

The diseases listed above have magical properties because they are the products of magical preoperational thinking. One of the symptoms of so-called schizophrenia is the presence of delusions defined as false beliefs that defy all evidence to the contrary. The diagnoses of any DSM clearly fit the definition of a shared delusion. Consider the following sentence from *DSM-IV*:

Manifestations of the disorder (Oppositional Defiant) are almost invariably present in the home setting, but may not be evident at school or in the community. Symptoms of the disorder are typically more evident in interactions with adults or peers whom the individual knows well, and thus may not be apparent during clinical examination. Usually individuals with this disorder do not regard themselves as oppositional or defiant, but justify their behavior as a response to unreasonable demands or circumstances. (p. 92)

Were the political consequences of this statement not so serious it would be laughable or perhaps pathetic in its lack of logic and scientific standing. Could cancer or perhaps a broken leg appear and disappear according to the setting in which an individual moves? While a disease might be misdiagnosed or even overlooked by a physician, it would never be assumed that it cannot be seen by the doctor trying to detect it. But a purposeful set of adaptive attitudes and behavior of an individual do change depending on the setting and the individual's motives as he evaluates the usefulness and morality of his own position vis-à-vis any given set of figures. Only a magically maintained delusion does not collapse in the face of such logic. But the question here does not involve the sickness that controls psychiatry. The question concerning any delusion involves asking What do individuals and groups gain by maintaining such beliefs? My answer is that such thinking creates political power for psychiatry, power that can be sold to the highest bidder. In the case of conflict between children and adults, particularly students and teachers, ADHD and Oppositional Defiance Disorder automatically justify the actions of the authority in controlling the behavior of the child.

As discussed earlier the ability to define 'what is' and 'what should be' is necessary for successful political action. The power to resolve conflict between individuals and govern requires the ability to get the conflicting parties to agree with the judgments of those mediating or governing the conflict. Authority must have moral justification in its exercise of power. In a democratic and open society authority renders judgments based on an open and honest discussion of descriptive facts. In a closed society moral judgments pose as descriptive facts and authority acts on the basis of its presumed inherent superiority over inherently inferior others. I-Thou is replaced by I-It.

Psychiatry is structured along the classic lines of dictatorship and the closed society. Individuals diagnosed are seen totally in terms of a moral label and the more severe the diagnosis the more complete the condemnation. To be labeled with any mental illness but especially severe diagnoses such as schizophrenia is to be cast into the role of nonperson. Only those diagnosed and those involved in the mental health field as critics of its politics can understand the political consequences of being defined as a schizophrenic. The convention is to say, "He has ADHD or Oppositional Defiant Disorder," but "He is schizophrenic." I will delay a fuller discussion of the degree to which those diagnosed as schizophrenic or psychotic are persecuted and tortured by institutional psychiatry until Chapter 7.

It is difficult to overestimate the power of the psychiatrist and other experts in diagnosing mental health and illness as expert witnesses providing service to the courts, governmental offices, corporations, and other social structures wielding great power. The power possessed by a combination of government, psychiatry, and the wealthy international drug companies is awesome. The "clinicians" working for this conglomerate appear cloaked in the expertise of the scientist and the power of the M.D., Ph.D., or even M.S.W. degree. They bask in society's confidence and faith that they are indeed inherently superior *both in their judgment of the facts and the facts themselves.* The clinician provides a diagnosis of the parties involved in conflict and in so doing creates a moral hierarchy of the contestants. The clinician appears to have established the facts of the case making it easy for the judge to render a verdict or a politician to exercise power. But as I have outlined the facts have disappeared and exist only as an illusion.

Once a clinician has rendered the diagnosis there is no longer any need to describe the thoughts, emotions, and motives of an actual human being whose actions have taken place in an actual set of interpersonal and political relationships. There is also no longer any need to use these descriptions and make actual predictions of behavior that might take place in actual situations as yet unknown. Those involved with predicting human behavior know how difficult such predictions are and how little we understand about human behavior in general let alone what might occur when a person confronts situations and events not yet in existence. The mentally ill cannot be trusted to make rational decisions in the here and now, and since psychiatry in *DSM-IV* insists against all the evidence that schizophrenia and the other serious mental disorders are incurable, they can never be trusted to make rational decisions in the future.

When the clinician speaks not only does the need for facts disappear and unproven theories emerge as proven truths but the values and moral preferences of the clinician and those individuals and institutions for whom he labors move from the realm of the subjective and personal to the impersonal and objective. Moral values, which are always the subjective opinions of individuals and, however based on facts, never in themselves facts, now are transformed into facts and given existence above and beyond the opinions of any given individuals. Like the presentation of morals in religion as coming from God and written in stone, the moral pronouncements of psychiatry are often treated as if they are beyond dispute or refutation.

The psychiatric diagnosis, true to its roots in medieval religion and other examples of closed societies, pretends to get at the essence of the person, defining them in the eternal truths provided by the god(s). The law judges criminality and who should enjoy political freedom. Governments define treason and who should be citizens. Religion has the power to define sin and heresy and therefore determine who shall receive grace and enter heaven. But psychiatry tells us who should be heard and comprehended, taken seriously as a human being, and admitted as an equal into the dialogue of humanity. Psychiatry increasingly has the power to determine who shall appear as an equal before a judge, government, the clergy, or their fellow human beings.

Seth Farber (1998) traces the roots of psychiatric diagnosis to the notion of universal sin underlying the power of the medieval church. Today, everyone is in a state of psychiatric deficit, whereas our forbears found themselves in a state of perpetual sin. Szasz's (1970) most trenchant analysis of modern psychiatry traces its roots in and resemblance to the Inquisition. The Grand Inquisitor and the clergy are replaced by the psychiatrists who must convince their patients to accept their illness and dependence on them just as the church convinced the faithful to accept their inevitable sins and need of the clergy.

As an interesting aside, Szasz describes the work of the witch prickers, a group within the hierarchy whose job it is to prove beyond a doubt that the accused was a witch. The witch pricker searched the body of the accused for a wart, mole, or other "mark of the devil" and failing that stuck needles in the victim's body searching for a place that would not bleed. The failure to bleed proved the church's case. It is my contention that the modern witch pricker is the psychologist with his Rorschach inkblot test and other projective tests that are believed to examine the unconscious of the patient and discover pathology relevant to diagnosis. Robyn Dawes (1994) confirms that these tests lack reliability and validity and are no better than random guesses at predicting patient behavior. I am ashamed that I ever participated in a debacle that never fails to get the goods on these hapless individuals whose any and every answer become indicative of one type of pathology or another.

Early in my career when I still had faith that there was real meaning to what I discovered using tests, I was confronted with a gay man who as he leered at me responded with graphic pornographic responses to my inkblots. Shaken, I brought the protocol to my supervisor who allayed my concerns about drawing universal statements concerning the pathology of the patient by saying that in this case his responses were merely to the situation at hand and could not be generalized. Sometime later I discovered that a child I tested with an intelligence test had had a stomachache and these results as well reflected a momentary truth and not the essence of his intellectual functioning as is regularly assumed by those using intelligence tests. I realized that every test might reflect little more than thoughts, feelings, and behaviors of the moment and current situation and that drawing generalizations from them that became diagnoses reflecting lifelong pathology and brain injury was destructive to the patient and all concerned.

THE POLITICAL CONSEQUENCES
OF PSYCHIATRIC IDEOLOGY

It is simply beyond the province of this book to detail the debasement of most of the social institutions of our society by the forces of organized psychiatry. Examples abound that demonstrate the seeming powerlessness of judges to decide in cases of adoption, child placement, or the sentencing of criminals without the testimony of expert witnesses from the mental health system, psychiatry in particular. Criminals might go free if psychiatrists make an adequate enough case for mental illnesses that seemingly account for the behavior of the accused. Individuals innocent of any crime might be incarcerated and forced into treatment by testimony accusing them of being mentally ill. The legal system seems to increasingly view the rights and privileges of its citizens through the distorted lens of psychiatry.

The inability of the legal system to separate the rights and privileges of citizens from the personal motives and history of the perpetrator is all but complete. In a civilized society the motives and states of mind of individuals accused of crime can always play a role in creating extenuating circumstances in evaluating guilt and in sentencing procedures. However, the political issues in defining an individual's rights and responsibilities as a citizen cannot be wholly conflated with the psychology of the individual without compromising those rights. *Our society has allowed the status of the individual as citizen be replaced by the status of the individual as patient.* The folly and dangers of this transformation are compounded by the fact that psychiatry does not demonstrate the facts that might help understand the motives of the accused but present a moral judgment posing as a fact.

Any given crime can be treated as an illness and the treatment, both its course and length, determined exclusively by the "experts" assigned to the case. Any individual can be diagnosed and treated as a criminal. Once assigned to psychiatry and placed in a "treatment" facility neither the diagnosed individuals nor the public are protected by constitutional guarantees as to how they will be treated or when they will be released. The political tenor of the times will determine whether individuals might be released for the same crime in days, weeks, years, or never. The release will be predicated on the severity of the illness, the faith that the treatment has worked and the psychiatric opinion that the diagnosed individual is better or even cured.

But a patient cannot be cured of a label or of a disease that does not exist. The public must hope that the released patient is indeed no longer violent or intends to commit additional crimes. The diagnosed patient who has committed no crime must hope that his cure will be divined by his "therapists" since there are no markers or symptoms of the illness other than the unwanted behaviors that led to a diagnosis in the first place. Unlike an assessment of a medical disease there are no lab reports demonstrating reduced levels of pathogen, no X rays of shrunken tumors, no healed organs, and so on. The lack of objective evidence of cure or remission and the power of the psychiatrist to label make it possible for virtually any individual to be incarcerated and "treated" against their will, making psychiatry a potent political force indeed.

If psychiatry is pseudomedicine then the hospitals where patients are placed are not really hospitals. Psychiatric hospitals have locks on the doors and bars on the windows making them prisons not hospitals. No matter how serious the diagnosis of a medical disease a patient can refuse treatment and leave the hospital even if it is against medical advice. Not so the psychiatric patient. Once diagnosed, an individual who has neither been charged nor convicted of a crime can be held and treated against her/his will. It is interesting that occasionally a patient will walk away from a mental hospital and the public and political establishment will be as outraged as if a convicted felon walked away from a prison. People are supposed to be able to leave a hospital if they wish to. The outrage felt by the public exists because there is an implicit understanding that the mentally ill are to be treated as criminals and the mental hospital is in fact a prison.

If there are no true psychiatric diseases and psychiatric hospitals are more like prisons than medical establishments, then what can be said of psychiatric treatments, especially when they are forced on a patient? From my perspective, psychiatric treatments have as their primary goal changing unwanted behavior into wanted behavior. In the case of forced treatment the individual is being asked to change behavior that he wishes to continue and replace it with behavior of which his captives approve. To me, this defines torture and not treatment. (An old saw concerning psychiatry goes: Psychiatry is the profession where symptoms the patient wants are replaced with symptoms he does not want.)

The increased use of forced hospitalization and treatment (incarceration and torture) represents one of the most flagrant examples of violations of our constitution and the dangers of an emerging dictatorship. The leadership of this emerging plutocracy are a combination of governmental offices including those concerned with public health and large pharmaceutical corporations whose economic health are in no small measure based on the sale of drugs, euphemistically called "medicines." Szasz (2001) refers to this emerging dictatorship as either a "therapeutic state" or a "pharmacracy."

The agents of this closed society are the medical establishment with mental health professionals and psychiatry in particular as the proximate agents of enforcement. Groups of supposedly concerned relatives of the mentally ill often provide the political justification of forced treatment by lobbying Congress and placing their message in front of the public. The media never seems to ask or care about the fact that many of these groups receive much of their funding from the drug companies. The original leadership of these organizations comprised of genuinely desperate parents and relatives of those labeled "mentally ill" often have long since abandoned the organizations that they helped found. Few also seem interested in asking just how much of the genuine suffering of the mentally ill is a product of their treatment by the mental health system; that is a real issue that I will discuss.

Those suffering the type of unwanted thoughts, emotions, and behavioral patterns that end up being diagnosed can be held for psychiatric evaluation and treatment if they commit a crime or otherwise become a public menace or nuisance. But a person can be committed for treatment if worried or frightened, and desperate relatives seek psychiatric care for a relative who refuses treatment. The justification for this incarceration is to be found in the growing use of "right-to-treatment" laws that basically state that mentally ill persons have a right to be treated but it is in the nature of their illness that they can neither recognize that they are ill nor be trusted to act intelligently on their own behalf. The psychiatrist determines who lacks the ability to recognize their illnesses and thus must be in the privileged position of determining who is or is not treated.

A second set of forces operates to increase the number of individuals subject to forced treatment. Medicine exists in both a public and a private sphere. Typically, an individual seeking medical help contracts with a physician for his services. Under this arrangement both parties are bound by the contract into which both voluntarily enter. The doctor works for the patient and is bound by rules of confidentiality. In their public role physicians work for the government as public health personnel. Public health doctors are concerned with protecting the public from highly communicable diseases such as plague and smallpox as well as diseases such as anthrax that can result from acts of terrorism.

In recent years highly publicized incidents involving people diagnosed as mentally ill committing crimes has turned the concept of mental illness into a public health issue. The public, fearing crime, has been led to imagine that all those diagnosed as mentally ill might be dangerous and therefore should be kept under close surveillance and if in the opinion of the psychiatrist be treated if necessary. In the schema of the authoritarian society the mentally ill increasingly play the role of the despised minority and feared and hated scapegoat. At present the public accepts and even demands that psychiatry has the power to treat people against their will, and the number of such cases continues to rise.

I make clear that in many specific cases such as those involving the prevention of a suicide or helping an individual who is truly helpless to protect herself/himself the notion of protective custody is both appealing and compelling. *However, these decisions must be made with full awareness that they are political and not medical.* They must also remain the exception to the political rule rather than the model. In a system in which everyone fits into one or more diagnostic category and the power of the expert can apply these elastic labels to any citizen, there exists a system capable of great tyranny. Where treatments are by definition forms of torture and the torture can be directed against individuals guilty of bad thinking, wrongful expression of emotion, patterns of speech, and acts of overt behavior, the possibility of totalitarianism looms large and menacing.

I turn now to a discussion concerning the evidence that psychiatry might be actually dealing with biological diseases wrongfully classified as mental diseases. This discussion proves critical because increasingly the treatments that Shorter (1997) considers smashing successes involve the chemical and mechanical alterations of the living brain. Several issues must be addressed. If there is no evidence proving that an individual has an organic brain disorder of one type or another, then what justification exists for alterations of perfectly normal brains? If there are no brain problems under treatment, then what effects do these intrusions into the brain have? If there are true brain problems, are these treatments safe and efficacious? Finally, in those situations of forced treatment what is the nature of the tortures being applied to the persons of the incarcerated?

PSYCHIATRIC DISORDERS AS
BRAIN AND GENETIC DISEASES

The psychiatric establishment christened the 1990s the "decade of the brain." The advent of psychiatry's new renaissance followed several decades in which scientists began to have some genuine success in understanding the anatomy and physiology of the brain. Psychiatry, in consort with large and powerful drug companies, capitalized on the success of neurobiology and neurochemistry and by employing very effective advertising and public relationships techniques convinced the public and the professional communities that psychiatric diseases involved brain disorders, often with genetic predispositions. It was simultaneously argued that these biological diseases required medical interventions involving alterations of either brain chemistry or the structure of the brain itself.

I contend that an examination of the available scientific evidence fails to support the contentions that any mental illnesses or disorders have either a genetic predisposition or an underlying brain disease. It is equally true that evidence is lacking to refute the genetic and biological hypotheses but then critics of the biological theory of mental disorders are not trying to justify the use of drugs or brain surgery. If mental illnesses are not, or do not, involve medical conditions, then the drugs given to "treat" these problems are not medicines but just drugs. Altering the brain's structure or function takes on a very different meaning if the diseases for which they are intended treatments are not literally diseases but metaphorical in nature.

The lack of proof for the medical model of psychiatry comes from the fact that there are no known medical or biological tests for any of the major diagnostic categories diagnosed behaviorally. No patient diagnosed with any of the "disorders" discussed earlier nor those diagnosed with "Schizophrenia," "Major Depressive Disorder," or "Bi-Polar Disorder" is ever sent for any recognized, routinely employed laboratory test. *Indeed, the* DSM-IV *makes clear that no such tests exist.* Moreover, when drug companies advertise their treatments for these and other disorders they are forced by law and ethical considerations to state that these disorders "may" involve chemical imbalances in the brain. There seems little doubt that if these companies could make genuine claims of brain difficulties they would certainly do so.

There is something morbidly laughable when a commercial for a serotonin reuptake inhibitor suggests that there "could be" a chemical imbalance involved in depression, social anxiety disorder, premenstrual dysphoric disorder, chronic anxiety disorder, and post-traumatic stress disorder and that the drug in question acts to restore the imbalance. How can the therapeutic claim be made for the drug if the chemical imbalance may or may not exist? Can all of these separate so-called diseases involve the exact same chemical imbalance and be treated with the same drug? Am I and the other critics aware of the issues being raised here the only ones left feeling incredulous and surreal while watching these commercials that bombard the viewing public day after day?

A robust literature now exists that brings into dispute the claims of biopsychiatry and the drug companies that depression is the result of low levels of serotonin or that schizophrenia is a product of high levels of another neurotransmitter, dopamine. One of the earliest and most comprehensive in this growing literature—that of Sarbin and Mancuso (1980)—examined fifteen hundred studies purporting to find biological and other markers for schizophrenia. Their critique included the introduction of competing studies with results that disconfirmed a number of reported studies. Criticisms were also levied at the methodologies of a number of studies as well as reinterpretations of the conclusions of many. The authors concluded that no markers were found for schizophrenia and that in all cases the diagnoses were based

solely on behavioral indicators. They concluded that the search for proof that
schizophrenia is a true medical disease is similar to the search for the unicorn
and likely to be just as successful.

The ongoing work of Peter Breggin (1997, 2000), Peter Breggin and
David Cohen (2000), Ty Colbert (1996), Al Siebert (1999), Laurence
Simon (2000b), Eliot Valenstein (1998), and a host of others provide compelling evidence of the following: The pattern of behaviors diagnosed as
mental illnesses lack credible proof of being correlated with any consistent
chemical or anatomical deviations.

It is virtually impossible to follow the number of discoveries concerning various forms of brain damage that appear, are touted as the proof that
schizophrenia or some other disorder is a brain disease, only to disappear
from the literature as quickly as they appeared. Either subsequent study fails
to verify the discovery or else large numbers of individuals seem to possess
the newly discovered biological marker of diseases. For example, K. Zakanis
and colleagues (2000) examined the literature involved with examining
brains of schizophrenic patients for evidence of temporal lobe deficits, a recent discovery that had the psychiatric world convinced that it at last could
prove that schizophrenia is a brain disease. Their review demonstrated that
some studies found no deficits, a minority revealed some deficit, while still
others revealed augmented function and structure rather than a deficit. The
authors concluded that the current evidence disconfirms the hypothesis of
temporal lobe deficiency. Two hundred years of studying the blood, urine,
brains, and other body parts have yet to produce any viable evidence of
brain problems in the mentally ill.

The public has been led to believe that many mental illnesses, especially serious ones such as schizophrenia and major forms of depression, have
a proven genetic predisposition or causation. Such evidence has been provided by studies of monozygotic and dizygotic twins and larger studies of
children who were adopted as a consequence of their mothers having been
hospitalized for mental illness. Studies such as those by Jay Joseph (1999a,b,
2000) call into question both the methodology and the conclusions of all of
the important genetic studies done on mental illnesses such as schizophrenia.

Twin studies are often unreliable because of the small samples available. Results demonstrating a purely genetic cause of the disease is called
into question because many of the twins studied were not removed from the
homes of their psychotic parents until they were of an age when they might
have been affected by their parent's behavior. In addition, it is known that
twins are treated more alike than nontwin siblings, creating still another environmental counterargument to the genetic hypothesis.

The adoption studies usually quoted in this realm are the Finnish and
Danish adoption studies. In these studies the rates of emerging cases of
schizophrenia were compared in groups of children put up for adoption

from parents hospitalized for mental illness and children from homes with no indications of mental illness. Sample sizes were now larger but were no less equivocal in their results. While children were removed from their parents' care the ages of separation varied greatly, making it possible that their behavior was affected by their association with their parents as much as it might have been affected by genetics.

Moreover, Joseph (1999a) points out that the Finns have a long-standing prejudice against the mentally ill and demonstrate as strong a belief in eugenics as their medical counterparts in the United States. The children of the schizophrenics were not only stigmatized but also were often placed in homes with known criminals or other family members who were themselves mentally ill. Such factors also create problems for those trying to advance a specifically genetic argument for schizophrenia. Finally, Joseph's reanalysis (1999b) of the statistical data showing a difference in schizophrenic rates between groups of genetically similar and genetically different children suggests that the reported differences could have resulted from chance. However, even if statistical significance was reached, the differences between groups was so small as to argue for an environmental or very weak genetic effect in explaining schizophrenia.

Evidence for a genetic explanation for mental illness has come and gone with the same frequency as biochemical and anatomical ones. Erica Goode (2001) evaluates the current status of the genetic hypothesis of mental illness. For example, she quotes Dr. T. Conrad Gilliam, codirector of the Columbia Genome Center at Columbia University, on the results of research into genetics and mental illness over the last decade, "The jury is still out." After interviewing a number of leading scientists in the field, Goode concludes that they have given up the search either for a single gene or for an explanation that does not include environmental factors interacting in complex ways with genes. In short, we do not know why people behave in the complex ways that they do.

Schizophrenia is not an illness by any of the evidence that now exists. Schizophrenia is a moral label for a complex of patterns of behavior that are alarming, unwanted, and difficult to understand. Schizophrenia is a way of being in the world and it may well turn out that asking questions about the genetic and biochemical substrate of schizophrenia is the same as asking why one is a psychiatrist. Put that way it is an interesting but daunting question. Do we as yet know enough to explain and predict the mode of a person's being in the world? The answer is obviously not; but in the world of the pseudoscience of psychiatry the deeper, more difficult philosophical and empirical questions concerning personality and its development do not get asked. If they are not asked they can never be answered. I will return to some of the philosophical issues bedeviling clinical psychology and psychiatry in Chapter 7.

TREATMENTS: SAFE AND EFFECTIVE?

If mental disorders are not real illnesses but instead are moral judgments of patterns of unwanted, hard-to-understand behavior, then those psychiatric treatments involving the brain are not treatments at all. I suggest that they are, in actuality, control mechanisms and punishments for deviant behavior. The more severe the diagnosis, that is, the harsher the moral label, the harsher the punishment. Robert Whitaker (2002) makes clear that in the past each and every physical treatment of those labeled "mad" involved the induction of terror and pain. His book is mandatory reading for anyone interested in the dismal political history of institutional psychiatry.

Whitaker along with Peter Breggin (1997) and a growing number of other researchers make a compelling case that in our modern era each and every chemical and physical treatment leads to a disabling of whatever is normal brain function for any given individual. I suggest that the only reason damaging a person's body and brain can be referred to as "a safe and efficacious treatment" is because the therapists involved really believe that their patients are morally defective and their diagnoses imply that. I begin my discussion with the so-called chemical therapies.

Interventions involving chemicals or physical alterations of the brain cannot be assumed to be medical treatments and therefore are no different from the pleasures or relief sought from alcohol, marijuana, or any other drug, legal or illegal. The same references provided earlier that question the validity of the organic disease hypotheses of mental illness come to the conclusion that the drugs provided by psychiatrists and other nonpsychiatric physicians correct no chemical imbalances in anyone's brain and cure or ameliorate no known problems in brain functioning. Rather they work in general ways affecting the mentally ill and the mentally healthy in highly similar ways.

For example, serotonin reuptake inhibitors, originally prescribed for human beings with depression, are prescribed for a wide variety of emotional upsets in *humans and animals alike.* Dogs upset with long hours alone in apartments are apparently soothed and calmed by the same drugs given to millions of human beings labeled "depressed," "anxious," "socially insecure," and the like. Apparently it is not in a canine's makeup to live alone for long periods of time but their adjustment to a human schedule has been made necessary by their symbiotic relationship with our species. Are we to label these animals mentally ill for their emotional responses to a lifestyle to which they cannot adjust? Are the drugs that interfere with the production of emotions that motivate them to urinate or defecate on the carpet expressions of mental illness? Are we to believe that Prozac is a cure for their mental disturbances or some chemical imbalance in their canine brains? Absurd! But such is psychiatric logic and its partial basis provided by the economic needs of the companies selling these drugs.

Psychiatric drugs, like all the drugs that human beings have been taking to alter their states of consciousness from the emergence of our species, have their value measured by the degree to which they help those associated with their use. One measure of their value involves the degree to which their users feel differently and better than if not taken. Another measure involves the degree to which those involved with the user are pleased with its effects on the user. Still a third might be the advantage provided by society at large and especially those selling or providing the drugs. Finally, any assessment of the use of drugs must include a discussion of the price paid for their use by all concerned. I will delay a fuller discussion concerning the price society is paying for the use of psychiatric drugs until Chapter 6, but here I will consider the cost to those who use drugs in terms of their safety and effects on the health of the user.

I deal briefly with three classes of psychiatric drugs: neuroleptic drugs given with and without patient acceptance to schizophrenics and others diagnosed as psychotic, antidepressants given to those diagnosed as seriously depressed, and stimulant drugs such as methylphenidates and amphetamines given to children diagnosed as learning disabled and ADHD. There are several conclusions that can be made of all psychiatric drugs. The first is that they alter normal brain chemistry or the as-yet-unknown abnormal brain processes that might be associated with various diagnostic groups and they all work by disabling the functioning of what is normal for any given individual's brain. The second conclusion is that in disabling the functioning of the brain all psychiatric drugs produce a variety of significant neurological impairments of which some might well be permanent. *Given that none of these drugs are a genuine treatment in any medical sense, it can be concluded that in the aggregate the damaging effects of these drugs represent one of the most significant iatrogenic disease processes in human history.*

I begin with the antipsychotic drugs collectively known as "neuroleptics." The great breakthrough in psychiatric treatment came in the 1950s with the accidental discovery of a class of drugs known as "phenothiozines." Farber (1996), Valenstein (1998), and Whitaker (2002), trace the discovery of these drugs and their early use in psychiatric hospitals to calm and make the psychiatric patients docile and easier to manage. They all quote from the scientific journals of the time that the phenothiozines were perceived as a chemical lobotomy and not as any cure or amelioration of abnormal brain chemistry. Schizophrenia was (and still is) seen as an incurable disease and that the best that could be hoped for was to keep the patients calm and, perhaps even more important, make things easier for their caretakers. It is clear that history was rewritten during the 1990s with the notion that neuroleptic drugs ameliorate the abnormal brain chemistry of the psychotic patient rather than aid in keeping the patient population docile. I add that these treatments also punished those referred to as "schizophrenic" for the moral transgressions their behavior represents.

The whole range of antipsychotic drugs are in general of more value to those who live or work with patients experiencing psychosis than they are to the patients themselves. Most psychiatric patients despise how these drugs make them feel and part of the proof of this is the fact that there is virtually no black market for them. One of my patients put it best when he referred to the drugs he was given as "handcuffs in a bottle." Patients regularly complain of difficulty concentrating or experiencing the smallest actions as requiring a massive effort of will.

In his critique of psychiatric research David Cohen (2000) points out that once a person is labeled "schizophrenic" their testimony as to how they experience their treatment (or any other aspect of life) is discounted and seen as merely the symptom of their disease. It is rare in psychiatric research on the effects of these drugs that patients are asked about their subjective experiences of the drugs that they take. The psychological effects of these drugs are often defined as the symptoms of the disease. A patient that I worked with for many years swore that her hallucinations did not begin until after she began taking a phenothiozine drug. Such stories are common among patients but utterly discounted by the average psychiatrist prescribing these drugs.

The neurological effects of antipsychotic drugs are devastating on a majority of those taking them (Breggin, 1997; Breggin and Cohen, 2000; Valenstein, 1998). Estimates are that as few as 25 percent and as many as 65 percent of all patients taking neuroleptic drugs develop a disfiguring and disabling brain problem known as "tardive dyskinesia." An unknown, but significant number develops a deep painful set of feelings that relate to unwanted movements of the limbs known as "akathesia." An estimated 1 percent of users develop a fatal disease known as "neuroleptic malignant disorder." While many patients accept that they have no choice but to use these drugs or be hospitalized, few are told the truth concerning the devastation these drugs bring to their lives. Since the "decade of the brain," the rise in managed care, and the increased power of the drug manufacturers, even fewer are ever told of any alternative explanations or treatments for the patterns of behavior that led to their diagnosis.

Cohen (2000) and others point out that as soon as drug companies develop a new drug for a mental disease that they claim has fewer side effects than the drugs that they replace they will become more open and forthcoming as to just how devastating the older treatment could be. Until that point they will do all they can to prevent negative findings to be published. Joseph Glenmullen (2001) and Whitaker (2002) have published the results of investigations concerning the attempts of drug companies to not only prevent negative results from being published but in controlling and compromising the research done in this area of concern. At present there are a flood of newer antipsychotic medications being touted as safer than older drugs but there is no substantive evidence that they are any less dangerous than those they have replaced.

The second great "triumph" of modern biopsychiatry involves the endless propaganda that the sadness, hopelessness, and despair that has been labeled "depression" is a brain disease involving a chemical imbalance of neurotransmitters. The public has been informed by an endless media blitz that depression (known within psychiatric circles as "the common cold of psychiatry") is easily treated by the use of a new generation of antidepressant medications known as "serotonin reuptake inhibitors," or "SSRIs." Anecdotes, aided by a number of testimonies by high-profile celebrities such as author William Styron and television reporter Mike Wallace, abound as to the success of these drugs in treating depression. Sales of the drug skyrocketed after psychiatrist Peter Kamner published his book *Talking to Prozac*, which suggested that the drug (the original and first successfully marketed SSRI) was capable of changing human personality and society itself. However, it is not clear from real research just how these drugs work in relieving depression, just how many individuals find genuine relief in them, and, finally, just how safe the drug, prescribed to tens of millions of Americans, actually is.

While clearly not a treatment (as we have seen depression is not a disease and evidence is lacking as to its cause being a brain problem of any kind) SSRIs are apparently tolerated and enjoyed by many more patients than the neuroleptics prescribed for those diagnosed as psychotic. It appears to be of real value to many of those taking it. While the literature on SSRIs is confusing and contradictory at best, it is clear that it is neither as safe nor effective as advertised. For every anecdote that SSRIs have changed a person's life, there seem to be an equal number of anecdotes that SSRIs create intolerable feelings of excitement, anxiety, akathesia, and other hard-to-classify subjective complaints. Recent court decisions in Great Britain have forced the drug companies to admit that the SSRIs are extremely addictive, a fact denied until the courts examined research to the contrary. Large numbers of those who are prescribed these drugs discontinue their use.

Valenstein (1998) reports an unusual study in which several of the researchers involved in the development of the SSRIs took the drugs to assess their own subjective reaction to their invention. They reported symptoms of asognosia, a neurological condition in which individuals become incapable of recognizing their own distress and disease processes. Janet Garland and Elizabeth Baerg (2001) report cases of "amotivational syndrome" in teenagers prescribed two popular SSRIs. They write, "A frontal lobe syndrome characterized by apathy, indifference, loss of initiative, and/or disinhibition has developed in some adults with SSRI therapy but has not been previously reported in the pediatric population" (p. 6). It is possible that many individuals adjusting to life on psychiatric drugs do not feel better but simply either do not feel anything or do not react to their own distress or life problems. Another of Cohen's (2000) criticisms concerning research into the effects of psychiatric drugs is the general lack of query into just what kind of life is lived by those treated with drugs. Is their life restored to one that is rich and meaningful or does the patient exist in a limbo of drug-induced apathy? Rarely is an improved life the case with schizophrenics treated with antipsychotic medication. The same might be the case with many taking SSRIs and other antidepressant drugs.

A theoretical linkage between SSRIs and violent and suicidal behavior has made its way into several high-profile court cases (Rogers and Waterhouse, 2001) including the high school massacre in Littleton, Colorado, by two students, both of whom were taking SSRIs. Breggin (2000) and a growing number of others point out that the pharmacological effects of these drugs are similar to cocaine and may well induce agitation into the subjective state of a depressed individual. As rage is often a component of depression, the SSRIs and cocaine, both stimulant drugs, might well help create an increase in dangerous behaviors.

A. R. Praeda and colleagues (2001) report that 8.1 percent of 533 admissions to Yale University Hospital in a fourteen-month period were for *mania or psychosis caused by an antidepressant*. Stuart Shipko (2001), a psychiatrist writes, "It looks like about 1/3 of all patients on SSRI's develop clear cut akathesia, most but not all of which stops when the drug is stopped" (p. 1). Whatever the eventual outcome of the current debate over the safety and effectiveness of the antidepressants it is clear that they are not the panacea for depression or any other so-called mental disease that they are promoted to be.

I turn next to the rapidly developing controversy over the use of stimulant drugs such as methylphenidates and amphetamines in treating millions of children labeled as "learning disabled," "attention-deficit disorder" (ADD), and "ADHD." Breggin (1999a,b, 2000), Breggin and Cohen (2000), Brian Vastag (2001), and others have concluded that these stimulants act like cocaine and are more addictive than cocaine and they cause significant damage to the brains and general health of the children taking them. ADD/ADHD are moral judgments, not diseases. There is no evidence supporting the claim of brain or biochemical disturbance in the children prescribed these drugs known on the black market and by the large number of recreational users as "speed." Therefore the use of these drugs on children represent one of the most cynical low points in the whole desultory history of psychiatry and their patrons in the drug companies.

The handwriting may already be on the wall for the use of stimulants in children. Research suggests that they are far less effective in helping schoolchildren achieve success in school than their proponents claim. Any positive academic effects are more than offset by the side effects that include migraine headaches, loss of appetite and weight loss, sleep disturbances, high blood pressure, and heart disease.

Moreover, the Dallas law firm of Waters and Kraus, the same group that successfully sued the tobacco companies, has brought a class action lawsuit against Novartis (the manufacturer of Ritalin, a methylphenidate), the American Psychiatric Association, and CHADD, a supposedly independent support group of people involved with the disease (O'Meara, 2000). The lawsuit will demand that the named defendants not only prove that ADHD is a real disease but defend against the claim that a conspiracy existed to have millions of children diagnosed as ADHD in order to sell more drugs.

I close this section with a brief discussion of electroconvulsive shock therapy (ECT). This is a process of passing an electric current through the brain of individuals suffering from a variety of mental disorders but most notably depression. Daniel Smith (2001), a journalist, writes of shock therapy, "Electroconvulsive therapy was once psychiatry's most terrifying tool—blunt, painful and widely abused. It is now a safe and effective treatment for a wide range of mental illnesses" (p. 10). Once again a member of the media pronounces as safe and effective a supposed treatment without a meaningful discussion concerning the evidence that ECT is neither safe nor effective.

It goes without saying that Smith and Shorter (1997), in whose history ECT receives the same uncritical evaluation, never question the underlying myth of mental illness. ECT does something to those who receive it but whatever benefit that might accrue does not represent cure or amelioration of a medical condition. An examination of how ECT works reveals a plethora of explanations, none of which are sustained historically and none of which deals honestly with the evidence that many individuals experience long-term memory loss and various forms of brain injury as a result. Lost in all of the discussions is the use of ECT in forced treatment, making it clearly a form of torture rather than a treatment and giving lie to Smith's belief that the bad old days of ECT use are past.

Nathaniel Lehrman (2001), a psychiatrist, writes in rebuttal to Smith, "Two seemingly contradictory facts therefore characterize the treatment: (1) it causes undoubted brain damage manifested by memory and thinking difficulties of varying intensity and duration, and (2) it can temporarily relieve the depression of many patients. The temporary improvement is due to the brain damage and confusion cause by the treatment" (p. 1).

Leye Jeanette Chrzanowski (2001) reports that the American Psychiatric Association's own task force survey found that some 41 percent of psychiatrists responding answered yes to the question Is it likely that ECT produces slight or subtle brain damage? She quotes Stanley Samet, M.D., as saying in *Clinical Psychiatry News*, "As a neurologist and electroencephalographer, I have seen many patients after ECT, and I have no doubt that ECT produced effects similar to those of a head injury. ECT in effect may be defined as a controlled type of brain damage produced by electrical means" (p. 4). At a staff meeting at the mental health clinic where I worked for many years our chief psychiatrist said of the suicidal patient under discussion, "I'd like to get her into the hospital for some shock therapy. It'll scramble her brains enough for her to forget how to be so crazy."

How can physicians induce brain damage in individuals they claim are already suffering brain dysfunction and claim that it is treatment? My answer lies in the reality that any *DSM* represents moral, rather than medical judgments and that these deviant and morally deficient beings must actually deserve what is being done to them. They are being controlled and punished and the more severe the diagnosis, the more severe the punishment. I further develop this thesis in Chapter 7 when I discuss schizophrenia.

Linda Andre, herself a survivor of ECT, has formed an organization of hundreds of individuals who tell of being disabled by the supposed treatment after being convinced by their physicians that it is safe and effective and that any memory loss is minor and temporary. Each can tell a story similar to the testimony provided by the individual who writes the following:

I really don't know who can help me. . . . I have suffered from depression for over the past ten years. I have been to many doctors . . . and finally, electric shock treatment was prescribed by one of these "medicational experts." That was two years ago and my life is completely destroyed. . . . I had 12–18 treatments. . . . I suffered terrible migrane headaches, nauseousness and horrible memory loss. I woke up at the last treatment and was freaking out and was admitted to the psych ward at the hospital because I was so disoriented. . . . My boss noticed my performance decrease . . . and after nine months was fired from my job. I was with them for 8 years. I lost all self-esteem, was even more suicidal and continued to get worse. . . . I had a 3.8 GPA in college and now can't even remember a face or what I had for dinner yesterday. I'm scared of the future and how much worse it's going to get.

PSYCHIATRY AS A "SMASHING SUCCESS"

If one reads a celebratory history of psychiatry such as the one authored by Edward Shorter (1997) or books devastatingly critical of the field such as those by Richard Gosden (2001), Jeffrey Mousaiff Masson (1988), Thomas Szasz (1970), or Robert Whitaker (2002), one reads exactly the same history. Only the ending is different with celebrants proclaiming that the new biologically oriented psychiatry is scientific, moral, and produces at long last safe and effective treatment for mental diseases. In both types of manuscripts one reads of the rise of horrendous institutions such as Bedlam in England and others all over Europe and the United States in which patients were tortured, physically and mentally destroyed, and from which they rarely emerged better than when they had entered.

One reads of the endless theories that were presented as truthful and scientific without a shred of real evidence that not only flourished but also supported a variety of ineffective and/or frankly damaging treatments. I close this chapter by discussing the dreadful and recent era of biological psychiatry in which prefontal lobotomy flourished in Europe and the United States. Invented in the early 1940s by Ignaz Monaz, a Portuguese psychiatrist, lobotomy involved cutting through the skull of the patient and severing various amounts of tissue from the frontal lobes of the patient. Patients did indeed show fewer psychiatric symptoms, such as anxiety and intense fears, and they did, in general, become more docile and easier to manage by hospital personnel and family members.

However, the procedure also took the humanity from the bulk of these individuals, turning them into passive vegetables rather than human beings struggling to overcome problems in living. Monaz won the Nobel Prize for medicine for a procedure first hailed by the media as a miracle cure for mental illnesses that later became synonymous with butchery and the abuse of power. The individual credited with lobotomy's downfall was Walter Freeman, a neurologist, who used an ice pick to sever the frontal lobes of individuals by entering the brain through the orb of the eye. Freeman kept a record of 3,439 lobotomies that he performed in his career. (A total of between 40,000 and 50,000 were performed in the United States alone.) He committed his atrocities in hotel rooms and his patients' homes as well as in hospitals, making it hard to know just how many of his patients died or were left completely crippled by a procedure that cut differing amounts of tissue from each victim.

What is important to note is that there were few, if any, protests by the medical or the psychiatric community against the procedure or the actions of Freeman and his associates. Only slowly did psychiatry accept the ultimate discreditation of the lobotomy and the theory on which it was based and then mostly because of the introduction of the chemical lobotomies provided by the new neuroleptic drugs. Nothing has changed in psychiatry since its inception. It is my opinion that psychiatry is based as it is on a lie that it will never repudiate. Its science and morality are compromised by the complete conflation of moral judgment with descriptive fact. It increasingly draws its resources from large corporations whose main motive is the bottom line of their ledgers.

Psychiatry is the only branch of medicine that has motivated the emergence of grassroots organizations comprised of individuals who refer to themselves as "psychiatric survivors." While there are many support groups helping individuals cope with a variety of dreaded diseases, the survivor movement is the only one supporting individuals for the effects of their treatments and fighting against the doctors themselves. It would be as if there were oncology survivor groups rather than cancer survivor organizations. For example, Support Coalition International coordinates the activities of over one hundred organizations of survivors in fourteen countries and publishes a journal that is mailed to more than 25,000 individuals. This, in itself, should be proof that psychiatry is anything but a smashing success, that the field cannot be reformed, and that it is a danger and a threat to every individual and the democratic society each seeks to maintain.

CHAPTER 5

Psychotherapy II: Psychoanalysis

INTRODUCTION

I introduce this topic in personal terms because I have a long-standing, ongoing, complex relationship with the ideas and the field of psychoanalysis. This book is, at least in part, a personal attempt to make a contribution to the theories and practice of psychoanalysis, endeavors with which I have been ambivalently involved for over thirty-five years. I have been intimately involved with psychoanalysis and psychoanalysts as part of my graduate training, my many years of work in mental health clinics, and as an analytic patient. Yet, in spite of twice being accepted to psychoanalytic training programs, I withdrew early in the experience for a variety of reasons. Some of my motives I understood and still find completely valid and others, which I barely understood at the time I acted upon them, still lead me to wonder if I did the right thing. As a result I am both an insider and an outsider in relation to the analytic community—a position that permits me an individual perspective on the problems and strengths of this multifaceted and fascinating enterprise.

I limit my discussion of psychoanalysis to this one chapter, which forces me to schematize, compress, and gloss over important issues more than I would like and more than the topic deserves. Sigmund Freud, the agreed-upon founder of psychoanalysis, clearly used the term to represent both a set of theoretical formulations and a type of psychotherapy. Over the many years of its existence psychoanalysis has meant many things to many people and in effect represents a very large number of theoretical formulations and a wide variety of modes of psychotherapy. The standard introductory textbooks in psychology, and even those created for introductory courses in personality theory, rarely describe analysis as anything but syn-onymous with Freudian formulations. However, an examination of some of the modern versions of psychoanalysis reveals little in common with Freud; however, their adherents might protest otherwise. For me to reach my goal of demonstrating the pro- and antidemocratic elements of both theories and practices I will be forced to cover a lot of ground in very little space.

Edward Shorter, whose history of psychiatry was discussed extensively in the last chapter, presents psychoanalysis as an unfortunate hiatus and a distraction in psychiatry's triumphant march toward its current glory as a biomedical specialty. Shorter confuses Freud and his circle of disciples with psychoanalysis and like so many critics of psychoanalysis glosses over the many subtleties and contradictions in Freud's work as well as modern ver-sions of analysis such as the interpersonal and intersubjective versions of the enterprise. I am of the opinion that there are numerous elements within the psychoanalytic community and literature that not only can provide the building blocks of a democratic and humanistic psychotherapy but also in-fuse mainstream and other elements of psychology with new life and vigor. Moreover, I agree with Philip Reiff (1966) who suggests that Freud's output represents the first genuine reform of psychiatry whose history and present directions are based on the "dead theories" of biological reductionism.

I am also of the opinion that psychoanalysis is in deep trouble. If it does not confront the authoritarianism, pretentiousness, and pseudoscientific as-pects of its past and present not only may analysis not survive but probably does not deserve to. Unless psychoanalysis rejects its links to psychiatry with all that psychiatry politically represents and joins with the best of the human sciences to become a science true to its subject matter, analysis will continue to be a beleaguered field embodying some of the worst and most conserva-tive aspects of the larger field of psychotherapy. It will also continue to be comprised of practitioners charging large fees to wealthy clients and geo-graphically isolated in large urban areas such as New York City. I offer the fol-lowing as evidence for my claim in addition to the personal comments made to me by practitioners in the field.

First, a recent article in the *American Psychologist*, perhaps the most in-fluential mainstream journal in psychology, dealt with the future of the field of psychology. Its authors (Robins, Gosling, and Craik, 1999) suggest that psy-choanalysis has very little, if any, future because their empirical research has revealed that it has virtually no serious standings at present in the academic community training the next generation of psychologists. They write,

Mainstream scientific psychology has paid little attention to research published in the preeminent psychoanalytic journals over the past two decades. Moreover, there have been relatively few psychoanalytic dissertations or psychoanalytic flagship ar-ticles over the past several decades. Psychoanalysis seems to be a relatively self-contained camp, perhaps interacting more directly with research in psychiatry and with scholarship in the humanities. (pp. 123–124)

The general reasons given for psychoanalysis' imminent demise in this article, and virtually all similar articles, is the fact that it is not a science and its scholarship is not scientific enough.

Second, articles appearing in a variety of newspapers and journals all report that the largest medical management corporations will no longer pay for psychoanalytic treatment because it is a form of education and not a medical procedure. I highlight this point because it relates to the larger issue of third-party reimbursements to all forms of psychotherapy in the present climate of psychiatric ideology, which has convinced the public that mental illness is a problem caused solely by broken brains best fixed by drugs euphemistically called "medicines." If managed care pays for psychotherapy at all it must be short term and demonstrably more effective than "meds." Psychoanalysis is trying to adapt by training individuals in a variety of analytically oriented psychotherapies but this might well be the end of the enterprise as it has evolved since Freud's era.

FREUD, PSYCHOANALYSIS, AND POLITICS

I begin my discussion of psychoanalysis and politics as well as my main contentions concerning the field's political endeavors with a discussion of the work of Sigmund Freud. I will avoid discussing his life as it appears in many of the biographies that exist (for example, Gay, 1988) and especially seek to avoid discussing his person or history as a hero or villain, god or thing. I do think it important to discuss his role in the development of psychoanalysis as a cultural and moral movement as opposed to the science it was supposed to be, but in this I will avoid the invective which so often accompanies such discussion.

During my years as a student and trainee I became aware that Freud was venerated in terms fit for a god. One could not criticize the main Freudian ideas without it being suggested that one had some problem requiring years of psychoanalysis to overcome. The value assumed in the writings of other analysts was based on the lineage of the author with either Freud himself or one of the disciples with whom he surrounded himself. I will never forget recommending a book to a well-known analyst who asked by whom the author had been analyzed. Her reply to my ignorance on the matter was in effect that she never read a book unless she knew with whom the author had been in analysis.

In recent years it has become fashionable to excoriate the master and attack him in terms usually appropriate for the truly villainous. There are many criticisms of Freud's ambitiousness and his authoritarian dismissal of theoretical competitors that are historically accurate. I contend, however, that the rage with which they are generally presented seems motivated by disappointment in his being human rather than the god they, and perhaps he, hoped he would be. Similarly, any failings in his theoretical oeuvre are greeted with derision and contempt and are indicative of the fact that nothing in his output is of any value whatsoever.

Freud's intellectual output was vast and the sum of his efforts and his disciples changed Western civilization. The notions that we human beings are motivated by affect as much or more than intellect and reason as well as the fact that we are capable of deceiving ourselves so well as to possibly believe our own lies alone makes Freud's canon overwhelmingly important. He developed multiple theories of normal and abnormal behavior, the rise and fall of civilizations, and the relationship of the individual to society. He also developed a type of relationship between patient and therapist that served both as a form of therapy and a methodological tool of studying the human mind and its development.

I contend the following: His enormous canon contains many inconsistencies and contradictions and the importance of his work for political democracy and genuine science was found in his view of the therapeutic relationship rather than his clinical theory of mental illness. I develop the hypothesis that if Freud had derived his clinical or scientific theory from the moral and political grounding found in his view of the therapeutic relationship his ideas would have promoted democracy far more than they ultimately did. I suggest as well that the psychological theory he would have been forced to develop would have been far better grounded in science than the one he ultimately settled on.

Freud, suggests Reiff (1966), was one of the important moralists of the twentieth century. However, Freud believed himself to be one of the most important scientists of the century and his theory of the infantile sexual roots of mental illness his great contribution to science. I begin with the moral Freud and will then briefly discuss Freud the scientist. Finally, I will suggest that to the degree his disciples and followers emulated his scientific attitudes and concepts they foster the authoritarian society and create little of real scientific worth. To the degree that his descendants made the morality of the human relationship their primary concern, they make a contribution to democratic, humanistic, and open forms of society and are able to create a real contribution to a possible science of psychology.

At the heart of Freud's therapy lies the notions of the free association of ideas by the patient and a therapist concerned not only with hidden meanings contained in these verbal productions but the emergence of transferential and countertransferential reactions between patient and therapist. As the therapist listens to the patient's free associations they listen for signs of defensiveness and infantile conflicts. Defenses, according to Freud, involve denials and distortions of the truth concerning their motives that are based on fears and wishes stemming from infancy and early childhood. The job of therapist is to find ways of interpreting the true meaning of the patient's speech so that these patients can understand these hidden, repressed, and unconscious meanings. The end goal of these new insights—insight being the ultimate goal of treatment itself—allows patients to deal more honestly and truthfully with those desires and the false beliefs that hide their wishes and fears from their consciousness evaluation and control.

Freud believed that inevitably the patient transferred infantile wishes and fears onto the person of the therapist and these distortions and social defenses also had to be interpreted to the patient and ultimately resolved between them. One of the great dangers in the treatment involved the therapist's unconscious response to the fears and wishes of the patient with his own pathological infantile material. Hence the therapist had to be a well-analyzed individual capable of recognizing and refusing to act on those fears and wishes of his own that were stimulated by the patient. If the therapist lacked insights into the manner in which the therapy had become hijacked by the patient's pathology, the therapy became distorted, compromised, and ultimately reinforced the patient's pathology rather than new searches for mental health. With these ideas Freud had laid down the groundwork for a theory of psychology based on the bidirectional nature of social relationships in which the relating participants were complex psychological beings both capable of shaping the relationship.

For Freud mental illness existed as a number of conditions. The first involved psychological states in which the instincts or desires of the id, the repository of instincts, and/or the demands of the environment overwhelmed a regressed, underdeveloped, or otherwise weak ego. The ego is comprised of human intelligence and the skills required to survive and satisfy id needs. Pathology also existed whenever individuals failed to understand and resolve infantile wishes, fears, and unrealistic childhood moral demands adopted as defenses against dangerous desires. Psychoanalysis was successful to the degree that egos were strengthened and truth vanquished untruth thereby allowing reason to prevail against irrationality and unbridled desire.

I argue that Freud was mixing his metaphors. Factual truth about the source or etiology of pathology may have little to do with removing pathology since pathology is basically another name for bad or immoral behavior. Endless examination, and even understanding the past, can actually help patient and therapist avoid examining current behaviors that are the actual source of the patient's miseries. The past is important to the present to the degree that its manifestations are to be found in the present, particularly as the past shapes the modes of present experience and affects current relationships.

What Freud had proposed, however, was a moral–political relationship whose real goal is rooting out what he was in effect calling evil (pathology) by use of free speech and scrupulous honesty on the part of the therapist.

Transference and countertransference are both motivated by pathology in Freud's system and hence in my reinterpretation they are motivated and sustained by deception, blackmail, threat and application of force, manipulations, and a refusal of both parties to deal honestly with both themselves and others. I believe that the model proposed by Freud to help others overcome bad behavior—behaviors that are the product of authoritarian political systems based on fear, intimidation, and deception—was to expose the patient to a democratic and humanistic political system. Goodness and good relationships would defeat badness and replace bad relationships. The truth about 'what is,' represented by increased insight that would grow from the therapy, was in effect grounded in moral–political goodness rather than the other way around. Individuals would become better scientific psychologists about their own lives, thoughts and feelings, and relationships because their science was grounded and motivated by their growth as moral philosophers.

However, instead of insight and the search for truth remaining secondary to the moral, social, and political development of the patient as a result of experiencing a morally humanistic and democratic relationship, the reverse took place in psychoanalysis' historical development. Freud focused his clinical theory of mental illness on the intrapsychic struggles and conflicts of the individual with only secondary reference to the social matrix enfolding the individual. Therapy often dealt with uncovering the past roots of intrapsychic conflicts rather than their current manifestations. This reversal has had the effect of warping the potential democratic nature of the therapeutic relationship and creating a fragmented science comprised of warring camps arguing whose theory of childhood best explains mental illness and justifies what type of psychotherapy.

Freud was ever the scientist and unfortunately never took his own advice about analyzing his own stance as a scientist. He developed a theory of therapy that helped patients see how they see but never examined the underlying visions of how he saw as a scientist. Like so many of the scientists discussed earlier he unwittingly identified with the model of science which suggests that the scientist has a privileged position from which truth can be ascertained and that he was above and outside the social and political forces that were to be his subject matter. Freud became the model of the authoritarian scientist who believes that not only was his methodology the only genuine means to the truth but that his theory of human behavior was the truth and not to be tampered with in any essential manner. Donald Spence (1994) develops the thesis that much of psychoanalytic theory generates the facts rather than the other way around as demanded by empirical science and that much of analysis is overblown rhetoric rather than science.

There are several interlocking qualities and consequences of Freud's scientific posture, theory, and the politics thereof that still bedevil the current climate of psychoanalysis. First, as Rieff (1966), Thomas Szasz (1990), and others make clear, Freud not only developed the body of the theory of psychoanalysis, largely by himself, but surrounded himself with disciples; individuals who helped him develop and propagate his theory but did not dare change any significant aspects of his main contentions. In the course of time psychoanalysis became a closed community, a way of life, and a social and political movement for its adherents.

When individuals such as Alfred Adler, Carl Jung, and Karen Horney challenged any of Freud's main contentions they quickly found themselves on the outside of the inner circle looking in. Szasz (1990) demonstrates how dissidents were dealt with by Freud and especially by his acolytes, individuals of often limited intellectual creativity but whose loyalty to the master was total and unquestioning. Dissenting individuals became the other. They were often diagnosed as mentally ill and subjected to vicious personal attacks posing as intellectual and medical opinion. Freud managed to make his ideas publicly visible and popular by the creation of a community loyal to his thoughts. He ultimately stood at the helm of an authoritarian, closed community paradoxically committed to a therapy that helped individuals seek the truth about themselves and their lives.

Freud also adopted the psychiatric medical model as the ideological underpinning of his canon. Analysis was a treatment and the goals of treatment involved rooting out and relieving mental illness, disorders, and pathology. It is clear (Frosh, 1999; Jacoby, 1986; Reiff, 1966) that Freud was more interested in his creation as a tool for the scientific study of human beings and ultimately as a means of changing humankind but he simultaneously developed it as a treatment through which he earned his own living.

I have argued that the terms *mental illness* and *pathology* are demeaning moral labels for unwanted patterns of thinking, feeling, and adaptive behavior. Therefore, when an analyst "diagnoses" either a patient, or in this case a dissident colleague, they are acting as the Grand Inquisitor and rooting out heresy, apostasy, and other forms of forbidden disbelief. *Every diagnosis is an act of significant countertransference*. It is interesting that Freud, who believed that all religion was a defensive form of mental pathology, not only established an authoritarian community but a secular religion comprised of a hierarchy of secular priests.

Psychoanalysis demands of its practitioners many years of ongoing personal analysis. As discussed earlier the rational for this procedure is clear and makes complete sense: "Sick" people lacking insight cannot be trusted to make good therapists. I suggest that there is a second reason for the unending therapy required of analytic candidates and practitioners: Therapy can act as a confessional with analyst acting as moral priest to the analysand. In such a procedure sins of deviance and heresy can be rooted out and corrected before there is serious challenge to the dogma of the "head cleric" of the movement.

Many of those rejected by early psychoanalysis for heresy established their own schools of psychoanalysis and paid Freud the highest of compliments by similarly creating schools and communities organized along the same authoritarian lines. Each currently existing analytic community claims to be the true version of analysis. Each requires its candidates to spend years in therapy with one of its own training analysts regardless of how many previous years of treatment the candidate has had and regardless of proof that the treatment will make one bit of difference to the quality of treatment to be provided. Acolytes must be loyal to the principles of the religion they will practice and the personal therapy is designed to root out and cure the sin (pathology) of false theoretical belief.

Each subsequent variation of psychoanalysis also emulated Freud in seeking to establish its own version of the etiology of mental illness. Each tried to justify its method of treatment by its view of human development and each demonstrated the same authoritarian commitment to the truth of its theory. Each demanded of its analyzed acolyte faith in his/her master's genius. For Adler, childhood feelings of inferiority created neurosis. Horney opined that too much intense basic anxiety was the culprit. Object relations theorists claimed that inadequate attachments to mother or failures to properly separate created the fatal childhood flaw that drove the neuroses and psychoses of the adult. Each theory became ensconced as dogma and each school a claimant to being either the true psychoanalysis or as worthy to wear Freud's mantle. Each school demanded years of psychoanalysis with one of its senior analysts as part of training to be an analyst.

The theory of infantile sexuality that Freud insisted was the Rosetta stone (Spence, 1994), which explained the etiology of all mental illness, contributed many problems to the historical development of psychoanalysis. Freud insisted that the roots of mental illness be found in the traumata of early childhood (as did all the other variants on the same theme that followed his theory). The specific trauma in Freud's narrative involved the child's difficult negotiation of the Oedipus and Elektra complexes. Children are born as sexual beings and eventually the innately determined course of libidinal development creates a dangerous and unacceptable incestuous desire of son for mother and daughter for father. The boy must renounce his desires for mother under the murderous castration threat by father by identifying with his father's values and prohibitions. In this way the boy comes to reject his forbidden desires for mother, develops a masculine identity, and by internalizing father's moral prohibitions and values, develops his own superego. Failure to negotiate this labyrinth of crises results in one type of neurosis or another.

The girl's psychological journey was similar to the boy's, with several interesting wrinkles in the narrative. The girl not only wants to possess father but his penis as well. One of the tragedies of being female involves the discovery that one has been castrated and must contend with inevitable conflicts concerned with penis envy. The girl's journey is reached when she finally realizes the hopelessness of her situation, identifies with her mother, and ultimately accepts her innately passive and intellectual and moral inferiority to the male whose masculinity is defined by activity and superior intelligence and adaptational skills. Frank Sulloway (1979) suggests that Freud's descriptions of the instincts that comprise the id and the inevitable conflicts that result from the fixed nature of their development prevented him from ever developing a true psychology. Freud was, to the end, a "crypto-biologist."

There are several serious intellectual and moral–political difficulties created by this and other theories based on early childhood traumata. First, they demand that we see childhood (or even biological nature) as the primary source of adult difficulties, thereby denigrating later events as significant sources of unwanted behavior. Analysts could take the position that later trauma depended for its effect on a relationship to earlier trauma. Patient complaints concerning all manner of social injustice and authoritarian abuse could be ignored or downplayed as being manifestations of sensitivities created in childhood. Not only were such complaints derivable from infantile conflicts but they were also a function of mental illness or pathology and hence did not need to be taken seriously. Erich Fromm (1980) believed that psychoanalysis' turn from a potentially revolutionary to a conservative social process was a function of therapists treating social injustices as manifestations of childhood pathologies.

Similarly, any or all of patients' complaints toward their therapists could be interpreted as having their origins in early childhood and became products of transference and thus were lacking in reality. These ideas permitted all manner of power on the part of the therapist—victim blaming and scapegoating of the patient—and, in general, helped create a moral hierarchy in which the "mentally healthy" doctor stood above the "mentally ill" patient. Just as therapists challenging Freud's theory could be dismissed as mentally ill so could patients unhappy with either their treatment or the person of their therapists. Under these arrangements both the theory and the therapy comprising psychoanalysis could be made immune from criticism either from within or without the field.

Moreover, the truth that Freud believed would set patients free and would result from treatment often became the truth as the therapist, and not the patient, saw it. Patients disagreeing with their therapist's interpretations were told that their own viewpoints represented resistances created by their illnesses and transference distortions toward their therapists. Therapy must proceed until both the resistances were overcome and the transference resolved.

In this way not only were therapists kept true to the scriptures created by their masters but patients as well were indoctrinated into the religious analytic sect.

Reliance on a dogmatic hierarchical notion of individuals differing in their mental health also permitted a wide variety of other hierarchical god-thing stories to be incorporated in any given psychoanalytic formulation. For example, feminists (Benjamin, 1998; Chodorow, 1978; Lerman, 1986) have long attacked or tried to modify Freud's incorporation of the Judeo-Christian view of the inherent inferiority of women into what became a secularized version of earlier religious narratives. Horney's losing feud with Freud was over this very issue as she insisted that women want the power and prerogatives that the penis metaphorically and symbolically represents. There is no innate wish to be men or hatred of being women, but if such feelings exist they are due to injustices in culture and not to either Godly decree or possible consequences.

Seth Farber (1998) argues that psychoanalysis incorporated much of Christian theological dogma concerning the innate moral failings of humanity. I would add that psychiatry, in general, focused on human weaknesses and failings rather than on strengths and successes, and psychoanalysis is very much the product of psychiatry even if it relies on a psychological rather than a biological model of human weakness. As of this writing most psychoanalysts appear to be more disturbed by the loss of patients, prestige, and income to the new biological psychiatry rather than by the growing number of diagnostic categories of sin=disorder being heaped on every inhabitant of the planet or the growing loss of democracy inherent in forced treatment of patients.

PSYCHOANALYSIS AND THE REALITY WARS

There are two types of reality wars now raging in the academy, especially in the social sciences and the humanities. Both reality wars are highly relevant to a discussion of psychoanalysis. The first type involves the historical and endless philosophical discussion concerning the nature of reality. This type of debate has been given new life and intensity with the intrusion of cognitive constructivist theories such as those of Jean Piaget and by the influence of postmodern theories, particularly those involving social constructionism. Piaget demands that we see our experience of reality to be constructed and reconstructed in the interaction of individuals and their environment throughout development. The child is not given reality but constructs the meaning of things. Things mean different things to an infant, a toddler, an older child, and an adolescent.

Social constructionists suggest that our individual realities are the products (in part or totally) of the power and linguistic games played between individuals in any given culture and society. Many feminist critiques of psychoanalysis contained many elements of social constructionist theory within them. Gender differences, it is argued, are more a social-linguistic reality than a reality created by biology (or God). What is socially constructed can be deconstructed and reconstructed along democratic and humanistic lines. The work of Lev Vygotsky (1978) attempts to take Piaget's theory of cognitive development and demonstrate how intellectual growth takes place within social interactions; it is best fostered by an understanding of how the social affects individual development.

It is interesting that Freud's ideas concerning the analytic relationship are potentially models of postmodern social constructionism and that the patient's search for a different set of truths to live by conforms nicely to the postmodern tool of change, deconstructionism. Lynn Segal (1999) suggests that one reason feminists were, and still are, so drawn to psychoanalysis despite Freud's view of sexual and gender differences is the power to change society inherent in the use of analytic tools affecting the development of insight into how we see what we see. As I will suggest, restoring deconstruction to the center of analytic theorizing and therapy may yet change the tragedy of what so much of analysis was and still is.

The second type of reality war involves arguments concerning specific facts rather than those concerning the nature of reality itself. If the first knowledge war involves how we know something is true, the second involves what we know to be true. As long as people see the world through the same set of moral and intellectual visions their disagreements tend to involve differences that are incompatible. When individuals disagree about 'what is' based on different underlying visions the differences in 'what is' tend to be incommensurate and not just incompatible.

Differences of both types were at the root of many analytic disagreements but were most often expressed in terms of the second type of reality war. For example, analytic insistence in examining the infantile roots of mental illness led patients to examine their past lives and not how they examined their past lives. It led various schools of therapy to argue endlessly about which theory of infantile etiology was correct but not did not lead them to examine these conflicts from a perspective that required a justification of searching for an answer to human unhappiness in childhood to begin with.

The two types of reality wars are deeply interrelated. For example, we can ask if it is true whether the human view of reality is a function of social construction, just as we can inquire into the etiology of human mental pathology. Social constructionists might well argue that the very search for truth presupposes some underlying political, moral, and cultural bias and as such any facts that we come up with are never value-free but at least in part reflective of some individual or group's self-interest. At their extremes, opponents of postmodern thinking still claim that science, when done correctly, is essentially value-free and that reality is directly knowable.

At the other extreme postmodern thinkers challenge scientific assumptions and claim that all facts are a function of some theory and that all theory is in essence a narrative that satisfies a variety of social and individual needs. At its extreme this position states that no science is really possible, especially in the area of human behavior and social relationships, and that psychology and psychoanalysis belong with the humanities and not the sciences. It is this wing of philosophy that suggests that Freud was a much better literary figure than scientist and that psychoanalysis is better understood in its form and function as hermeneutics than science (Ricoeur, 1970).

I stake out a middle ground in this debate. I believe that if we separate our moral judgments from our descriptions and examine our hidden assumptions as best we are able we can establish an agreed-upon body of evidence that is more than the product of our wish fulfillments. Unless we can assume some superiority of science over the humanities in explaining how things work and assume that our theories are more than "just so" stories not only will we be unable to set any standards of truth but we will have totally blurred the line between truth and fiction and, for my concerns here, madness and sanity. However, I do not believe that our ability to define scientific truth will ever be anything close to absolute or that our theories will ever be free of bias. Human beings cannot ever see the world free from their human perspective and the internal mechanisms that guide cognitive construction.

It is my contention that a number of those referring to themselves as "psychoanalysts" have begun to analyze the manner in which they know the world rather than the nature of the world they think they know. But for the moment I discuss the continuing knowledge wars over what are to be the facts that explain mental pathology and the correct means of curing these mental diseases and disorders. I then return to what might be called "postmodern psychoanalysis."

Perhaps the earliest of the psychoanalytic knowledge wars (of the second type) involved what might be the question What did Freud know and when did he know it? Freud originally developed a theory of childhood sexuality and its effects on later mental health that he called the "seduction theory" (Masson, 1984, 1988; Spence, 1994). Based on various recovered recollections from his own childhood and combined with reports from his (mostly female) patients in treatment, he concluded that real sexual abuse in childhood had taken place and was responsible for the adult maladies from which these people were suffering.

However, shortly thereafter Freud concluded that his own memories of childhood sexual abuse were faulty and that his patients' reports were also not to be trusted. He concluded that his patients were not remembering actual abuses but wish fulfillments in the form of dreams and childhood fantasies. The patients were recalling affectively loaded constructions related to their Oedipal and Elektra complexes and not actual events. Guilt was removed from those originally held responsible for the abuse and placed on the child who could not be actually guilty for their imaginings, as these were the inevitable products of innate libidinous desires and ultimately of mental pathology. The child was responsible for constructing these false memories but no one was guilty of any abuse.

Which Freud was and is to be believed based on this change of heart? It makes an enormous difference which scenario is accepted as true. In the first theory a patient's mental woes are the result of a social experience involving a terrible betrayal of the trust of an adult especially in the case of a loved one. Not only is insight required but justice must be done, in this case justice involving an odious crime against an innocent child. In the second scenario there are no crimes, no apologies, or any restoration of a sense of justice and legal convictions of real criminals necessary. All that is required is insight into an unavoidable childhood misunderstanding and the development of more mature and accurate ways of interpreting the world in and around the self.

Controversy concerning Freud's conversion to the Oedipal theory from the seduction has never been fully resolved. There are those critics who feel Freud made both theories up and badgered his patients until they agreed with him one way or another. Frederick Crews (1996, 1997), Donald Spence (1994), and others believe that the interpretations of sexual abuse that Freud drew from his case material leaves much room for many other nonsexual conclusions. My own reading of the famous Wolf–Man case leaves me filled with doubt concerning either sexual abuse or the sexual wishes that Freud concludes explains the material. Crews points out that the so-called wolf man himself repudiated Freud's conclusions.

Had either Freud or his disciples and later followers been less concerned with the absolute truth concerning the childhood etiology of mental illness and more concerned with how we know what we know, psychoanalysis might today be on a surer footing within the scientific community as well as in its own camp. There would probably be fewer hours spent on wondering which Freud to believe or if Freud could be believed about anything. There would certainly be less of the kind of political viciousness that led feminist groups to use Freud's picture on dartboards and more reasoned discussion on the issues he raised (Segal, 1999).

Psychoanalysts would be less embarrassed by the work of Adolf Grunbaum (1984) who demonstrates that any theory that posits infantile roots to adult behavior, pathological or otherwise, can never be scientifically tested and therefore accepted only on faith. Perhaps if Freud had stayed longer with issues related to how we know what we know and how interpersonal pressures can affect memory, research similar to John Kotre (1995) and Elizabeth Loftus and Kenneth Ketchum (1994) would have been done by psychoanalysts, and psychoanalysis' latest debacle and embarrassment, the recovered memory controversy, could have been avoided.

Freud reified many of his own concepts, among them id, ego, super-ego, and mind itself. Processes that can only be described with verbs became things denoted with nouns. Among the processes so reified was the notion of unconscious mental processes that became the unconscious, a place where endless activity took place particularly between the id, ego, and superego. The conflicted activity of these agents within the unconscious, the most important of which took place in infancy, is for many analysts the real source of adult mental illnesses and it is the release and reorganization of such unconscious conflict and warfare that represents the cure that insight would provide.

Freud raises the most profound questions concerning human functioning when he demands that we understand the degree to which we are capable of hiding our own intentions from ourselves, to say nothing of others. But for scientists to accept this view of ourselves does not mean that we have to accept Freud's model of the mechanism explaining how repression and self-delusion operate. Psychological activity is process, and while we may experience ourselves as objects describable with nouns, it does not mean that these are the most fruitful of metaphors to use as we try to understand human behavior.

Freud's model precludes a more social–political understanding of the causes and effects of repression. Perhaps the real source of repression is the fear of attack by others or the awe we feel when confronted by authority re-gally bedecked during ceremonies involving pomp and circumstance rather than an escape from painful and embarrassing emotions and drive states. Perhaps a better explanation for the reason we can lie so well to ourselves is that it makes us better liars toward others and therefore more able to reach our political goals with others within authoritarian political structures. We can also ask if the phenomenological experience of repression and defensive beliefs are experienced in the same way as beliefs experienced as true and without defensive embellishments.

Questioning Freud's mechanism of repression can help us give up the notion of the unconscious as a repository of old memories and the nineteenth-century view of memory as a file cabinet of old pictures. We can then accept that the same memories might be cognitively constructed and reconstructed over and over again both as a function of individual's current needs and a mode of cognitive development. It seems to me that all of these critical questions must be raised and answered if psychoanalysis is to be the science it must be if it is to survive. However that has not yet happened in any general way as much of modern analytic and other dynamic therapeutic activities continue to be haunted and embarrassed by operating within Freud's model of pathological origins and the unresolved controversies I have outlined.

Late in the 1980s, the exact date eludes me, I had lunch with some colleagues and one of their guests, a woman who announced with much obvious pride that she was a feminist and a psychoanalyst. During the lively conversation that followed she made the following pronouncement: Any woman with an eating disorder had been sexually abused during her childhood and abuse is the direct cause of her pathology. Most patients do not remember the actual abuse as they have been repressed but it is the job of the analyst to cure her patient's eating problems by reconnecting to her the sexual abuses and traumas of her childhood. She went on to suggest that she referred to her patients as "sexual abuse survivors."

When I asked, in utter amazement, for the evidence of her conviction I was told that the evidence is provided by the dramatic recovery of the repressed material and the emotional conviction with which these memories are finally presented in the clinical setting. To hear these women weep with pain and relief over the discoveries of their lost childhood is more proof than anyone might need to verify her claim. She also suggested that my skepticism was born of my inability to handle the enormity of these new discoveries, that I was a man and that perhaps I was unconsciously or consciously on the side of the abusers. The latter remark ended my part in the conversation and over the next several days I put all thoughts of it out of my awareness.

Over the next several months I became aware that my luncheon partner was not evincing an idiosyncratic belief but that she reflected a growing and powerful movement within psychoanalysis and the general therapeutic community at large. Not only was psychoanalysis to be a vehicle for the cure of the suffering of sexually abused women but it was also to be an engine of social change and increased social justice. This engine would not find its expression on an overt political level but through the results of specific therapeutic interventions.

The media became frenzied over disclosures by the therapeutic community that not only had uncounted millions of women been sexually abused as children but that millions more innocent children were being abused in their nursery and public schools, by their day-care workers, and by parents and relatives. Fueled by popular books found in mall bookstores, endless interviews of experts on television and radio, and by expert witnesses at high-profile criminal trials, the Salem witch trials of the late 1700s were put to shame. Interestingly, the experts presenting these discoveries had not first published their data in peer-reviewed professional journals, in books, published by university presses, or in books for professionals but rather in trade books where the public would become aware of their contents even before the experts' professional peers and colleagues.

Freud believed that patients were cured of their neurotic agony when they gave up the distortions of their defensively created beliefs and were better able to accept everyday misery. The therapist was enjoined not to become involved in a patient's life outside of the treatment. The patients were warned not to make any major life decisions until progress had been made in resolving major distortions and transferential issues. His was a cautious approach that took into account the difficulty of helping a patient overcome resistance to change and the ease with which defense, fantasy, and wish fulfillment created distortions to replace those already resolved.

The new warriors of analysis were not to be inhibited by any Freudian caution. Having decided that their patients were actually abused they returned analysis to the original seduction theory. Patients were seen as the innocent victims of betrayal and abuse and no longer fit the model of the active agent generating sexual desires and concocting fantastic solutions to deal with the consequences. Whereas the Oedipal model of mental illness left genuine victims of abuse without hope of justice and retribution and ended up blaming the victim, return to the seduction theory allowed a naive realism to dominate the proceedings.

The passive victims of abuse no longer needed to have their ego skills strengthened and defensive distortions corrected. They required heroes to protect them—banish any doubt that distortion might have played a role in their newly found memories—and, most of all, advocates to help see that the guilty were punished and the justice required to restore mental health achieved. Demonstrating the same certainty as Freud in being intellectually correct our heroes also announced in no uncertain terms that they were on a moral crusade and would not make the same mistake as Freud in requiring difficult demands of the patient. (In a very real sense this intellectual and moral position defines the death of psychoanalysis as Freud conceived it. It has often been suggested that if Freud had not given up on the seduction theory, at least in part, there would not have been a psychoanalytic movement because there would have been no need for it. All that would be required in the case of rape and abuse would be law enforcement and perhaps some counseling or support groups to help the victims afterward.)

For example, Laura S. Brown (1994, 1997:449), a leader in what might be termed the "abuse memory recovery movement," tells the psychological community and the world at large that the goal of treatment is subversion of a society. Males who are either insensitive to or active in the abuse of women politically create the rules of this society. Moreover, she writes that she is motivated by the concept of "tikkun olam, the Hebrew term for healing of the world," and "informing social justice practice." Brown clearly sees herself and her compatriots as involved in a religious movement and pursuing a social cause justified by its inherent holiness. Hers, and those who cast themselves as members in her cause, is not Freud's goal of intellectual rightness but one of moral righteousness.

An immediate casualty of this newest of crusades was not only any vestige of genuine science within the analytic community but any desire to follow

Freud's lead and make psychoanalysis into a general science. As a result almost all of the problematic conceptual problems raised by newer theories of how short- and long-term memories operated—related controversies as to how repression actually worked, if in fact it existed as Freud originally claimed it did—are ignored.

Most important, many of these therapists refused to even consider the possibility that at least some of the memories recovered in treatment might be a function of the treatment itself. Trapped by their own sense of moral righteousness and the problems created by a view of illness based on infantile abuses, a genuine social theory of human adaptive misery is lost. Equally lost is the political stance of the therapist as it might figure in an examination of the countertranference of the therapist.

Science and medicine replaced the church as moral arbiter of society for two basic reasons: First, because of the technological developments and visible health improvements it brought about, and second because it proved to those educated in scientific modes of reasoning that supernatural forces and places like a literal heaven and hell could not actually exist. Without its ability to promise rewards for goodness and punishments for the wickedness and without its truth statements, the church lost much of its moral authority. The church certainly retained its capacity to make moral judgments and define right from wrong but its political power to enforce behavior with other than moral suasion was lost.

I have argued (Simon, 2000b), as has Perry London (1986), that psychotherapy is inescapably a moral activity and one that must be directed toward moral goals. But therapy must also be based on science. Science not guided by a strong moral philosophy is like any other human activity: simply dangerous to all concerned. But psychotherapy must be more than a set of moral demands and judgments. The therapist cannot be just another "cleric," albeit a secular one. There must be some scientific basis to guide those procedures involving what Michael Mahoney (1991) refers to as "human change processes." The therapist cannot be an expert in morality since morality is based solely on opinion and any adult's opinion is as equally valid as any other. I agree with Barbara Held (1995) that the therapist must have some real and practical knowledge to impart to the patient about his suffering and what to do about it or else go out of business.

Brown and the others involved in the religiously based, fervently and righteously promoted moral crusade dealt another serious blow to psychoanalytic and other dynamic therapeutic goals of becoming part of the sciences and not another inferior religion or what Szasz (1990) refers to as a "form of base rhetoric." But as I have also argued when science and other searches for the factual truth disappear morality also suffers. The therapeutic search for justice unleashed by those in the analytic movement associated with recovered memories not only ignored the need for facts and truth as science demands it but ignored the need for facts as required by the law and criminal justice system.

Based on the testimony of the experts on childhood sexual abuse, families were destroyed and people who were falsely accused and found guilty went to prison. Even when convictions were overturned, it was too late—the damage had already been done. Ironically the victims of this therapeutic tyranny formed an organization to fight what they saw as their tormentors and in so doing most probably created a haven for real sexual abusers. While there has always been a problem for sexually abused children and survivors to have their cases heard and have justice done, I believe that psychoanalysis' hijacking by the morally righteous has not only set back the cause for which they supposedly stand but irreparably harmed psychoanalysis, as well as dynamic psychotherapy.

It is often hard to establish the truth about events in childhood and especially traumatic ones where the only eyewitnesses are victims, and in this case children, who might be enduring unbearable physical and emotional pain. But there are fewer problems testing the truth of therapies that explain their patient's complaints with theories of devil worship and possession, abduction by flying saucers, and especially past-life experiences. As the mainstream of psychoanalytic therapists sat by not speaking out as moral fervor and righteousness replaced scientific objectivity as the vehicle of social change and therapy, the door was opened for therapies based on any and all forms of fantasy and personal wish fulfillment. Many within the analytic community have simply given up on the idea of psychoanalysis as based on or being a genuine science. The consequences of this are extremely serious for psychology, psychoanalysis, psychotherapy, and the politics of the society with which they impact.

Perhaps the greatest damage caused by this movement was to the patients themselves. Morality, in general, and therapeutic morality, in particular, demand that individuals be treated as ends in themselves and not as a means to the ends of others. Throughout morality's history there have been numerous psychoanalysts who have used their patients as a means toward one end or another. There is no choice that patients are a means toward the financial well-being of the therapist. I have already discussed the problems created when patients become a means toward establishing the truth of their pet theories. But in this case the patient also became a tool in the therapist's moral vision of justice, the structure of the family, and the relationship of the sexes.

THE FAILED POLITICS OF PSYCHOANALYSIS

Psychoanalysis has had as its various goals the development of a general theory of psychology, the development of an effective therapy of mental disorders, and the overall improvement of the human condition. I believe it has substantially failed to achieve all three goals and this chapter has detailed some of the reasons why its potential has not been realized. The failures related to each goal has its roots in the failures of the other two. Psychoanalysis has changed our society in many ways but as will be discussed in the next chapter not necessarily for the better. These failures in achieving what I believe to be the field's enormous potential in all three endeavors relate to factors already discussed. I argue that if psychoanalysis is to realize its goals it will have to be successful in all three.

Psychoanalysis, until recently, has successfully avoided creating a theory of human behavior that was based on the demands and assumptions inherent in its view of treatment. It has consistently failed to make explicit that the analysis of transference and countertransference simultaneously involves an analysis of the kind of politics that should operate within the therapeutic dyad. The kind of therapeutic relationship envisioned by Freud is clearly both humanistic and democratic.

If psychoanalysis had begun with a political analysis it would have been forced to ask how democratic and humanistic interactions help change mental pathology. Simultaneously, logic would have forced it to inquire as to the types of political interactions responsible for shaping the mental illnesses being treated. Its scientific theories would have inquired directly into the bidirectional nature of individual development as it takes place in authoritarian and democratic political structures at the level of family, school and psychiatric clinic, and private therapists' offices. Psychoanalysis would envision itself as a science and a treatment concerned with its role at the individual and societal level. It has failed to achieve such a status.

For example, Stephen Frosh (1999) examines Freudian and a variety of post-Freudian theories for their value in helping create new political systems that will help change the moral–political nature of our society. His test of the usefulness of each theory, which includes, among others, the object relations theories of D. W. Winnicott and the work of Melanie Klein, involves the degree to which the theory actively promotes social change rather than accommodation to existing power structures as well as the theory's description of an individual capable of being a political agent.

It is beyond the scope of this chapter to detail the reasons Frosh finds fault with virtually all of the theories he evaluates for either one or both of his criteria. His critique of Freudian theory parallels some of those I have discussed: his failure to deal fairly with women and his reliance on a biological view of human beings as driven by an id conceived of as essentially an alienating and evil force. His critique of Winnicott is based on Winnicott's view of the infant as a passive, blank slate whose development is solely at the mercy of the success or failure of the good-enough mother. He is most interested in the work of Klein whose theories were concerned with the differences between male and females as a result of development and whose conception of the infant is a very active partner in the mother–child relationship.

Frosh's work is essential reading for those interested in the relationship of psychoanalysis and politics. However, he still focuses on the theories of development proposed by each analytic contributor. Frosh fails to primarily address the issues raised here by focusing on the nature of the therapy even after making it one of his criteria for the usefulness of the theory. More seriously, he never addresses the need for these theories to be tested according to some criteria of scientific validity. It seems to me that the theory of Klein-based as it is on Freud's notion of the death instinct and which credits virtual newborns with murderous impulses toward mother's breast, requires more than a little criticism. The biological drama that she proposes in which the breast and male penis are equated in the mind of the child simply flies in the face of virtually anything described about infancy by developmental psychology.

Psychoanalysis has still not taken seriously that it is a form of education; one that helps its patients experience themselves and their history from the forms of understanding that result from newly established modes of adaptive subjectivity. Similarly, the field has not yet come to grips with the fact that forms of adaptive consciousness can never in themselves be diseases. Psychoanalysis still refers to itself as treatment and the people it services as mentally ill, disordered, and pathological without realization that all such terms and their specifics as appearing in *DSM-IV* degrading moral judgments that create a moral hierarchy between patient and therapist. Acceptance by the patient of the diagnosis is acceptance of moral and intellectual inferiority and represents a serious and dangerous countertransference of therapist toward patient. Moreover, a society of individuals defining themselves as mentally ill and defective are hardly the human stuff of which a democracy can flourish.

If psychoanalysis has not separated its judgments from its descriptions and has not begun its descriptive understanding of its patient's modes of 'being in the world' it has also continued to rely on or proliferate theories of human behavior based on early childhood experiences. It still largely ignores the whole range of political interactions that have shaped a patient's view of reality up until and including the moment he or she enters the analytic office seeking help. Finally, while aspects of evolutionary theory, feminist theory, and the larger important contributions of mainstream psychology and psychotherapy have begun to infiltrate some analytic training programs, by and large the curricula of these programs are museums filled with relics of the past and monuments to the godlike theorists who are seen as worthy to be called "psychoanalysts."

Thomas Kuhn (1970) points out that a field of study is not a science until its founders are seen as part of its history and its theories no longer depend on the authority of their creators. Psychoanalysis will not be a real science until the ideas of Freud, and all the other major historical figures of analysis, are established as part of a much larger framework of ideas. Both Freud and his heirs must be seen as a worthy historical figure and not as god or villain to be endlessly debated both as to their scientific and moral value. Psychoanalysis will not be a genuine science until its ideas and theories stand on their own without the authority of their creators and when these ideas have been tested against each other as well as those outside the mainstream of analysis.

Before discussing intersubjective and relational theories of psychoanalysis I briefly describe Russell Jacoby's (1986) history of psychoanalytic forays into the political arena. He describes the life and times of Otto Fenichel and his colleagues who fought against psychoanalysis' evolution from a tool of social change into a fashionable medical treatment for upper-middle-class patients. Fenichel and his group had lived through the horrors of World War I and by the 1920s became fully aware of the potential social disaster created by Adolf Hitler's rise to power. Fenichel and his associates aligned themselves with the socialists and communists, who were at that time both the natural enemy of Fascism and the hope of progressive intellectuals throughout the world.

Fenichel was never able to marry the ideas of Karl Marx and Sigmund Freud. His political activity was cut short when he was forced to emigrate to the United States, a place hostile to Marxists of all kinds. He died a bitter man when he discovered that in America Freudian ideas had become the bedrock of treatments for the wealthy and upper-middle classes to better adapt to their comfortable existences. Fenichel is best known today for his 1943 *Psychoanalytic Treatment of the Neuroses*, a book that closely follows the Freudian line and gives aid and comfort to those forms of treatment with the most politically conservative goals.

INTERPERSONAL AND INTERSUBJECTIVE PSYCHOANALYSIS

In recent years a variety of psychoanalytic theorizing has emerged, which simultaneously treats both the therapeutic relationship and the theoretical underpinnings of mental illness in very different ways from earlier forms of analysis. These trends can be understood to be the result of postmodern and feminist thinking and can have the potential to transform the entire analytic enterprise. It is not clear, however, just what directions these turns in psychoanalysis will take or if in fact these ideas will have a wide impact on the general practice of psychotherapy as it courts ever deeper relationships with biopsychiatry. I summarize, all too briefly, the trends that make this either a very hopeful development in theory, practice, and politics of psychoanalysis, its logical historical terminus, or perhaps both.

I begin with that branch of psychoanalysis dealing with the social–moral–political nature of the therapeutic relationship. The interpersonal and intersubjective school of psychoanalysis is inspired by the legend and written legacy of Harry Stack Sullivan (1953) and developed through the work of Lewis Aron (1999), Jessica Benjamin (1998), Stephen A. Mitchell (2000), Thomas Ogden (1994), Donna Orange (1995), R. Stolorow and G. Atwood (1992) and others. Benjamin (1998) summarizes the change in philosophy and direction of this new branch of analysis, "In current relational analysis we see a reversal that restores the analyst's subjectivity as a fallible being and the analysand's subjectivity as one who can know and speak with authority" (p. xii). The interpersonal school reconfigures and extends the concept of transference and countertransference. The therapist and patient coconstruct tranference as well as all aspects of the relationship between them. Therapists accept Sullivan's notion that they are participants in the relationship as well as observers. There is an acceptance that both the therapist and the patient are also embedded in the culture in which they both have developed and live and as such must constantly deal with the ongoing events that currently shape them as well as understand their individual legacies of the past.

Moreover, the behavior of the participants is understood to be a function of their subjective experiences rather than as a function of id drives or any other impersonal, mechanical, or biological factors. Carlo Strenger (1991) argues that under this regime of thought, reasons can be seen as legitimate forms of motivation. Each individual's subjective experience is embedded in a different locus and level of development and hence each is capable of different types and levels of insight.

There is no place called "the unconscious" but, rather, insight is a function of how many perspectives an individual can bring to bear on their own past life and modes of experience. Hopefully, the analyst possesses the greater number of perspectives and can more easily focus on how each member of the dyad knows the world, as well as what each member knows of himself/herself in relation to each other and the world. It is the therapist who more easily focuses on the ongoing interaction between himself/herself and the patient, but an increase in the patient's awareness is one of the goals of therapy. What is unconscious relates more to our procedural memories rather than our declarative memories. The job of analysis is to turn the goals, expectations, and affects associated with unexamined and mislabeled procedures into verbal declarations capable of examination and, if necessary and through choice, change.

Therapy is a dialogue between individuals. It is not a master attempting to reveal truth to a subordinate. The patient increases self-understanding and sense of subjectivity by being an active partner in an ongoing dialogue free of judgments, blackmail, or a struggle to see who knows more. The patient is no longer told that disagreements with the analyst reflect pathology and "poor reality testing." In effect, psychoanalysis becomes a journey of self-discovery for both patient and therapist. Important to interpersonal thinking is the notion that the openness and fallibility of the therapist permits the patient to identify with another being as human, albeit one from whom there is something important to learn and emulate. Conversely, the therapist affirms the legitimacy of the patient's conscious experience allowing the patient to experience himself/herself as an object of respect and a person with whom the therapist identifies.

There is much more to these newer trends in psychoanalysis that needs to be developed than can be accomplished here. I will return to these and other analytic ideas when I develop my own notion of psycho"therapy" in Chapter 9. Suffice it to say that it is my opinion that the interpersonal, intersubjective school of analysis is developing a description of the psychological nature and consequences of democratic and authoritarian political relationships and the uses of interpersonal power even as they hold on to the notion of treatment of mental illness.

The second aspect of this new trend of psychoanalysis bears on the nature of what the therapist knows. The theories of the past, which were treated as truths to be revealed, have given way to the idea that theories are merely narratives that can be used to help the patient develop new perspectives on the narratives that brought him into treatment in the first place. Psychoanalysis as science gives way to analysis as a hermeneutic endeavor in which the dialogue between therapist and patient is one of understanding how one's personal life narrative guides one's interpretations of self and others as well as using new narratives to broaden and change one's interpretive style and capacity. The goal of mental health in this framework is to help the patient develop greater narrative coherence rather than greater empirical ability as scientist.

Strenger (1999) summarizes this trend when he writes, "We have simply settled for giving up notions of truth and scientific respectability that were once central to psychoanalysis. Instead, we relish in a newly gained space of freedom in which we can build our therapeutic conceptions along our favorite ethical view of life" (p. 610). He goes on to suggest that psychoanalysis would treat Freudian theory from a literary-hermeneutic production rather than as a scientific theory capable of empirical verification. He justifies this approach as he writes, "The playful use of concepts ranging from the primal scene through the symbolic order to projective identification can be justified if we argue that psychoanalysis is a cultural form of life that construes experience. What matters is whether these construals are ethically, aesthetically satisfying and whether they do not impede therapeutic progress" (p. 611).

I agree with Strenger and those who focus on the moral and ethical aspects of the therapeutic relationship and begin the process by affirming the consciousness and subjectivity of both participants. But I believe that if psychoanalysis removes itself from the sciences and gives up justifying its procedures and success rates from a scientific vantage point it will be forced to accept its theories on faith and become just one more religion, albeit a loosely organized and rather anarchistic one at that.

WHY PSYCHOANALYSIS?

Strenger (1999:613) asks "Why Psychoanalysis?" in response to a paper by Mauricio Cortina (1999) who attempts to use attachment theory as the theoretical justification of analytic treatment. In addition to problems involved with testing this or any theory, Strenger questions why this or any other developmental theory justifies the use of psychoanalysis over Rogerian therapy or any of the other hundreds of treatments that can be used based on the same model. Given Strenger's decision to relieve psychoanalysis of its scientific responsibilities and admitted burdens by moving to a hermeneutic approach that might utilize aesthetically pleasing stories instead, I think the question Why psychoanalysis at all? might be the better question.

Given its history as a dogmatic religion and pseudoscience, why should it be accepted as an undogmatic religion or literary art form belonging more to the humanities than to the sciences? If psychoanalysis gives up its search for the truth, I believe it does not deserve to be taken seriously or even exist and, ultimately, will not. The tragedy will then be the loss of psychoanalysis as the most nuanced and sophisticated attempt to understand the politics of human relationships in psychological terms. It will also mean a failure in developing a sophisticated theory of human development and interaction that begins with descriptions of individual human consciousness as they function in the context of ethical and unethical, democratic and authoritarian modes of political relationships.

I believe it is time for psychoanalysis to do the following:

1. Recognize that its true discipline is psychology and not medicine and especially the dead science of psychiatry. In this way it can best separate its judgments from its descriptions and avoid the moral hierarchies that will most impede its attempts to be an ethical and moral enterprise.
2. Recognize that it must be a science and give up theories based on hero worship and the cult of personalities while embracing the exciting developments taking place in psychology as the larger field tries to join with the best of the human sciences in developing an effective theory of human behavior.

3. Accept that psychoanalysis is just one of many forms of human intervention and like all the rest has no claim to be superior to any other except
   perhaps in its attempts to base itself in ethics and morality.
4. *Give up psychoanalysis as it has been since its inception.*

I will return to develop these themes in Chapters 8 and 9.

CHAPTER 6

Psychotherapy III: Psychotherapy and American Politics

INTRODUCTION

I have several goals for this chapter. I wish to further develop and tie together some of the themes discussed in the last two chapters and relate them to the overall effects of the mental health field on the politics of American society. I include in the present discussion everyone involved in the practice of helping individuals deal with her or his psychological miseries and problems in living. I include psychiatry, psychoanalysis, and all of the remaining types of psychotherapy and psychological interventions purported to help those struggling with mental illness. Because of the great overlap in these fields—psychotherapies of all varieties represent the nonmedical arm of psychiatry and most nonanalytic forms of modern psychotherapy are still derived from psychoanalysis—there will be some redundancy between this and earlier chapters.

Since the individual and society represent a duality, that which changes a large enough number of individuals changes society. A change in society, its organization, economics, and politics transforms every individual comprising that society. My main contention in this chapter is that psychotherapy is now a vast and exceedingly powerful enterprise, perhaps better referred to by Tana Dineen (2000) as the "Psychology Industry." This industry not only reflects the political moral values of our society but also, in large measure, shapes them as well. No longer does therapy change the consciousness and selves of one patient at a time. The topic of mental illness is now front and center as public health issues and, as such, is regularly discussed by politicians and others involved with public concerns. In addition the field in general has enormous resources to reach out to a public fascinated with its collective and individual health.

The totality of the mental health field is comprised of a variety of professional organizations, hundreds of competing types of treatments, and hundreds of thousands of individuals with a bewildering variety of academic degrees and preparations working in and for every cultural institution comprising our society. Clinical personnel work with individuals of every age group. They tell parents how to raise their children so that they will be mentally healthy and offer their services to help those children and their families who are already mentally ill. They work with families, changing the composition and interactions within families.

It appears that virtually no school system in our land can operate without the services of school psychologists, individuals most often trained in the arts and science of clinical services. These individuals act as a resource to principals and teachers, providing them with the supposed psychological reasons for the failure to learn through the use of tests that assess the intellectual levels and mental health and illness of the student populations. If necessary they will offer their or a colleague's services to the families of those children afflicted with depression, anxiety, learning disabilities, ADHD, and any other *DSM* illnesses that might be diagnosed. These services are most often provided in the private practices of the school psychologist and in a hospital clinic or a freestanding clinic.

Our public libraries and the huge bookstores crowding our shopping malls have large sections of trade books written by clinicians of every stripe that attempt to instruct the reader on which mental illnesses and disorders account for their private and public unhappiness. These books discuss how mental illnesses create the failures in business, family, and self that make life miserable. They simultaneously attempt to offer the reader insights, wisdom, and strategies to change from mentally ill to mentally healthy and thus restore their lives to health, wealth, and happiness. In their variety they suggest that psychiatric drugs, herbs, vitamins, exercise, meditation, changes in diet, or any of the hundreds of forms of talk therapy that litter the American landscape will reduce mental illness and increase mental health. Moreover, the media counts a generous number of clinically trained experts and gurus among the endless number of talking heads that incessantly inform our society.

None of the advice, wisdom, and services offered by psychotherapists, mental health experts, and clinicians of all types and stripes comes free. Psychotherapy and mental health services are big business and represent a sizable portion of monies paid out for health care by individuals, third-party insurers, and the government to individual practitioners and institutions offering mental health care. The war to establish parity of payments to psychologists and social workers with psychiatrists by insurers has long been won. Each year the lobbying efforts of professional organizations, private individuals, and other friends of the therapy industry move ever closer to the goal of establishing parity between the mental and physical health divisions of medicine.

It should be clear to even the casual observer that an enterprise composed of respected professionals having influence at all levels of society will greatly influence society and its practices. Moreover, when the personal economic, social, and political standing of these individuals in society depends on their continued success as clinicians and mental health experts, one can predict that their efforts to remain visible and increase their numbers, power, and influence will be considerable indeed. I suggest that psychotherapy has been successful in changing the direction of the politics of our society and that like psychiatry these changes are too often deadly to democratic forms of government.

I must make several points clear before going on to discuss how and why I believe that psychotherapy and the mental health field are damaging our democratic institutions. Benjamin Beit-Hallahmi (1974) expanding on arguments first developed by Thomas Szasz, indicts psychotherapists for their insistence that their efforts are morally neutral and ignore the reality of and behave collectively as an agency of social control. More recently, Nicholas Rose (1999) makes a strong case for the fact that the governing of the human soul in Western culture has passed from the organized church to institutional psychotherapy. Rose, however, does not lament this passing of power in that he believes that psychotherapy is the better agency to see to it that our citizens are prepared for life in a democratic society.

I agree with Rose in principle but not in the actual practices of the field. I disagree with Beit-Hallahmi's implied contention that it is inherently negative for psychotherapy to be a form of political control, although I agree with his disturbance over the field's denial of its implicit politics. Every functioning organization that seeks to influence people's behavior and their development can be neither morally neutral nor nonpolitical. The duality of individual and society precludes that possibility. My argument against therapy involves the continued denial that its activities are inherently moral and political and making its political and moral effects invisible to its adherents. If the mental health field were to make its moral and political goals explicit, if those goals were truly geared toward the development of a humane, fair, and democratic society, and if it were to use and develop the best of the human sciences to reach its goals, then I would applaud its efforts along with Rose. But that is not generally the case as I will now try to demonstrate.

I also make clear before developing my critique of the field that I use broad brush strokes in my effort. The field of psychotherapy is both vast and fragmented, the latter requiring some discussion of its own. There is no possible way to describe and discuss every form and school of psychotherapy, so my general comments might well not apply to some therapeutic enterprises. More important, I strongly invoke the same contention I made earlier about individual psychiatrists: A large number of clinical psychologists, social workers, and other types of practitioners create democratic and humanistic relationships with their patients and struggle to maintain an appropriate scientific stance toward their subject matter. However, their success in these endeavors is in spite of, rather than because of, the underlying visions and philosophy of their chosen field.

THE POLITICS OF PSYCHOTHERAPY

In the previous chapters I critiqued both psychiatry and psychoanalysis against a backdrop of abstract therapeutic encounters and generalized interactions between psychiatrists and patients. I will repeat and extend my beliefs as to how the mental health field corrupts democratic, humanistic, and open societies but I do so in relation to an actual and very public event. On September 11, 2001, hijacked commercial airliners filled with civilian travelers rammed the Twin Towers of the World Trade Center in New York City and The Pentagon in Washington, D.C. A fourth hijacked commercial airliner crashed on the ground in Pennsylvania, killing all of its passengers, unlike the other locations where thousands of civilian workers died in terror and pain from fire, smoke, leaps from buildings, or from the airplanes themselves as they entered the workspace of the buildings. Ultimately, the Twin Towers collapsed, killing thousands of citizens and hundreds of firefighters and policemen and causing fires that destroyed several more large office structures as well as many local businesses. In all, America lost more people that day than they did on December 7, 1941, when Japan attacked Pearl Harbor.

Within hours the president of the United States, the Congress, the governor of New York and the mayor of New York City, the media at large, and every person with whom I came in contact, as well as myself, constructed the following meanings concerning the events of the day. We agreed that our country had been attacked by terrorists of unknown origin and that the attacks were reprehensible, dastardly, and one of cowardice. While a discussion among my colleagues revealed some who believed that American foreign policy had possibly played a role in these events, there was universal agreement in our grief for the victims and belief that the people responsible should be made to pay for what were now being called "acts of war" and "criminality." A military action in Afghanistan followed almost immediately and while the action was marked by various protests from pacifists, an overwhelming number of Americans supported the political and military decisions made by their government.

The fighting abroad had little direct affect at home and most Americans returned to their usual activities following the advice of political leaders to show the terrorists that they could not stop normal American routines. The public was encouraged to shop, eat out in restaurants, go on trips, and otherwise support the recovery of the economy, already showing signs of a recession and further damaged by the attacks. It is hard to know just what the general psychological response of various individuals was to the attack at varying times following the attacks although I assume that in many cases they were similar to my own. My own experience involved great anxiety and disbelief as I watched the towers burn and fall, accompanied by great sadness for the victims and rage that these events had taken place. My feelings were followed by relief when I discovered that my immediate family was physically safe and suffering no more than the same emotional upset, confusion, and turmoil as I was. I was further relieved when informed that the spouse of one of my colleagues who was working in the Trade Center was alive and well.

Later discussions with friends and colleagues revealed my emotional response to be typical, although the intensity of emotional reactions seemed to vary from person to person as well as how individuals expressed and dealt with their feelings. It became clear later on that those who were on-site or who lost loved ones during the attack experienced emotions appropriate to those situations. Horror, terror, grief, rage, and the extreme anxiety of not knowing if friends and relatives had actually been lost were typical of those reported in the hours and days following the tragedy.

An outpouring of respect and admiration for the policemen, firefighters, construction workers, politicians, and others working at "ground zero" emerged, as did a general sense of community and comradery among those living in and around New York City. In addition, there was such an outpouring of charitable giving to aid the victims and families of those directly affected by the disaster that charitable organizations literally did not know what to do with all of the money. I leave my description of events and political and emotional reactions from those involved in this historic occasion recognizing its inadequacy but feeling that I have created a bit of the backdrop for what followed from the mental health community.

Within hours of the catastrophe the mental health system and the media that, in general, support them so unquestioningly went into action. Hundreds of psychotherapists flooded ground zero to offer their services to the survivors and their friends and relatives unbidden and unasked for. The federal government sent in an unknown number of grief counselors, psychologically and therapeutically trained individuals whose appearance was first made after the rash of school shootings at Littleton, Colorado, and elsewhere. It was clear from the beginning that these individuals came as professionals offering their services as experts in mental health and illness and not simply as members of the community willing to share the grief of their neighbors.

A flood of newspaper, television, and radio reports followed the great tragedy, quoting mental health experts with various backgrounds concerning the epidemic of mental health problems that were about to afflict the country. A professor of psychiatry at Washington University is quoted as saying that "tens of thousands of people could be legitimately diagnosed with post-traumatic stress disorder . . . though this represents the tip of the iceberg. Our nation's sense of security has been replaced with the new emotion of vulnerability." Politicians were told that most at risk are America's children. "The first words five-year-old Eva said when she was introduced to me were 'my daddy died,'" said a psychiatrist at Cornell Weill Medical College. "Any failure to offer preventative interventions and treatments may have devastating consequences of impairments in social, academic and emotional functioning now and in the future."

Geraldine Sealey (2001) of ABCnews.com headlines her article "Fragile Psyches: Mental Health Counselors Gear Up for Potential Crisis in New York." Among those quoted is Harold Takooshian, a Fordham University psychologist who intones, "Everybody I know in the mental health community in New York is gearing up for later this year for the suicides and nightmares." Finally, an article in *Newsday* by Beth Whitehouse (2001) quotes a clinical social worker as saying, "Everybody who knows anything about trauma will be getting these cases. *It's going to be cataclysmic* " (p. 7; emphasis added).

It is not necessary to quote further from the hundreds of "experts" who make the same unquestioned claims and predictions. Psychiatrists, psychologists, and psychotherapists are notoriously poor at making accurate predictions and, as yet, have been unable to demonstrate a strong record of success in helping patients with whatever mental illnesses might represent as problems in living. Numerous studies suggest that the success rates of psychotherapy are similar from school to school and therapy to therapy. Moreover, research reveals that therapy is no more effective than similar interventions by clergy, good friends, or other forms of support of nonprofessional groups or untrained individuals. Clearly, any of the predictions made are not grounded in science, especially predictions of widespread social and individual catastrophe.

However, my goal here is not to further document from a scientific perspective the nature of the "house of cards" (Dawes, 1994) that my field is nor to discuss the arrogance and ignorance of those writing and providing the material for these stories. My need is to discuss the effects of this assault on the democratic institutions of this society. I suggest that the behavior of the mental health field in this instance is representative of behavior that has become a social norm and that the total effect of these experiences are sapping the energies of our society and advancing the development of a type of closed society or pharmacracy discussed earlier.

There are several interlocking factors responsible for psychotherapy's contribution to a closed rather than an open society, which are demonstrated in the field's reaction to the events of September 11, 2001. First, the entire field is predicated on the notion that whatever form of therapy is practiced and however those forms are justified by theory the goal of treatment is the amelioration and/or cure of mental illnesses or disorders. Therefore the field is not only based on a lie but on a lie that *defines virtually any citizen upset in any way over these events as morally damaged and neurologically impaired.*

Second, the focus of virtually all forms of psychotherapy is on the individual rather than the society in which she/he lives. To the degree that cultural institutions are the focus of therapy the discussion is limited to family and perhaps grade school and then to the manner in which these institutions create mental pathology *within the individual.* The third factor is related to the second. Therapists pay scant attention to the politics of their relationship to individual patients and then only in terms of the pathology, not the political stance of the patient.

Changing a patient's consciousness inevitably defines changes in the degree of personal political freedom experienced by the patient, the moral obligations that the patient feels constrain her/his freedom and the personal goals that define the direction of the patient's life. Those changes in the individual reverberate throughout every relationship in the patient's life and are necessarily paralleled by changes in every relationship. Success or failure in therapy is often determined more by the reaction of the family and friends to the changes in living initiated by the patient as a result of therapy than anything going on in treatment.

I have long been amazed by the degree to which therapists ignore the manner in which the immediate political relationships in the patient's life inhibit change the patient might wish to make as a result of therapy. This is especially true of children who can make no changes in their own lives without parental approval and assistance. I am equally amazed at the indifference many therapists show when helping a patient initiate changes that are devastating to the lives of all those with whom the patient is connected.

Moreover, therapists also fail to consider their political relationships with society beyond their target audience of patients. The therapeutic community is visible to and involved with those for whom they often work: schools, hospitals, large corporations, and, ultimately, the government that either funds various public institutions or hires mental health personnel directly. All of these complex political–moral relationships become invisible. The therapists insist that they are only restoring the mental health of sick patients and need not consider their underlying visions and political values as they affect and are affected by the community of which they are all an integral part.

I argue that the therapy industry generally attempts to define the nature of freedoms and proper relationship to authority for the public at large.

However, the degree of freedoms sought for any given patient changes depending on the patient's prior standing, status, and power in the community; the severity of the diagnosis made (often, in part, a function of the patient's status); and the institution where the patients are "treated." Of course this all depends on just how aware the therapist is of her/his own god-thing narrative and the manner in which this informs his reactions to the patients with whom she/he works.

Since therapists are often as embedded in the hierarchy of the society that employs them, and as Beit-Hallahmi (1974) makes clear, many therapists work far from the top of the power hierarchy of society; the god-thing narratives that guide their work are quite invisible to them. I have never heard a discussion among therapists whose focus is the role their own political and economic status plays in their work with patients. Some of the most unhappy individuals I have met are therapists (and teachers) whose salaries and societal recognition is barely above those with whom they work. As is common in such situations the professionals shift their personal feelings of resentment toward society onto the patients (and students) who represent the therapist's own sense of failure.

The fourth factor involves my belief that most therapists also pay scant attention to the notion of mental health or even the absence of mental illness. The average therapist is so focused on individual pathology that she/he never stops to define what being cured might mean either in individual or social terms. They simply do not ask what changes might be taking place in a community of well-treated and cured individuals or who might benefit as these changes in society take place beyond or instead of the patients. Therapists rarely have discussions concerning which of the dominant values of society affect the goals that define for them their patient's successful recovery. I begin my analysis with the first factor but attempt to relate all of the factors to each other. Again the constraints of this volume make a sketch of the issues a necessary evil.

My primary question is this: Can a society comprised of individuals who believe they are permanently morally, intellectually, and neurologically sick, damaged, and defective wage war, create peace, and hold together as a democracy comprised of confident, independent citizens? Can these same individuals live creative, independent lives as members of a community while permanently dependent on mind- and brain-altering drugs? As of this writing there are still individuals able to function according to the needs of a democracy. However, between an estimated 30 and 50 million adults now take SSRIs and other mood- and thought-altering drugs, and between an estimated 3 and 10 million children are given amphetamine-like substances for the mythical mental illnesses that interfere with their functioning at home and at school. What will happen if and when the mental health field convinces a majority of our citizens that they are defective and require a lifetime of drug ingestion and/or psychotherapy? I hope we do not have to find out.

Convincing people that they are defective also convinces them that their problems are not between them and others but within themselves and others. Conflicts between individuals are ignored and so, too, are the politics practiced between them. Therapy focuses on the sick individual and not the "sick" relationships that might help *create and maintain* the individual. Change becomes the responsibility of the individual who becomes focused on improving the self as an autonomous but defective agency. If analyses of the abuse of power take place at all they take place on the micro level of the family rather than the macro level of the whole society. Social injustice and the corrupt practices of authoritarian leaders are ignored. Individuals are not helped to understand their individual misery as a function of their place in the social hierarchy or as it relates to their mode of dealing with themselves.

So much of what psychoanalysts such as Karen Horney (1950) describe about the intrapsychic dynamics of the "mentally ill" involves a tyranny of the self along classical totalitarian lines. Moreover, individuals never learn that perhaps the real relief they seek can only come from developing political strategies that will help them change their place in the social institutions that have defined them or even change the nature of the institutions themselves. Would the American Revolution had ever taken place if the aroused citizenry took their drugs and turned inward on their fears and personal shortcomings?

Moreover, when individuals accept the definitions of themselves as intellectually damaged they often accept the places set for them within the hierarchy of an authoritarian, closed society. Not only does this mean accepting that authority is truly superior to themselves but that real freedom belongs to their betters higher on the social ladder as well as the moral responsibility that goes with those freedoms. When individuals become content with their lot and accept as true the historicisms and myths that define the inevitability and unchanging true nature of their beings, society can become quite closed. Under such circumstances democracy can be perceived as dangerous and those that propose it the enemy. These conditions inhere in much of the rhetoric of the mental health complex following September 11.

I briefly discuss the specific diagnosis most frequently invoked after the September 11 attacks, post-traumatic stress disorder, (PTSD). *DSM-IV* defines the symptoms of PTSD as follows: "The person has been exposed to a traumatic event in which both of the following were present: 1) the person experienced, witnessed, or was confronted with an event or events that involved actual or threatened death or serious injury, or a threat to the physical integrity of self or others[;] 2) the person's response involved intense fear, helplessness, or horror" (pp. 427–428). The symptoms of this mental disorder include (and I am abridging the list) recurrent and intrusive distressing recollection of the event; recurrent dreams of the event; efforts to avoid thoughts, feelings, or conversation associated with the trauma; feelings of detachment or estrangement from others; difficulty falling asleep; hypervigilance; and exaggerated startle response.

The idea that our reaction to the acts of terrorism is trauma and represents illness is just another attempt at utilizing medical metaphors incorrectly and forgetting that they are metaphors. The idea of trauma as a medical concept implies an assault on the body and subsequent change in the body's normal functioning. Clearly, this involves medical judgments based on clear evidence of bodily harm against well-established standards of physiology and anatomy. Trauma in the context of a social catastrophe demanding great changes in human adaptive responses is a concept of a very different order. PTSD is a moral judgment and invoked en masse as a distinct political act.

The diagnosis strips most of the meaning of the event for these offending individuals who accept the moral labels offered them. Is not vigilance necessary when individuals do not know if further attacks are imminent? Is it appropriate to sleep soundly and hence be totally vulnerable unless individuals feel safe? Can the world mean the same thing after such events as before? And if the world and one's life are seen the same, is that more or less pathological than living in a world whose meaning is forever altered and requires new modes of adaptive response? Moreover, the *DSM* description of those individuals diagnosed assumes their victim-hood. Peter Marin's (1981) description of his work with Vietnam veterans mirrors my own. Many of the soldiers suffer from guilt over the horrendous things that they did under wartime conditions for which they cannot experience absolution and redemption.

The use of PTSD as a moral–political concept has an interesting history. The diagnosis was created (diagnoses are never discovered) during the Vietnam War. It replaced earlier judgments made about men whose emotional reactions prevented them from carrying on their functions as soldiers. Prior to the rise of the pseudoscience of psychiatry, men who cried, trembled, and failed their fellow soldiers, country, religion, or society on the battlefield were labeled "cowards" and generally were put to death. With the rise of psychiatry the reactions of these men were relabeled with pseudomedical terminology. During World War I it was "shell-shocked;" by World War II the term had evolved to "war neurosis;" and finally, in our own era it is "PTSD."

General George Patton destroyed his career during World War II when he slapped and called a soldier diagnosed with war neurosis a coward. The power of psychiatry to redefine the morality of our society was already greater than that of a general prosecuting the war. Of course, just as this redefinition of morality continues, the media, the public, and even the professionals involved did not understand that the conflict between the general and the doctors was moral and political rather than scientific or medical. If seen as a moral conflict one can think clearly about it and both question and debate the moral assumptions involved. Who is the saner or moral individual; the one who fights, kills, and dies or the one who cries for his mother and home? It is not my purpose to debate these issues here and decide whether "hero" or "coward" is the applicable moral judgment; rather, it is to make clear the possible effects of diagnosing the entire American population as mentally ill because they are upset and angry over the attack on their country.

I need not repeat my argument that what are being described as symptoms of an illness are, in my thinking, the adaptive reactions of individuals experiencing a complex, highly unusual, dangerous, and terrifying situation. These individuals are not being traumatized but are being called to action to save their lives and the lives of their friends and relatives and members of their community. They are being asked to cope with unknown threats that may or may not reoccur. They must mourn the deaths of familiars and strangers and perhaps of the community and lifestyle of which they are a part. They are being called to behave according to the morals and politics inherent in such situations.

Citizens under attack have needs to satisfy and problems to solve under difficult and highly ambiguous circumstances. The public is confronting immediate and profound change, the experience of which, according to Eric Hoffer (1963), renders existing adaptive skills useless. Under such circumstances anxiety, however painful, is an appropriate emotional response in that it motivates a search for new answers, modes of response, and even new leadership and forms of social organization.

The emotions demonstrated by these individuals are not sicknesses to be cured; instead, they are evolutionary products that exist to connect them to their situation and fellow community members as well as to provide the motivation to deal with their situation. I agree with Nico Frijda (1986), Carroll Izard (1977), Richard Lazarus (1991), and Martha Nussbaum (2001) that our emotions are essential to our intelligence, fully integrated with our cognitive capacities that alone do not motivate us to action. It is time we rethink the emotions and give up the Enlightenment notion that we are rational creatures and that the emotions represent weakness and irrationality. Certainly, the therapeutic attempt to equate terror, rage, guilt, shame, and grief with trauma is both without truth and dangerous to our survival as a society and a species. (I also wonder how anyone can make a moral judgment about a child grieving the loss of a parent that neither the child nor the adults in her or his life can begin to explain.)

Psychotherapists who do not understand mental illness in terms of social, moral, economic, and political interactions also do not understand their own role as political agents within the lives of the individuals with whom they work and the institutions with whom they and their patients function as dualities. The therapist's transformation of the social institutions with which they work became clear to me with my own work with children during my many years as a psychologist with a large mental health clinic. Parents brought their angry, recalcitrant, frightened, rebellious, academically failing children to the clinic seeking explanations for their behavior and help in dealing with them.

These parents were interviewed about their child by a social worker and then sat by as the child was tested by a psychologist and ultimately diagnosed by a psychiatrist. The inevitable choice of treatment was either individual or group play therapy for the child and perhaps counseling for the parents. The child was treated while the parent sat in a waiting room. There is nothing wrong with this arrangement in the mind of the treatment team and clinic; doctors often must treat sick patients independently of the relatives who bring them for therapy. But as time went on I became increasingly concerned about the role that I, and the institution that employed me, was playing in the lives of these people in terms of the family's dynamics.

Not only was I ignoring the dynamics within the family which provided the context of the child's behavior but I was doing nothing to change the very dynamics and relationships that determined the adaptive demands toward which the child (and all members of the family) was struggling to meet. I was also ignoring the larger social dynamics that had and still were determining the behavior of the adults in the family. For example, I worked with a group of women who had been abandoned by their authoritarian husbands and left with debts and insufficient economics to take care of their family. The social development of these women had not only deprived them of education and marketable skills—in part because they were women—but they had never been taught to be authorities toward their children or any other relationships in their lives. Their families lived in anarchy except during the outbursts of rage when these women often used physical discipline in an attempt to control their children.

Not only was I most often ineffective in helping these children but I discovered that my successes could be even more destructive than my failures. Children often came to like and trust me even more than their parents. They spoke to me of their fears and angers and sought advice from me rather than their parents. I discovered that I was undermining what little effective relationship these children had with their families as well as what little authority the parents might possess. I was successful, in part, because I did not love these children as did their often frantic mothers and fathers and did not get upset when they confided some of the things to me that would have made me frantic were I to have heard it from my own children. My demands that the clinic place these children in family treatment fell on deaf ears, as there was no protocol to diagnose a family, only the individuals comprising the family.

My refusal to see any more children except under conditions in which I could help families deal democratically and humanistically with their children rather than as totalitarian or anarchistic structures came as a result of two events. The first incident that strengthened my resolve to think socially and politically came as a result of a losing battle to change a therapy of a mother and two of her children who were seen by the same analytic therapist. He saw them not as a family but separately each with their own separate diagnosis. In addition they were treated under the ruling that the mother could not know what was transpiring with her children as that would compromise both confidentiality and the transference with the children. I could not bear to see the emotional pain and degradation inflicted on the mother as her role with her children was undermined as well as the overall damage being done to this family.

The second event that turned me forever from working alone with children unless they were orphaned or no adult authority was available (and then I referred to myself as "rent a dad") came when I finally convinced one of the fathers who had abandoned his son to meet with me and the child for some sessions. At a critical juncture in one of our discussions the boy finally decided to speak to his feelings but hesitated for fear of upsetting the father (whose usual response was to run away from anything emotionally painful). "It is all right," said the father as he offered to leave the room. "He trusts you more than me." I realized that this was true and that their relationship was the very "pathology" that needed "curing." The father was stunned when instead I left the room. In all the previous treatments with which he did become involved he was the one to leave and the therapist who was no relation to the child remained. How many uncountable families have been so disrupted by we mental health experts?

I resolved never again to play a role in which I took a parental role, under the deception that I knew better because I was treating a sick child, or to do anything again to undermine the functioning of a family or social structure of which I was a paid outsider. If parents do not play with or communicate with their children then changing those interactions can, if the parents so wish it, become the "therapeutic" goal. In addition, my influencing of family structure and function is done without diagnosing any of the family members but instead trying to understand the politics within and without the family interactions. I now try to alert the American public to what is being done to their society as a result of the massive attempt to diagnose millions and millions of their children as suffering from ADHD, Oppositional Defiant Disorder, and, since September 11, 2001, PTSD.

I have another and more personal question concerning the politics of the professionals who begin diagnosing their fellow citizens after a social disaster such as occurred on September 11, 2001. From what privileged platform did this name-calling take place? Were these "diagnoses" made outside or above the role of citizens the professionals share with their "patients"? Were not the professionals servicing their clients suffering from the same emotions of disbelief, rage, confusion, and anxiety as their clients and, hence, from the same mental illnesses of those they were trying to treat? Are not the therapists as citizens equal to their fellow citizens and if so on what basis do they morally judge the fellow members of their shared community? Does not psychoanalysis warn us that when we cannot stand outside the problems we share with our clients that we must be vigilant for the types of countertransference that most damages the therapy and both members of the therapeutic dyad? Certainly those therapists participating in the diagnosis of their fellow citizens do not raise such questions, as the politics inherent in their efforts remain invisible to them.

Tana Dineen (2000) and John McKnight (1995) provides insightful analysis into the mechanisms involved in psychotherapy's (and other professional group's) redirection and reorganization of American society. Therapists have become integral members of society by convincing ever-greater numbers of citizens that they ultimately need therapists to even live their lives. I agree with McKnight when he opines that not only are these beliefs untrue but they mask the reality that it is the therapists who have the greater need, that is, for the unwavering loyalty and dependence of their patients.

I have argued throughout this book that the authoritarian politician must find ways of convincing their followers to accept their legitimacy or else resort to violence in order to maintain leadership. The church convinced the masses that it represented the only true means of the moral life and salvation; psychotherapists have largely succeeded in convincing the public that they must depend on mental health experts to live lives free of mental illness and demonstrative of mental health. The myth that the patient (or student, parishioner) needs the therapist (or teacher, cleric) rather than share a mutual need, or in fact that the authority needs the client (in any capacity) more than the reverse, allows an authoritarian hierarchy to thrive.

No longer are families and communities expected to mourn their losses together and plan the means of getting on with their lives. Instead, they head off singly or as isolated families to experts from outside their communities and restructure their social ties around the empty, unproven theories of individuals whose very notion of intervention requires focusing on the past, and the individual. No longer are communities expected to organize politically and either protect themselves from external danger or from their own authoritarian leadership. No longer are we as a society expected to rise to the occasion and debate a collective response to danger and immorality that can help make us both a safer and morally better society. Instead, we are to assume the position of individual victims and seek our answers in a therapist's consulting room.

The public's acceptance of therapeutic myths is now aided by the fact that increasing numbers of professionals and lay individuals now spread the gospel of mental health and seek to enforce its dictates. For example, numerous teachers now regularly diagnose their students with ADD/ADHD and other mental disorders and either recommend or seek to enforce compliance with either therapists or, worse, psychiatrists and pediatricians prescribing methylphenidates, SSRIs, and other psychotropic drugs. Long lines of children regularly line up at the school nurse's office to receive doses of their so-called medications. The public and politicians of several states have seen fit to either pass or discuss passing laws against teachers either diagnosing children or recommending drugs, although none of these states peer below the myth of mental illness itself.

The politics of the therapists are essentially authoritarian although hidden within the moral, often pious declarations that they seek merely to treat mental illnesses and disorders of their clients and patients. Rarely do therapists admit to their need of their patients, thereby establishing the necessary equality that democratic structures require. No matter how outraged psychologists become toward psychiatric biological reductionism and the overuse of psychiatric drugs they still refuse to recognize the essentially dehumanizing, dependence-producing effects of psychiatric diagnosis.

Rarely, as I have argued throughout this volume, do therapists question the lie on which the entire field depends for its existence. Like the authoritarian political structures that historically have preceded it, the individuals who enter the political structure of the therapeutic industry find that they must embrace and admit to the diagnostic terms that define their essence while accepting the goodness of their therapists. Unless these arrangements become the defining aspects of the relationships of those comprising the therapeutic community the whole structure topples and dies.

The politics of the therapeutic relationship change dramatically with changes in the settings where therapy takes place and make clear the importance of recognizing the therapists' relationship to those more powerful in society than themselves. I have worked as a school psychologist and as a staff member in a variety of hospital and freestanding clinics and, over my thirty-five-year career have maintained a private practice. While I have never heard it openly discussed nor have I found literature on the matter I claim that the patient–therapist relationship and its goals are vastly different in a private-practice setting and an institution of any kind. The language is the same: Mentally ill patients are being treated for their illnesses and the goals of therapy are still directed toward the patient's experience and expression of emotions. However the political dynamics of private practice where the patient hires, pays for therapy, and can fire the therapist are quite different than when the therapist has his work paid for by a third party, particularly one on site.

In a private practice where clients have money and more of the middle- and upper-middle-class trappings of success, the goal of treatment is quite often helping patients justify an increase in the expression of the emotions that define personal needs. Working with those at or near the top of the power hierarchy permits the therapist more easily to join with the "gods" rather than with the "things" of any societal "god-thing" narrative. Such narratives are invisible and unspoken to all concerned. I can relate my own experiences with wealthier, more successful clients to case studies described by Stephen A. Mitchell (2000) and Carlo Strenger (1998). While it may be true that people are diagnosed for the purposes of insurance companies paying part of the therapist's fees, their diagnoses are never referred to as the therapeutic work proceeds. These patients are never called the bad names that invariably accompany those at the lower end of the power structure of society.

For example, Strenger describes his work with a beautiful young woman who travels all over the world making critically and economically successful documentary films. She describes a life with few social attachments except with the gays in her hometown and a vigorous sadomasochistic sex life with a wide variety of partners that is both emotionally fulfilling and extremely dangerous. Over the course of time Strenger helps this young woman, who sees him only when she is in Israel where Strenger lives, develop a satisfying explanatory narrative about her behavior involving her early relationship with her passive mother and cruel and dominating father.

The details of this explanation are of little concern here except to note that I judge them to be the work of an educated and facile mind passionately concerned about his patient and in love with his work as analytic therapist. However, the topics of guilt and shame are never queried of the patient, or discussed by Strenger. Moreover, the patient is never questioned as to her feelings of obligation to anyone but herself. It is the construction of her own self that is the focus of the treatment and not the construction of a social or political self that comes under scrutiny. Strenger accepts the patient's goals as his own, is wholly respectful of his client, and at no time does he ever diagnose her with any of the *DSM*'s dehumanizing labels.

I am not suggesting that either I would or Strenger should try to impose a lifestyle on this or any patient; our goals for democratic and humanistic social interactions forbids that. I am suggesting, however, that the patient herself might have intense needs for the very moral–political relationships that are so invisible during this well-written and interesting case study. With patients low on the social totem pole judgments abound and are used as the explanations of the very patterns of behavior that produced the diagnosis. With wealthier, more admirable private patients it is almost the reverse situation. There are few, if any, judgments and only theoretical explanations of behavior based on descriptions. *It is almost as if to explain all is to forgive all.*

Some years ago a former colleague living in a wealthy community asked me to lead a discussion for a group of parents at the nursery school attended by her child. I was stunned and left feeling surreal and uncertain as to how to proceed when told that the topic I should discuss were problems related to being wealthy and not knowing how to raise children who can have every material thing they could possibly wish for. I have often dealt with problems having to do with too little money and even real poverty. As I come from the lower working class and have never felt myself to be "blessed" with too much money, I had a difficult time for the hour's time it took to discuss these problems. I know few people who ever worry about having too much wealth nor have I met therapists who hope for a practice with poor patients. How often do therapists concern themselves with the problems of patients being materially wealthy unless money becomes a substitute for love and the social obligations of parenthood? How often are such politics confronted by a therapist asking, as they might about poverty and helplessness, about how it feels to be powerful and wealthy?

A critical issue involved in any discussion of psychotherapy is confidentiality. Confidentiality is critical to any relationship in which trust is sought and required. People simply do not share thoughts and feelings that are likely to be used against them, labeled as "weaknesses," and become either sources of intense shame and humiliation or even justifications of punishment. Moreover, in the political meaning of relationships confidentiality means privacy, a reality that defines in many ways the heart of democracy. I have no doubt that Strenger has hidden the identity of "Tamara" so well that she might not even recognize herself in his book and has received her permission to write about his relationship with her. I also have no doubt that whatever "Tamara" told Strenger as a secret stayed a secret with him.

The experience of working in a clinic especially with those lower on society's ladder of success, wealth, and power is distinctly different than working in a private practice with successful, wealthier clients. No individuals are lower in our society's hierarchy than those diagnosed as schizophrenic or psychotic. At the mental health clinic where I labored for many years I was part of a team, whose head was always a psychiatrist. One of the main preoccupations was diagnosis and using the diagnosis to justify the lack of progress made by the patients as well as the constant use of brain- and mind-disabling drugs.

The idea of increased freedom of opportunity as well as rights of privacy cease to exist in the politics of those on the "thing" side of the social curve. As part of the team even the therapists lack privacy, a disabling fact however invisible and ignored as it is. Patients are regularly told that their individual and private lives have, in effect, ended, as they will require a lifetime of treatment merely to be kept out of the hospital. The cases of these patients are discussed openly and everywhere including the lunchroom and the elevators. The patient's files are scrutinized by any who wish to so and are regularly visited by state and local officials as well as representatives of Medicare and Medicaid who fund the therapy for the poor.

I offer two painful personal stories to make my point about the politics practiced in public clinics dealing with the poor and those labeled as the "sickest" in society. I worked for some time with a woman who lamented her life as a permanent member of the mental health system. She described herself as intelligent and ambitious and was a college graduate who for some years had been a well-paid executive working for a large corporation. She stated that she was always riddled with guilt and felt that she had never been successful enough in life especially when it came to taking care of her mother and sickly brother. As time progressed she felt ever more burdened and exhausted by the pressure to do well in both her family and business life.

One evening, in a state of exhaustion and depression, she began to hallucinate that Jesus Christ and Satan (the patient had been raised a strict Catholic) were giving her advice about her life. Jesus told her to keep shouldering her burden, while the devil intoned that she should relax and take care of herself. These hallucinatory experiences continued for some weeks during which time she was hospitalized and diagnosed as "paranoid schizophrenic." The hallucinations ended when she decided that the devil's voice was really Jesus' and vice-versa. It was morally right for her to relax and lay down some of the burden she had carried for so long.

This woman never again had another crisis such as the one that had led to her hospitalization but she had internalized the belief that she was brain injured and would always be sick. She believed that she had to take her "medications" for the rest of her life despite her experience of them as disabling and disfiguring. She accepted as well that she had to see a therapist once a week to oversee how well she was following her regimen, which included doing nothing that might upset her or cause stress. She complained that she had no life but was terrified to do anything to recapture the life that was so difficult but rewarding to her. I suggested that she make plans to engage in just some of the activities that gave her pleasure and she excitedly began making plans for a luncheon at which she would invite some old friends.

As the day of the luncheon arrived she became elated and excited and had trouble falling asleep one evening. The following morning she appeared for her monthly medication appointment and related her plans and the fact of her sleeplessness to her psychiatrist. When I arrived that afternoon I discovered that the patient had been removed from my care, given an increase in her neuroleptic drugs as well as a prescription for a sleeping pill. She had been instructed to give up plans for her luncheon, expect not to see me again, and never hope to do more than stay out of the hospital. After venting my rage against the clinic and those who had removed this woman from my care without consultation with me, I sat and wept for my patient.

The second incident that for me demonstrates the political damage done to those in mental health clinics involves a therapist who rushed into my office after a student she was supervising reported a woman she was treating for child abuse. The patient had come for treatment, specifically seeking help for her lack of strategies in dealing with her anger when upset with her child. The woman was young, poor, and abandoned by the child's father and herself the product of a broken home and abusive parents. The patient had assumed confidentiality when she spoke of her problems and was stunned when the young therapist picked up the phone and reported her to hospital social services saying that this was the law and she had to follow it. I tried to stop the process set in motion but the clinic administration insisted that our responsibility be first to the state and not our patient.

I do not condone child abuse but neither can I accept a political process in which spies working for the state turn in individuals seeking help in changing their lives. It is the unexamined and denied authoritarian politics of the psychotherapeutic field that has allowed the principle of confidentiality and privacy to become so eroded especially in cases of the most powerless in society. Dictators hate and fear privacy in those they seek to control, as they do not know what disloyalties and plots might be hatched out of their sight. Priests and lawyers still have confidentiality, as the politics of their relationship to society are well-defined. Our field and its work are based on a myth and as such our political role in society has not been clearly defined and commitments made to democratic and humanistic political rules that would make confidentiality mandatory.

I turn last to psychotherapy and the notion of cure. It is one thing for an individual to give up a "pathological" lifestyle; it is another to replace it with a newer, "healthier" form of living. Since my own view of pathology is at least in part social, any change in an individual involves a change in the relationships of the individual with family, friends, and community. I have explored the difficulties faced by an individual when confronting a whole set of social–political relationships that are threatened by the change in that individual's behavior (Simon, 2000b) and will return to this theme in Chapter 9. Here, I briefly explore the changes seemingly advocated by the field of psychotherapy in relation to our society in general.

Sigmund Freud had a fairly good idea of what cure meant if therapy was successful both for the individual patients *and* the society in which they must function. The patients developed greater insight into both their animal nature and the defenses that hid their nature from themselves. While this freed the patients from the suffering created by their own lies and infantile fears, as well as the lies told them by institutions such as their church, patients were not promised happiness. Moreover, a successful analysis changed nothing about humanity's essential depravity, greed, and self-centeredness. Freud thought little of human beings and demonstrated a very

Hobbesian vision of their nature. In a letter to Oskar Pfister, Freud wrote, "I have found little that is good about human beings on the whole. In my experience most of them are trash, no matter whether they publicly subscribe to this or that ethical doctrine or none at all" (quoted in Meng and Freud, 1963: 36).

A successful treatment allowed a patient to become conscious of and accept their animal nature but exercise self-control nonetheless. In a real sense therapy strengthened the ego and made people smarter about themselves and the world. Society and civilization had to be maintained at all costs and remained a thin veneer protecting humanity from living again in the jungle. Once individuals understood the nature of their sexual urges and became capable of genital orgasm they were expected to have those orgasms in a heterosexual relationship. (Not only do some women's groups have dartboards with Freud's picture on it, but some gay groups do as well. Any sexual gratification involving the mouth or anus, or even masturbation, was seen by Freud as evidence of fixation and hence of pathology.) For Freud unconscious drives and instincts were the real danger to society as they were not under the conscious control of the individual and therefore would more likely lead to destructive acting out.

American psychology has never shared Freud's dark view of humanity nor his view of therapy having the goal of helping maintain civilization through the development and deployment of an intellectual elite. American therapists, for the most part, define the positive changes wrought by successful treatment in terms of changes in emotional experience and expression rather than intellectual growth. Their goals concerning their patients' changes in emotional expression and relatedness are generally inconsistent and ultimately hypocritical when seen from the lens of how differently the rich and the poor are often treated.

I have rarely met therapists, and have even more rarely read anything related to psychiatry, psychoanalysis, and treatment in general, who posit that a legitimate goal of treatment be a patient's search or struggle for intellectual superiority and creativity. In fact, the idea of struggle itself is often indicative of some form or other of mental illness. Therapists at present share with their academic colleagues an abhorrence of what is known as "elitism." They are part of a historical movement that Jose Ortega y Gasset (1957) referred to as the "revolt of the masses" in which the rebellion against corrupt authority is conflated with mistrust of any notions of superiority by anyone along any dimensions whatsoever. It involves a view of democracy that not only assures all concerned equal opportunity on a level playing field but equal success as well.

I am certainly against the kind of "god-thing" narrative that leads to the type of intellectual snobbism that intellectuals so often demonstrate. But being a snob and looking down one's nose at inferior beings while convinc-

Psychotherapy III   157

ing someone that they can never aspire to be as intellectually great as one-self is hardly elitism. Would anyone seriously buy tickets to an athletic event such as a basketball or a baseball game unless they expected to see the elite of the sport play one another? I think not. Michael Jordan and Derek Jetter are multimillionaires because they are the elite of their respective sports and rarely are voices raised against the huge salaries they command for playing a game that they both obviously enjoy.

The same elitism is frowned on in all too many classrooms and con-sulting rooms when it comes to intellectual superiority. What then is the mark of mental health for these experts whose therapeutic goals so differ from Freud's own? In our culture a shift has taken place in the notion of mental health from being insightful to feeling good. The primary object of all too many therapies is a change in emotion first and intellect second. *Our goal as educators and therapists, and increasingly for the parents that we influ-ence, is to help children grow up happy and safe from any painful or negative emotions regardless of the reason for the emotions.* Even cognitive therapies conceive of changing the interpretive skills of patients in order to service the emotions rather than improving developmental intellectual skills for their own sake.

Children in school are to have their self-esteem improved as a condition of learning rather than the other way around. Intellectual competition is frowned on as the naturally brighter might make those they outperform feel bad about their inability to achieve the same grades. It is interesting but my observation has been that children who feel they are being judged by the same standards as other children and given equal and fair opportunity to compete admire, rather than resent, those naturally more gifted than themselves. I hear little resentment for Michael Jordan's height advantage or what appears to be the innate skills of a Beethoven or a Heifitz. Instead these individuals become objects of admiration and their achievements set the standards toward which the rest of us tend to strive.

Ignoring the context and meaning in which emotions are aroused is destructive to a democracy that depends on the creative efforts of those in voluntary cooperation. Feeling good, or at least not feeling bad, ignores the individuality that emerges when individuals struggle to express their personal best. There are no standards possible in feeling good unless it is to discern who feels better and who feels best. Working individually with-out regard for either societal standards or individual achievement to help people feel better has resulted in a rise of self-preoccupation and narcis-sism (Lasch, 1976) as well as a "dumbing down" of the whole culture. The result has been a rise in individualism and a corresponding decline in individuality.

Therapists often help clients feel better by making them aware of their victimization by parents, teachers, and the general unfairness of society and life in general. Charles J. Sykes (1992) suggests that we are becoming a nation of complainers and whiners who resent rather than admire or seek to emulate the elite of society. I believe it is important for people to move from the self-hatred and despair that so often results from being victimized in authoritarian/totalitarian political structures. Psychological growth often requires the therapist to identify with and, when ample evidence is available, affirm an individual's pain and feelings of violation and injustice. But the goal of therapy and education must be to help individuals themselves move beyond victimization by escaping from or changing the painful politics that have entrapped them and seeking to restore justice denied.

During my whole career I have watched as therapists confuse pity with sympathy and empathy while convincing their patients to resent those who have victimized them by rendering them permanently mentally ill, brain damaged, and in need of a lifetime of chemical and psychological treatment. The patients are made to feel temporarily better by shifting responsibility for those aspects of their unhappiness that they themselves create while failing to develop necessary strategies for changing their own lives.

It is interesting that one can often hear the same therapists that pity their hopelessly damaged patients complain about the hopelessness of their own lives and careers as well as express the contempt they ultimately have for the people with whom they work. They are unaware of the connection between the god-thing narrative that defines their work and the fact that the work has become hopeless and unbearable. They fail to understand the dynamic so well described by Jessica Benjamin (1998) that a person's failure to affirm the dignity of those with whom one lives or works leaves one without a valued partner to affirm one's self.

Freud evinced a political conservatism. The successful patient found a place in society and ceased rebellion or "acting out" unconscious motives. However, Freud assumed that the ultimate adjustment of the patient would involve an honest acceptance of the leaders with intellectual superiority such as himself. Like Plato, Freud hoped for a society comprised of intelligent people ruled by a benevolent philosopher king. As I argued in the last chapter Freud's idea of a therapeutic relationship that allowed free speech and demanded scrupulous honesty between the parties involved would help individuals see through the pretenses they had adopted as a result of their abuse at the hands of irrational authority. However, Freud blinked and did not see his therapy as a universal form of individual education but only one that could benefit an intellectual elite. He failed to develop a psychological theory of democracy because he did not believe in it. But he did believe in intellectual excellence as one of the goals of treatment.

I agree with Beit-Hallahmi (1974) that most therapists also want to be the new rulers of our society but proclaim instead their love of humanity and democracy. They become quite upset when the reality of their politics is demonstrated to them. However, for all too many of those practicing therapy, success in treatment is defined by feeling good as a consequence of accepting whatever major societal values are being promoted. Their goals are anything but helping their patients see through the shams and pretensions of authority, especially their own.

School psychologists and others working with children confuse their students as they simultaneously tell them how valuable they are and how they should have "self-esteem" while diagnosing them as ADHD, intellectually retarded, and the like. I hear school psychologists rail against administrators and shoddy school standards and still work toward getting students to adapt fully to school demands. Yes, it is hard to be a political activist in a school setting but should not the role of the elite be to get the system, at least some of the time, to accommodate the individual rather than the other way around?

Philip Cushman (1995) echoes my sentiments when he criticizes so much of psychology's acceptance of our society's materialism and greed. He suggests that the result is an "empty self" that forever hungers for more goods and fails to recognize the deeper needs that go unfulfilled when material goods are substituted for love and creativity. I disagree with other intellectual critics who focus on the ills created in society by capitalism and the therapeutic blind acceptance of capitalism. Many critics of mainstream therapy demand that some form of Marxian socialism replace capitalism.

While Karl Marx was correct in his assessment of the plight of the poor and their mistreatment at the hands of the rich, his theory of social change is predicated on essentialisms, historicisms, and advocating violence toward a dehumanized view of anyone who is wealthy and powerful. Given that every major social experiment trying to create a Marxist society has been totalitarian and the horrors perpetuated by these regimes has been so destructive to all involved with them, I think it best to try to bring about social and economic justice by other means.

My own focus remains on the political freedom of individuals and their economic status, as vital as that is, as a secondary issue. My position therefore demands an open and free market system. I add, however, that our current economic system is not open but exists as a plutocracy, a growing dictatorship of international corporations that are wealthier and more powerful than the countries in which they are based. These companies are justified by "god-thing" narratives and include historicisms, essentialisms, and all of the other characteristics of authoritarian, closed societies. While a full discussion of this topic is beyond the scope of this book, I think it important that it be part of the professional discussions of therapists whose lives and work are as involved in the economics and politics of this society as their patients.

I close the chapter by reiterating my suggestions for my wished-for future of psychoanalysis. I believe that if therapists consciously take a moral–political position, one that I hope is committed to a democratic and humanistic society, the field can be a powerful force for social justice and the betterment of humanity. Without that discussion the field will be rooted in the bankrupt scientific theories and moral politics of psychiatry and will continue to ally itself with the worst in humanity and its politics.

CHAPTER 7

Madness and Other Forms of Being

INTRODUCTION

In this chapter and the remaining two I sketch my personal reconstruction of psychotherapy as a moral–political and psychological enterprise. I attempt to do more than simply repeat previously written arguments (Simon, 1986, 1998, 2000 a,b) and include where I can those contributions made to my thinking from elements within the fields of psychology and psychoanalysis. I have several goals for this chapter. The first is to discuss madness and those forms of madness that psychiatry calls "psychoses" and demonstrate my belief that madness and the psychoses represent nothing more, or less, than adaptive forms of consciousness or particular modes of 'being in the world.' In turn, it is my contention that the psychoses and the particular forms of psychoses referred to as "schizophrenia" are but two variations of wider varieties of madness.

Further, it is my contention that madness has shaped human history and its politics and is central to all human functioning despite its capacity for destructiveness and ability to create endless human misery. I contend that the majority of humanity is and has been mad and one reason that this is so is that they live in political systems that are models of madness. I am speaking, of course, of any and all political systems based on supernaturally justified god-thing narratives that evolve into authoritarian/totalitarian and closed societies.

I suggest that so-called schizophrenia is psychiatry's and modernity's prototype of madness and agree with Thomas Szasz (1974) that it is the sacred symbol of psychiatry. The behavior of those labeled "schizophrenic" threatens the social and economic adaptations now favored by Western society and its priesthood of modern science. *It is my belief that it is the madness within science that motivates the viciousness of the assault on the madness represented by schizophrenia.* Schizophrenia, as represented by a variety of patterns of adaptive behavior, is no more difficult to understand than the patterns of adaptive behavior demonstrated by the rest of us. The commonly held psychiatric belief that the psychotic cannot be understood is based on the political stance that turns certain individuals into the other, the "it," the scapegoat.

I see those labeled as schizophrenic forced into treatment and tortured by psychiatry as the triple victims of authoritarian god-thing politics. They are first victims of society at large and the particular manner in which families, schools, churches (all too often institutions practicing totalitarian politics justified by religious madness), and other social institutions have dealt with them. Second, they are victims of those who have sworn oaths to help them with the suffering created by their madness, namely, the mental health field. As I suggested in Chapter 4 the cruelty to those diagnosed as schizophrenic is often subtler now than in earlier times but still represents an unrelenting assault on the minds and bodies of those diagnosed. Richard Gosden (2001) and Robert Whitaker (2002) detail the historical continuity in psychiatry's dehumanization of those labeled schizophrenic. They describe medicine's continued goal of inducing terror and creating brain damage to control and pacify beings seen as animalistic and less than human while violating the basic human and civil rights of those diagnosed as schizophrenic.

Finally, the schizophrenic, like all who are mad, are also victims of their own politics of the self. I do not see this particular set of victims as either heroic or noble as do some of my colleagues with whom I share a view of schizophrenia as a socially constructed entity comprised of societal forces hostile to their existence. The solution used by the individuals labeled schizophrenic to their problems in living are, in my judgment, immature, self-destructive, and lead to a life that is tragic and full of unnecessary suffering.

My second goal for these final chapters is to bring into focus certain philosophical issues whose explicit discussion permits understanding of some of the intellectual reasons that have allowed psychiatry to wander so far from a genuine science of human behavior, of a moral humanism, and democratic politics. I will briefly discuss and demonstrate my resolution of the mind (brain)–body problem, the nature–nurture controversy, issues related to free will versus determination, and arguments over the split between self and object. I will in no way settle any arguments over these issues, which have troubled and held the attention of thinking people over the centuries, but will attempt to demonstrate that even a solution which creates controversy is better than psychology's, psychiatry's, and psychotherapy's pretense that these issues simply do not matter.

MADNESS AND SCHIZOPHRENIA

I use the word *madness*, as did R. D. Laing (1967), to denote an individual's particular manner of relating to the world in and around him/herself. I recognize that the term *madness* is a moral judgment as it reflects personal opinions that establish the worth and value of the types of adaptive behaviors and modes of consciousness and being under consideration. I make my judgment from the privileged position of a scientist. I recognize that my stance reflects my personal values: that science is a socially constructed and sanctioned set of activities and represents one of many modes of human adaptation. I recognize as well that millions of human beings relate to the world as scientists just as I do and that being a good scientist in the way it is used here in no way requires expert training or advanced academic degrees.

Science is but one form of many modes of adaptive understanding of ourselves and the world we live in. It is my judgment that science, based as it is on formal operations, guided by humanistic values, and operated as a democracy in which knowledge is organized as theory and open to debate and demands for empirical verification, represents the diametric opposite of madness. Science represents that balance between being both a willing participant in the world and a potentially critical observer of it. As a result the scientist/artist is in the world but never fully of it. It also represents an individual's capacity for loving, creative self-expression as a member of a democratic political structure or one who seeks to create democratic/humanistic relationships.

I warrant that madness is not a medical diagnosis but a socially constructed convention of a variety of individual modes of human adaptation. As already discussed there are no medical tests or known biological markers that differentiate the mad from the professionals (especially the mad doctors) who refer to the mad as "psychotic," "schizophrenic," or any other type of pseudomedical terminology. One set of particular modes of adaptation is labeled schizophrenia. I turn to *DSM-IV*'s definition of schizophrenia to help me establish my own criteria of madness and the basis in which psychiatry differentiates the madness of the patients designated as psychotic or schizophrenic from the madness that is psychiatry.

DSM-IV defines the characteristic symptoms of schizophrenia as delusions, hallucinations, disorganized speech, grossly disorganized or catatonic behavior, and negative symptoms, that is, affective flattening, alogia, or avolution. Delusions are false beliefs that defy all evidence and logic to the contrary. Delusions might involve grandiosity or persecution or both. Many delusions concern themselves with religious themes involving God, the Devil, and so on. In many of the delusions examined by mental health professionals, individuals often claim to be controlled by God and/or the devil or even be God and/or the Devil.

In recent years the delusions of the schizophrenic have become secularized and increasingly involve the Central Intelligence Agency (CIA), the Federal Bureau of Investigation (FBI), and other powerful governmental agencies. Modernity has added new delusions involving godlike and monstrous creatures from outer space. In other delusions individuals claim to be machines, robots, puppets, and a variety of things not quite human. In recent years delusions involving supernatural forces have been replaced by beliefs whose content reflects spaceships and aliens from other planets.

Hallucinations are claims of perceptual experiences that cannot be experienced by those sharing the same perceptual field. Most hallucinations are auditory, although visual hallucinations are not uncommon, and often involve the claim that God, the devil, space aliens, or members of the CIA are speaking to the individual. Any of the senses can be involved in a hallucination but such experiences tend to be less usual that those involving hearing or vision. The experiences of those hallucinating often match up well with their delusions. Individuals might be told by the beings with whom they converse that they are powerful, talented, and wonderful along some particular dimension or another (for example, a patient who was regularly told by God that she is an immortal poetess). These same invisible beings might also tell those who become psychiatric patients that they are vile, ugly, or evil, in short, the very opposite of the moral and physical judgments of perfection originally offered.

The delusions and hallucinations of the individuals with whom I have worked over many years seem to represent the same needs, problems, satisfactions, and solutions as my own and just about everyone else I know including those in the mental health field. The "pathology" of the schizophrenic involves explaining how the world and the self work individually and together as well as judging the ethics and morality of those same objects, events, and beings. The themes of the psychotic mind seem to follow my own inner concerns: They represent narratives that describe, explain, predict, and attempt to control the self and the world around it while achieving a self and a world to live in that are truthful, beautiful, and good. What we judge to be schizophrenia is the manner in which these individuals go about the business of being scientists and moral philosophers.

Those "diagnosed" as schizophrenic differ in what they see in the world, and, as important, how they see what they see, from those whose mode of being conforms to humanistic science and those who live with more ordinary modes of madness. There are differences in the narratives of those who end up being called schizophrenic. These differences are both in the content of the narrative and the manner in which the psychotic experiences and lives out the narrative. The content of the schizophrenic narrative is often a "god-thing" story of extremes. These individuals live according to constructions of self and the world that conform to extremes of closed, totalitarian societies. Their understanding of themselves confuse judgments with descriptions, are based on essentialisms, and predict the future according to extreme versions of historicisms.

The individuals are seeking to become or bond with God or other powerful and moral figures or are seeking the emotional relief of becoming an unfeeling mechanical device. They are desperate to achieve these aims because they hold a certain set of attitudes concerning themselves and the world in which they live. In general, it has been my experience that the same cognitive–affective truths that motivate the schizophrenic similarly motivate a variety of other serious "diagnostic" groups to be found in any *DSM*, including profound depression and the escape provided by the extensive use of psychoactive drugs. The attitudes held by schizophrenics is also held, but to a somewhat lesser degree, by those who demonstrate everyday madness.

The attitudes evinced by the schizophrenic, which they will relate to anyone with an interest to listen and understand rather than diagnose and judge, are:

1. a profound feeling of self-hatred, shame, guilt, and loathing that grows from the belief that they are in some way significantly, irredeemably, and essentially, morally flawed;
2. terror and rage toward a world and its inhabitants perceived as unalterably hostile to the existence of their sense of self and self-interests;
3. helplessness as a result of the belief that the self is unable to alter any of the terrifying aspects of the world and the moral flaws that render the self undeserving of life, love, respect, and a place of honor among one's fellow human beings;
4. hopelessness that grows from the conviction that nothing will ever change; these individuals believe that their destiny has been chosen for them and it is useless to try to alter their dreadful fates;
5. intense confusion and anxiety that emerges from the experience of a world perceived as ambiguous, deceitful, unpredictable, and ever ready to betray.

The second difference in the content of the schizophrenic narrative is the failure of the diagnosed individuals to make their stories conform to the usual god-thing narratives that direct the lives of those around them. Most religions punish those for disagreeing with the core explanatory and moral assumptions of their faith. Heretics, prophets, and those who create their own religions are often despised by the established religions of their own time. At present this seems to hold especially true for those who dare to oppose society's worship of scientism and be obedient to the psychiatric religion in particular. *Those diagnosed as schizophrenic are treated as they are because in effect they are anarchists and do not participate in those forms of madness that comprise society's dominant authoritarian/totalitarian modes of political interaction.*

The third difference of the schizophrenic's mode of experience from those preferred by science and society in general involves the diagnosed individuals' reliance on preoperational forms of thinking. The reasoning of individuals who get into trouble with psychiatry is often defined by a degree of preoperational thinking that is more frequent than our society and its intellectual guardians now permit. The religion of science promotes and maintains hegemony of formal operations and punishes those expressing themselves in preoperational terms unless they are children.

Those judged to be schizophrenic often experience their narrative literally and not only alter their beliefs but their perceptual processes as well. Their personal narratives become excessively egocentric, lack serialization, and often object constancy especially where other human beings are concerned. As a result they become their narrative and lose (or never develop) the ability to recognize their authorship of their personal narrative and gain control of it. Our culture is particularly hard on those who alter their perceptions of what society agrees is reality. I believe that our intolerance of those who claim to converse with God or other supernatural figures grows out of modernity's and psychiatry's general intolerance with and struggle to supplant religion as society's moral authority.

How and why does the psychotic re-create the internal dialogues that comprise so much of the content of the human beings' stream of consciousness so that they are experienced as interpersonal rather than as intrapersonal? I hypothesize that the use of preoperations is part of the mechanism that permits the transformation of an internal dialogue to be experienced as interpersonal but that is just part of the explanation. (I hypothesize that the psychotic's experience of being in a dreamlike or altered state of consciousness is also a function of perceiving from a preoperational perspective.) We have as yet no real explanations of how these mechanisms might actually operate but then we have as yet little understanding of the mechanisms behind any forms of thought, speech, or even basic motility.

I hypothesize that the motive behind the use of this unknown mechanism grows from the extreme terror and loneliness of the psychotic that results from so radical a rejection of the human race of which they are a part. One of the critical questions I ask concerning schizophrenia is Why do these individuals go their individual way in madness rather than do what most of us do, that is, adapt to the collective madness that defines most societies? My hypothetical musings result from my belief that those labeled schizophrenic are, in part, responsible for their own adaptive efforts no matter how unreflective these efforts might be.

There are still some further differences between those who might be diagnosed as schizophrenic and those who are not. *DSM-IV* lists as positive symptoms of schizophrenia disorganized speech and behavior. True to its scientisitic origins psychiatry ignores the emotional state of mind that might provide a motive for such behavior. It is my belief that the schizophrenic person is in a desperate state of confusion, anxiety, and terror as well as shame, guilt, and a variety of other painful emotions. Some of this desperation derives from the fact that most hallucinations are what Ghazi Asaad (1990) refers to as pseudohallucinations. The individual does hallucinate but knows that something is terribly wrong in their mental orientation toward the world. Some of humanity's greatest terrors and anxieties involve the fear that people are losing their minds or souls. I suggest that these emotions both motivate and are the unfortunate outcomes of the type of extreme god-thing narratives that define the experience of what is judged to be schizophrenia. I also believe that the speech patterns of many diagnosed as schizophrenic reflect the use of a kind of code in which the patient speaks truth as they know it but in a way that avoids painful confrontations with others.

Psychiatry insists that one of the criteria for the diagnosis of any mental disease is whether the offending behavior of the diagnosed is dangerous or harmful to themselves and others. Those displaying schizophrenic symptoms are almost always determined to be dangerous to themselves, and as many members of our society are taught to be more fearful of those who are deviant within it, the psychotic is assumed to be dangerous to others as well. The justification for involuntary hospitalization and forced treatment is precisely that the schizophrenic is so dangerous.

Having defined schizophrenia in this manner I return to the more general issue of madness. Schizophrenia is but one form of human madness and, I submit, at any given moment the bulk of the human race is mad. I have already made the case that the whole medical model of psychiatry, which dominates the mental health field and its psychotherapeutic applications, conforms nicely to the definition of delusion. The use of the whole collection of *DSM*s can only be justified by ignoring a mountain of evidence and the basic logic that demands recognition of the difference between descriptions and judgments as well as moral and medical judgments.

To the mind of the Enlightenment rationalists, such as Sigmund Freud, belief in God, gods, and the supernatural is proof of delusion and madness. How much damage has been done to the world and countless millions in the name of faith in supernatural forces? Why is it not madness to actually converse with the gods? Moses, Jesus Christ, and Mohammed, as well as many of those later recognized as prophets, created the conditions of hallucination when they isolated themselves from their fellow human beings in the wilderness, fasted, and otherwise created states of mind conducive to hallucination and other ecstatic religious experiences.

I find it fascinating that some of the same psychiatric experts who diagnosed most citizens of the United States to be mentally ill as a result of the September 11 attacks suggested that the terrorists, who crashed the planes into buildings killing themselves and thousands of others in the belief that they were morally holy and thus were guaranteeing their place in heaven, were not psychotic. By any of the criteria used to diagnose psychosis I believe these individuals to be mad. If they are not mad then by what right do we have to diagnose anyone as psychotic or schizophrenic? The fact that they share their thought patterns with perhaps millions of others hardly seems justification for calling the delusions and hallucinations of the individuals diagnosed as schizophrenic that I refer to as creating religions of one. How can we not include in our diagnostic name-calling the behavior of the Grand Inquisitor, his minions and followers, and all the religious fanatics that have created misery and havoc on a large scale from the ancient to modern times?

By this same logic can we fail to ignore as psychotic the dictators and their followers of just this past century and the hundreds of millions of deaths and the untold suffering resulting from the politics practiced? How can we study the regimes of Adolf Hitler, Joseph Stalin, Mao Tse-tung, Idi Amin, Pol Pot, Slobodan Milosevic, Saddam Hussein, and a very long list of others and not say that the dance between themselves and those who worship(ed) them was not madness? Laing (1967) wonders why it is the schizophrenic who is diagnosed psychotic rather then the rational bomber pilot capable of dropping a thermonuclear device on a city of civilians and killing millions of men, women, children, and the aged.

A study of human history reveals one set of beliefs after another that were held as true as matters of faith and resisted any evidence to the contrary. It is the hallmark of closed societies that beliefs are maintained in such fashion. Thomas Kuhn (1970) points out that today, as in the past, new discoveries are in effect treated as delusions until their adherents die off and are supplanted by a younger generation of scientists. Then it is the older ideas that are treated as delusional. I believe that in the not-too-distant future today's psychiatric models will be viewed with alarm and humor and people will wonder how those in our time could be so crazy as to believe *DSM-IV* to be true.

Anthony Giddens (2000) has suggested that the battle now engaged between the West and much of the world is a function of world globalization. Globalization is a process in which the goods, ideas, and values of modernity are exported to countries in such as way as to disrupt and disorganize the traditions and values of those countries. Certainly the export of Western psychiatry in a myriad of ways that include inclusion in *DSM-IV*'s the "International Classification of Diseases" must have a profound effect on those who would maintain their own religious delusions against the intrusions of modernity's delusions. I also suggest that those most upset by the Western notion of sin as mental disease and the growing control of world society by modernity's priesthood are the most theocratic forms of foreign political systems.

The human race is mad and apparently cannot adapt to the world without its madness. The problem is not the madness itself but the types of authoritarian/totalitarian and closed relationships and societies that madness helps create and which then in its actions leads to ever more destructive forms of madness. We are simply human and however difficult it is to formally define our humanity it is madness to ever assume that we possess the omnipotence, omniscience, immortality, and moral perfection of God(s). Moreover, we are living beings and no matter how hard we try we cannot accurately be described as machines such as computers, toasters, automobiles, and the like. To do so is not only scientifically inaccurate but, from the vantage point of humanism, morally and ethically wrong.

In this context I challenge the use of the word *breakdown* to describe the process of individuals demonstrating the adaptive modes diagnosed as schizophrenic. Machines such as automobiles and computers break down. People struggling to satisfy needs and solve problems might be said to "break out" in an attempt to escape intolerable situations and the emotions that define them. Unlike breakdowns, which are passive and the product of impersonal forces, breakouts reflect choices made by human beings. There is evidence to support the notion that if individuals are provided the right emotional help their breakouts can turn into breakthroughs, allowing these individuals to live more creative satisfying lives than before the breakthrough. I believe that every crisis in living represents an opportunity for change that can lead either to destructive madness or creative joy depending on the social and political choices made by those seeking to help those in crisis.

Bertram Karon and Annmarie Widener (1999) review the literature that compellingly demonstrates that *DSM-IV* is wrong when it suggests that those labeled schizophrenic are either incurable or beyond the ministrations of a wide variety of psychosocial therapeutic techniques. It seems clear from a variety of research efforts that perhaps two-thirds of all those diagnosed as schizophrenic recover without any therapeutic interventions, often to higher levels of social and creative functioning than before their breakout and crisis in living. Karon and Widener review the purported success of programs such as Soteria House (Mosher, Menn, and Matthews, 1975) and others working in private practice that give lie to the idea that the effective treatment of schizophrenia must involve drugs or other brain-damaging techniques.

I have explored earlier some of the reasons for human madness but would now like to expand that discussion to suggest some of the social conditions and individual experiences that might account for some forms of madness including the so-called disease of schizophrenia. I turn first to what I have elsewhere referred to as the "psychotic landscape" (Simon, 1986,

2000b), and then describe the kind of self-assessment that results from time spent in the psychotic landscape *especially at too early an age*.

THE PSYCHOTIC LANDSCAPE

I begin a discussion, that of necessity will be all too brief and too highly sketched, concerning the possible origins of madness and the particular form of madness known as schizophrenia. I am not trying to describe the etiology of a disease and therefore will avoid all words and concepts having to do with a disease or defect model of human functioning. I will not speak of "weak egos" or especially of "defense mechanisms." Those terms are as morally judgmental as any of the pseudomedical terms filling up the ever more bloated editions of any *DSM* that continue to appear with such awful regularity. I seek to explain schizophrenia from the point of view of individuals doing the best they can under what for them in their experience are difficult and desperate circumstances.

A brief discussion of what is meant by defense mechanisms is in order at this juncture. All defense mechanisms are adaptive acts employed by individuals lacking other or, what we might judge to be better, adaptive strategies. When human beings are experiencing what is for them unbearable pain and cannot change the situations and events that they perceive as the source of the pain they will then change either their perception of the source of the pain or the meaning of the pain itself.

Jean Piaget made us aware that when we cannot change the world we change ourselves instead. The motive to develop new skills is provided by the experience of being unable to satisfy our needs and solve our problems. Psychological defenses are accommodations made by individuals that professionals judge to be inadequate, dangerous to self and others, or at too much variance with society's preferred modes of adaptation.

I think it important to try to understand how individuals go about satisfying needs and solving problems as they experience the various situations and events that occur as they move through the time and space that make up their lived environments. I treat my attempt to explain the adaptive mode of existence we call schizophrenia no differently than I would try to explain the behavior of other individuals whose adaptive mode of existence involves being a psychiatrist, psychotherapist, teacher, or baseball player. All are modes of adaptive existence that differ in the degree of their social acceptance, the power and status that accrues with the various roles played, and the feelings that happen as individuals live within such varying styles of living.

In any such investigation I begin by asking what the individual modes of consciousness are and what the social and other historical experiences are that shape the individuals choice of adaptive behavior at any given moment in their life. I include in this discussion of individual human differences the roles played by biology in the development of individual patterns of living. I have already discussed the beliefs and emotions that define the self of the schizophrenic or any individuals choosing to slip from the human condition and seek life solutions involving god-thing narratives. I turn to some of the life, and especially social–political–moral, events that I believe play a role in the development of the schizophrenic form of being. I call these situations and events the psychotic landscape and state again that this is theory and speculation based on my own experiences and those whose life and therapeutic work shaped their perceptions to be similar to my own.

The knowledge of our own death is my first category of experience comprising the psychotic landscape although it is not death alone but the possibility of nonexistence and nothingness that terrifies us as human beings. Laing (1967) suggests that our greatest comfort and terror is contained in the sentence "There is nothing to be afraid of." How many of our collective and individual delusions exist to help us cope with or even deny the reality of death (Becker, 1973) and nonexistence? A huge, meaningful, and, sadly, increasingly ignored literature exists that deals with the existential meaning of life and death in psychological terms for humanity and the role such psychology plays in the genesis of individual differences judged healthy and pathological. Ernst Becker, utilizing ideas advanced by Søren Kirkegaard, suggests that the threat of death and annihilation are potentially most "pathological" when experienced by very young children.

What has not been explored adequately by the therapeutic community are the consequences of children experiencing their lives spent at the bottom of a variety of social–political structures as nonbeings, lacking affirmation for their individuality while simultaneously experiencing terror created by physical and psychological threats to their existence. While psychoanalysts have explored the importance of attachment in infancy in the development of individual differences, this inquiry has largely not taken the shape of questioning the political structure of childhood spent in a totalitarian system and treated as a thing, it, or the other.

Gregory Bateson (1978), Jay Haley (1976), and others comprising a group known as the "communication theorists" did create one of the now largely (and sadly) forgotten theories capable of explaining how the social powers controlling children's lives might attempt to force their charges to drastically alter their modes of adaptation. These theorists described the adaptive problems of children and adults once caught in relationships defined by double-bind messages—messages that are inherently contradictory and yet demanded compliance of the individual to some unrealizable moral standards.

The double-bind communication might take many forms but common to all is a set of contradictory messages that ask Who are you going to believe, me or your own experiences? The child hears the words *I love you* but experiences instead coldness and rejection. The message continues that if you believe that which you do not experience and live up to the standards of behavior set for you, you will be loved; but no matter how the individual struggles to conform to the demands made on him love never comes. Instead there is continued rejection and punishment, all of which is similarly denied as the child is told that what is being done is for his/her good and benefit. The child can neither win the prize that he/she desperately seeks nor even figure out the rules of the game.

I believe that the modes of communication described by Bateson are generic to political authoritarianism of all kinds. Double-bind and even more advanced forms of damaging types of communication are inherent to the mental health field when it functions as a totalitarian church. Children, and I focus on them because they are the most vulnerable to this form of tyranny with their immature cognitive capacities and inability to escape the hold of authority, are told how valuable they are as they are diagnosed with moral terms that conflate their whole personalities with defect and disease.

These children, and others so diagnosed, cannot deal with the confusion and terror sown as the professionals seek and define their essences as defective while endlessly telling them how worthy they are and how they should have high self-esteem. Many implicitly understand, even if they cannot articulate their knowledge, that what is being done in the name of their good is really for the good of parents, schools, and professionals hired to make them conform to the social structures that they must endure.

The second quality of the psychotic landscape involves the need to escape from evil. I define *evil* as behavior that creates pain and destruction in an individual by individuals who cannot or will not empathize with the pain they are creating. In the extreme form of evil the individuals creating pain in others for no other purpose than to create pain actually enjoy the suffering of their victims. Becker (1975) has explored some of the human pathology created when individuals try to escape from their awareness that evil exists either in human relationships, in general, or, more specifically, in themselves. If we cannot tolerate the idea of our nonexistence so too do we have great difficulty tolerating the idea that we are evil or morally beyond redemption.

Some years ago I listened to a lecture on the nature of monsters. A *monster* is defined as a being in human form that cannot identify with the pain it enjoys inflicting on its victims. Monsters, therefore, fit my definition of evil. We cannot tolerate the idea that we might be monsters, yet some of our greatest terrors in childhood are created by those, who as they play God and because they play God in our lives, become actual monsters. The human monsters that play God are still human and therefore cannot tolerate the idea that they do evil. They justify their actions by idealizing themselves as God(s) but instead dehumanize their victims, convincing them that they are the real monsters who perform acts of genuine evil. The Grand Inquisitor of the Inquisition, the chief psychiatrist of the mental hospital, the political dictator in his palace, the principal in his office, and the parent beating his child all operate along much the same line of human madness and, hence, become monsters.

The dynamics of madness created by living in a vertical social hierarchy based on god-thing narratives have numerous interpersonal and intrapersonal (a term I prefer to intrapsychic) consequences. Any individuals remaining true to the rules of the hierarchy must convince themselves to flatter, grovel, and, if necessary, worship those with more power than themselves while demanding the obedience of those with less power than they demand. All must convince themselves that they are less worthy than those above and that they are more worthy than those below while simultaneously justifying their obedience to those above and their abuse to those below. Each must deny in themselves those thoughts and feelings that might offend and bring down the punitive wrath of god–monsters above while splitting off and projecting their own feelings of evil toward those below. *The evil that must be denied, split off, and projected is that which is created by the definitions of the gods above and the real evil practiced on those below when we play god in their lives.*

It is interesting that those at the bottom of the hierarchy of power are those who become the scapegoats of the entire political structure above. If these individuals internalize the moral judgments used to scapegoat them, they might well become the very individuals that split off large segments of their own modes of adaptive functioning and become monsters to themselves. Those labeled schizophrenic often display such self-loathing; and the extravagant need to become godlike or an otherwise moral and powerful figure such as Jesus Christ, George Washington, or the czar of Russia flows from those efforts.

The third characteristic of the psychotic landscape involves the possible discovery that not only do our parents not love us but they might actually hate and despise us. Many of the children that I worked with who came from homes abandoned by a parent, most often the father, made up elaborate stories explaining and justifying the abandonment. Many of these parents walked out of their children's lives never to return. Birthdays, holidays, and other important occasions came and went without the children hearing from, receiving gifts from, or even receiving minimal recognition from the missing adults. It was clear to any that might observe the situation that these parents felt nothing for these children and did not love them according to any recognizable definition of love. These children blamed themselves, their mothers, circumstances, the gods, or anyone and anything but the absence of love to explain the behavior of the missing parent. The possible truth that they are unloved and forgotten simply could not be tolerated.

The final quality of the psychotic landscape involves the possible truth that all or most of life is an accident, that we do not live in a user-friendly universe and that if life has any meaning at all it is we who construct it. The idea that our life and our death may not serve any purpose beyond those that we create for them is intolerable to most in our species and is one of the leading candidates in explaining our creation of individual and collective forms of madness. The degree to which we create and live life in an autistic world of our own making to deal with the possibility that our suffering might contain no moral meaning and serve no higher purpose might also depend on when in our development we make such a discovery.

I close this section by noting that psychiatry and psychoanalysis have long noted the splitting that goes on within the psyche of those who demonstrate the adaptive forms of consciousness we label the most seriously ill or disordered. Laing (1969) referred to the selves of the mad as products of individuals who feel compelled to split huge portions of their inner life and experience them in the "not me" rather than the "me" where they more honestly belong. But all of this attention to the intrapersonal activities of those atypically mad individuals diagnosed as schizophrenic hides the splitting and alienation created by our more collective forms of madness.

We have split and alienated ourselves from nature, mind from body, self from object, male from female, the sacred from the profane, the individual from the collective, and the observer from the observed. All of these splits and divisions are morally weighted and organized into hierarchies that are used for political purposes. We see ourselves as above nature that is here for our personal usage and if necessary disposable. The mind is immortal, the body dust and a product of disposable nature. An ongoing struggle exists between the sexes in which descriptions based on gender are rife with moral judgments acting as descriptions. The self, marked by a holy soul provided by favoring gods, is situated above a lowly world filled with others less favored by the same powerful gods. As a result the strong devour the weak, the very Earth that sustains them, and ultimately themselves as well.

A PHILOSOPHICAL INTERLUDE

I continue my reconstruction of the field of psychotherapy by describing my solution to some of the philosophical issues I have listed, beginning with the mind (brain)–body controversy. I suggest that to the degree that psychology and psychiatry are mired in god-thing narratives and authoritarian politics the conception of mind and body will reflect splitting and alienation, one from the other. A vision of humanity as a house divided against itself, as a dualism rather than as a duality, is both the product and, in part, cause of a closed intellectual system filled with essentialisms and historicisms of one type or another. My goal is to restore my field to a genuine mode of scientific inquiry and a democratic/humanistic form of politics. Achieving these goals is impossible unless the underlying visions of an alienated and divided humanity are replaced with a conception of humanity that is organically whole and free of all god-thing narration. I follow this discussion with one concerned with issues related to human nature.

MIND AND BODY

There are many professionals in the camp dedicated to stopping the damage done by psychiatry who object to psychiatry's reduction of human behavior to a function of neurobiochemistry. I have taken such a stand in this book and provided evidence that the whole of the *DSM* reduces human beings to creatures without consciousness and without social, moral, and political context. I have suggested as well that there is neither logic nor empirical evidence to support biological psychiatry's most recent claims that the diagnoses in *DSM-IV* are brain disorders no different from epilepsy or Parkinson's disease. I stand horrified as a psychiatrist opines for the television cameras that a young woman who drowned her five children is no more responsible for her behavior than if she had had a heart attack.

However, I part company with many of my colleagues in the battle against the psychiatric abuse of power when they go on to assume that all individual differences are the result of social practices and that biology plays no role in the genesis of human differences including and especially those differences referred to as mental illnesses or disorders. While it is true that individual differences in adaptive behavior are not reflective of any known physical brain diseases, it is equally true that these differences, as well as all other individual human differences, are in large measure a function of individual differences in human biology. The reductionisms of biological psychiatry and much of clinical psychology reflect problems in the resolution of the mind–body and nature–nurture controversies.

My attempt to close the divide between mind and body begins with a statement by Anita Craig (1999) who writes,

We are born as bodies and die as bodies. Our bodies are also expressive unities: in other words, the significance of being embodied does not reduce to the heap of flesh and bones cremated on death. . . . As capable bodies we announce ourselves to the world in the position "Here I stand." In other words, through our bodiliness we are placed "face to face" not only among other bodies (as "things"), but also before others or "face to face" with them as Levinas emphasizes. (p. 206)

I unpack and detail some of the ideas contained in Craig's sentiment.

Our conscious experience, ultimately through development organized as a self, cannot be reduced to flesh and bones even as the self depends for its existence on flesh and bones. Consciousness, defined as an individual's purposeful response to meaningful stimulation, is the activity of flesh and bones and as such consciousness can neither exist without the body nor be reduced to the body. I suggest that we do not have minds as defined by nouns but instead we mind as denoted by verbs. *The body minds* closes the gap between mind and body created when we say we are comprised of a *body and a mind*. That we might experience our selves as a noun does not mean that such experience is anything but psychological activity that might still be better described with verbs.

We assume in our culture that the seat of conscious is the activity of the brain. Consciousness, or mind, is the psychological equivalent of neurological activity but is not reducible to it. Here we have a marvelous duality with as yet no explanation at all. If in my mind's eye I imagine an apple (I do not have *an* imagination but rather I imagine) I know that there is no apple in my brain but a series of chemical transmissions that on a neurological level represent the apple of my mind's eye. How my consciousness of the apple as an image that evokes feelings of hunger and a variety of emotions connected to apples exists in relation to the neurological and chemical activity is made manifest is a mystery. It is even a mystery as to why there was an evolutionary advantage to the fact that I experience an apple in all of its qualia to begin with.

However, I have no doubt that on a psychological level I experience the image of an apple (not a real apple) not the activity of the brain responsible for the image of the apple. The brain is incapable of feeling itself because if it did the self could not differentiate between neurological and psychological experience. Psychology is the legitimate field of study concerned with images of apples and all of the motivational, social, political, and other factors associated with these and all other images and experiences. Biology and its subspecialty neurology are the legitimate fields of study for the activity of the brain associated with images of apples. While there is an intimate relationship between biology and psychology, the two fields have their separate domains and methodologies and neither field can reduce the other to it or afford to ignore the relationship between the two enterprises.

I have yet to meet any ardent reductionist who fails to accept as legitimate the sentence "I have a brain." They accept their own experiences that they exist as an "I" that is the owner of the very brain that makes the "I" possible. It is the "I" that chooses where to have lunch and what to eat, that goes home to "his/her" family, engages in research and theory building, grows old and faces death. It is the "I" that dreams of a future both here on Earth or in the hereafter. It is the "I" that is credited with constructing and destroying, with the building and tearing down of whole worlds. No matter that physicists, chemists, and biologists have not been able to define and measure the self with the tools of their trade; *the self exists as a psychological reality for most of us with more certainty than does the moon, molecules, and atoms or even the existence of our own brains.*

If the self has psychological reality, then it is the self that makes decisions and it is the reality of the self that suggests to me that from a certain perspective we have free will and therefore can be held responsible for our actions. The idea of free will seems always to irk "scientific" psychologists and biological reductionists as they argue that the notion of free will destroys the scientific concept of determinism. I am not suggesting that human beings are not subject to the laws of physics, chemistry, and biology. We do not float Godlike above the world in which we are embedded. I argue instead that psychology and the self are not reducible to the laws of other fields, and if we are to understand the world and the laws that determine its operation, we will have to include psychology as part of the picture.

I argue, along with Isidor Chein (1972), that the past no longer exists to determine the present except that it has provided the antecedent conditions for the present to exist. For something to cause something to happen it must be in existence at the moment it makes its effect manifest. No matter the events of the past, every moment in time is unique and has never happened before in exactly the same way. The events of the present are determined by all of the forces operating at the moment they exist in the present.

Since all situations in the present are unique, the conscious human being must be free to decide how to act in the unique present, and to the degree that individuals choose to act one way or another, the consequences of their choices matter and make a difference in determining the direction the present takes. Therefore, human beings have "free will" and can be held responsible for their actions. It is true that the choices any individuals make depend on the rules governing their interpretation and construal of events and these interpretations differ as a function of maturity and past experience. This in no way negates my argument concerning free will of the self and my argument regarding individual responsibility. It does, however, permit us to ask about the social and political circumstances that most broaden and develop the individual's capacity to make informed choices.

It is another aspect of "I" that is the recipient of experiences that happens to "me" that leads to songs of joy and sorrow, praise for one's good luck and the endless complaints and queries of all human beings: "Why me?" and "It's not fair!" Yet these same reductionists will deny the validity of the "I" and "me" of subjects and patients as they claim that the behavior of these individuals is the product of mental illnesses and disordered brain chemistry. In doing as they do to their subjects and patients they are denying the validity of psychological experience and of the field of psychology itself.

I agree with Antonio Damasio (1994, 1999) when he argues that conscious experience and its organization into an experiencing self that functions both as agent and object of experience begins with the rhythms and sensations of the body. "I think, therefore I am" is no more or less true than "I am, therefore I think." The development of the experience of self, the emergence of identity, and what Damasio calls the "historical self" will be sketched in the next chapter along with what I refer to as the "emergence and development of the political self."

However, I believe that just as there are commonalties and differences in the human face I believe the same to be true for the human brain and all the other basic organs involved with information processing and meaning making. There are those who invoke the computer as a model for the understanding of human beings. The brain, it is argued, is like the computer's hard drive, and life with its social experiences provides the programming. However, the brain and body which provide the initial context for the development of a self that is socialized are unlike the hard drive of commercial computers, which are identical and add little in the way of differences in the programming that eventually finds its way into the hard drive. The same cannot be said for the "human computer."

The individual differences in the brains of various human beings are responsible for the fact that even before birth conscious experience differs from person to person. The interpretation of events and the emotions aroused by those appraisals are both a function of the events themselves and the colorings and intensities provided by innate differences in individual nervous systems. There appears to be a deep structure to human reactivity that differs from individual to individual and accounts for the emergence of differences in individual adaptive modes of experience. This suggests that even at birth the same stimulus event has different meaning for different neonates and demands from each a different adaptive response.

Jerome Kagan (1984, 1994) argues that infants differ in temperament at birth and that these differences predict various stable styles of functioning later in life. For example, infants strongly differ in their response to a balloon burst in front of their faces. Some infants react with a strong startle and fear response, while others appear interested and not the least bit upset by the explosion. Kagan has demonstrated that these differences predict later differences in children's styles of social interaction: The easily frightened babies tend to emerge as socially shy and slow to adapt to new surroundings and the least frightened infants develop a much bolder and assertive style of social interactions.

I hypothesize that temperamental differences might help explain why some children develop adaptive modes of being that are labeled as psychotic or schizophrenic. I suggest that these individuals have much lower thresholds at which they become emotionally upset and much higher thresholds before they become numb or apathetic when faced with threats of annihilation, double-bind communications, and other aspects of the psychotic landscape. Many of the individuals I have taught and worked with seem to respond to extreme threats to the self by going numb and apathetic, a response that makes less likely the choice of an adaptive solution involving madness. While these overt adaptive differences are, in part, a function of differences in the bodies and brains of individuals, none of these differences represent a medical illness or disease, real or metaphorical.

There is still another important difference between the "hard drive" of a human being and that of a machine. The computer's hard drive is fixed in its capacities before it receives its programming. The human hard drive is, in part, fixed. Damasio (1994) suggests that genetic hard wiring represents perhaps 50 percent of its capacity and is, in part, determined by the adaptive demands made on the developing individual. If this is so, then the human brain may add and lose capacity according to the same "use-it-or-lose-it" basis as human muscle and bone. It may well be true that the supposedly reduced functioning of the brains of schizophrenics seen in various electronic scans is a function of lives spent in mental hospitals and otherwise living lives lacking real stimulation and adaptive challenge.

HUMAN NATURE

Deborah Kleese (2001) discusses the varied and disparate definitions and uses of "nature" in relation to human functioning over the long history of our species. Throughout this book I have tried to avoid many of the uses of nature discussed in her article, especially those conceptions of nature that are both a product of and justification for closed political structures based on god-thing narratives. I have already suggested that the mind–body and nature–nurture controversies are the result of the splitting and alienation required by god-thing narratives. I seek to examine these controversies from a human perspective in which splitting is not necessary and a more holistic and natural explanation can emerge.

I have attempted to avoid the use of nature to define any human essence, especially ones which demand that we see human development as following some fixed historical course as it reaches for some teleological goal. I have especially avoided describing any human essences that are conflated with moral judgments that conceive of human beings as essentially good or essentially evil that can then be used to justify any type of political and economic policies. I have tried to avoid a view of human beings that separates them into a part that is natural and a part that is civilized and therefore conceives of naturalness as qualities that either precede or remain unaffected by socialization processes and the effects of human civilization.

I do not believe in searching for "real selves" that are waiting to escape the constraints that were overlaid by a corrupting society. I do not believe it is helpful to conceive of human nature as one of gentle moral innocence that must be freed by undoing all social constraints. Moreover, I have avoided any theorizing that conceives of the natural as wild, untamed, and dangerous and demanding the control of civilizing social forces. Much of the justification of the Inquisition and other historical periods of zealous religious activity that sought to control human beings with torture and painful death was supported with the view that human beings were naturally barbaric and savage. The destruction of whole civilizations perceived as uncivilized and peopled with "savages" marks much of human history and led Joseph Conrad (1988) to exclaim about that history through the voice of one of his characters, "The horror, the horror."

To this end I have been critical of the concepts of mental health and illness particularly when biology and genetics are employed to explain complex modes of social and adaptive behavior. The use of diagnostic categories conflates the descriptive with the moral and thus defines the essence of the individuals diagnosed as basically flawed and defective. The idea that complex patterns of behavior are under the sole control of the genes rather than under the control of a socialized individual with a biological history creates a teleological historicism that predicts the future course of their lives. Moreover, the assumption that the mentally ill are irrational and driven by emotion and need suggests that these individuals are without civilization, that they are in a primitive, natural state, and that this state is one of wildness and savagery in need of strong external control.

On the other hand, I have also rejected the notion that the human being is born a blank slate written on by the hand of social forces. I have suggested that human differences in reactivity are the product of biology, and now I further suggest that many of the similarities in human consciousness are also a product of the engineering of evolution and natural selection. I incorporate into my theorizing the work of modern evolutionary psychology as embodied in the works of Jerome Barkow, Leda Cosmides, and John Tooby (1992), David Buss (1994), Henry Plotkin (1998), and Robert Wright (1994). Modern evolutionary theory avoids the pitfalls of earlier versions of this genre of theory such as sociobiology that created an analogy between human beings and some animal lower on the phylogenetic tree such as rats or ants and demanded that we see human beings as larger versions of those animals. The results were filled with essentialisms, historicisms, and proposals for social policies that ignored the differences between human beings and these animals.

Modern evolutionary theory seeks patterns of behavior that are repeated across cultures and similarities of individual human reactions to these situations and events. It is believed that there are genetic predispositions for human beings to create various social structures and patterns of living that were advantageous to human survival during the million or so years after the evolution of Homo sapiens and their struggle to survive on the plains of Africa. Similarities in human behavior across various cultures assume that we possess similar needs or affective states that are aroused by both internal and external events. In short, the theory suggests that human adaptive consciousness has contained within it forces that produce similarities in motivating experience everywhere in the world. The body seems to contain predisposition to develop language (Pinker, 1994; Plotkin, 1998) and other cognitive structures as well as to respond with similar emotions to a wide variety of interpreted situations.

Few would argue with the above thesis when it comes to accepting that hunger, thirst, fatigue, and the elimination of physical pain as well as any other homeostatic drives represent universal needs and problems to be solved on both an individual and a societal level. That all societies must be involved in food production, distribution, and competition is easily envisioned. What is far more controversial, especially among those committed to a purely social explanation of human psychology, is the notion that some forms of social and political interaction might be generally or universally sought because of purely psychological needs. I share the fear of these dissenting individuals that such evolutionary ideas might become the basis of morally tinged essentialisms and be used politically to justify the efforts of some to control the life choices of others.

My fears notwithstanding, I still suggest that just as human beings are born ready to expect to adapt to an "average expectable environment" capable of sustaining and nurturing biological life they are born ready to adapt to an average expectable set of social circumstances capable of meeting some set of psychological needs as well. The wide range of political circumstances to which individuals willingly adjust and defend lead me to believe that human beings are born with a wide number of basic evolutionary needs and that these needs can be satisfied in a multiplicity of ways. If this is so we can query what these psychological needs might be.

I can also suggest that human beings might not be able to sustain their social relationships if these psychological needs and problems are not adequately resolved and that individual adaptations judged as pathological might be the result. It is also possible that whole societies might collapse if their political structures function outside permissible expectable social environments.

I suggest that there exist wide patterns of behavior that are motivated by evolutionarily created internal and reactive affective states. Human beings are everywhere in conflict and must resolve those conflicts. Honest negotiation of differences exist as often as deception and betrayal. Both styles of interaction appear to be motivated and reacted to with similar emotional states that define for individuals the meaning of such situations and provide direction for their responses. Human beings seem as capable of hate as well as love and grief is a universal response to the loss of those persons, places and things that are lost.

Carroll Izard (1977, 1979), Richard Lazarus (1991), and Robert Plutchik (1980) theorize that emotions such as love, hate, grief, joy, surprise, envy, jealousy, loneliness, fear, terror, pride, shame, guilt, and joy are the result of bioevolutionary processes and have important adaptive significance for human social interaction and general survival. In fact, I argue that part of our biological adaptive inheritance is the product of our long struggle to survive and flourish as social beings. Therefore it is as natural for us to be social as it is for us to hunt and gather in the wild or in Nature (spelled with a capital "N" and defined by Kleese, 2001, as the great outdoors untouched by human hands). Many emotions not only motivate us to behave in purely social settings but appear as specific facial expressions suggesting to others how they should respond to us.

I also agree with John Bowlby (1969, 1973, 1979, 1980, 1988) that most women develop powerful emotional ties to their offspring even during pregnancy and that infants are born with an emotional expectation of encountering human faces and various forms of social treatment leading to the development of reciprocated love and attachment. This belief in no way condemns as "unnatural" any woman's choice not to have children or treat their child in any way even if others or myself should judge such behaviors to be morally wrong. Certainly, I oppose any political attempts to force any such life choices on any woman in any manner whatsoever. However, I agree with those that suggest that early infantile experiences are important for human development.

My thesis concerning human nature suggests that when individuals meet and try to understand the motives of the other they are neither meeting a blank slate nor the sole product of an alien culture. All cultures reflect commonalties in the structure of social relationships and the politics that shape those interactions. We assume some idea of a common human heritage based on common human needs, motives, and expectations. We understand and can generally predict responses to offer charity and kindness, to steal from others, to respect whatever notion of privacy exists in the culture, to steal another man's wife, to tell a mother how beautiful her children are, and myriad other universal interactions. Are there any cultures that do not react with revulsion toward parents, especially mothers, who hurt or kill their children or soldiers who abandon their fellows on the field of battle? I believe that without some such notion of "human nature" there can be no genuine science of psychology either at the level of the ordinary individual or the professor and therapist creating a formal piece of theory.

The evolutionary thesis of emotion does not negate my agreement with social constructionists that all emotional expression is regulated by culture and that the expression of any given emotion might be demanded or forbidden by the moral standards of that culture. My thesis also will not suggest that there is something unnatural for any given human being to experience or express any emotion in ways other than any regulated by any particular culture be it family, religion, or society at large. Human beings ultimately construct their own appraisals of life and its constituent events and as such ultimately control which emotions they will experience and how they will express them.

I suggest that nature and nurture are dualities and not the dualisms made of them by the requirements of the various god-thing narratives contained in the religions and scientism of Western culture. To say we are products of the pressures of socialization is to simultaneously say that we are the products of nature; living in society as a part of a culture is as natural as our bodies or the birds and beasts of the forests. We are conscious beings whose basic modes of experience are as much the products of our inherited biology as they are the culture that of necessity begins to shape us as we drink in our mother's milk (Sowell, 1996). We are 100 percent a product of nature and 100 percent a product of nurture and *it makes no sense to question or separate nature from nurture in some vain attempt at discovering a human essence that can exist without one or the other.*

My statement that we are conscious beings shaped by biology and social relationships requires some discussion about the word *shaped*. I am suggesting that the word *shaped* masks two important aspects concerning the direction of human adaptation and the development of consciousness. The first is that both the social and the biological act on the development of individuals and the second is that consciousness is, in the words of Jack Martin and Jeff Sugarman (1999: 113), an "emergent, generative and reflexive" process whose development goes beyond what can be explained and predicted by focusing on biological and social factors. It is my belief that each individual responds to the biological and social pressures that impinge on them with decisions based on rules that are internal to consciousness itself whose nature and functioning have not yet been studied or identified.

We are bodies that include many behavioral and experiential potentialities that shape adaptive consciousness but only within an ever-present cultural and political context. But the developmental course of human consciousness is also a function of emergent rules contained in consciousness itself. We have, as yet, paid little or no attention to the possible internal rules governing the development of human consciousness, and therefore the creation of an effective understanding of the commonalties and difference in human functioning still lie in some distant future.

From this perspective the dualisms of nature and nurture break down and become as irrelevant as the dualisms of mind and body. The removal of these dualisms allows me to return to questions related to the relationship of psychology to the politics of human interactions. I have suggested earlier that the human form of consciousness seems to require an understanding of how things work and what is good and bad, beautiful and ugly. I suggest that human survival requires both types of understanding. Our need to become effective scientists and moral philosophers is a product of natural selection—one component of which is social evolution—and our necessary participation in culture. Human beings adapt to a wide variety of cultures and societies each of which reveals some political mechanism that permits conflicts to be resolved in ways that enhance the continuance of the society and its institutions. It seems no more or less natural for human beings to create and maintain democratic, open, and humanistic political systems than to live within the embrace of totalitarian, closed, and dehumanizing political structures.

Human emotions are the product of the totality of humanity's evolution and represent a significant part of the human motivational system by helping define human needs, problems, and, hence, the personal meaning of events and situations. The range of these affective states seems to allow adaptation to a wide variety of political systems as well as ensuring that any given individual will be both satisfied and unsatisfied with the adaptation. I suggest that at any given moment individuals might be in conflict with their peers, authority, and themselves over the relative balance between individual expression and conformity to the moral rules of that society.

My concern is with the manner of conflict resolution on both an interpersonal and an intrapersonal level and how the two levels interact and impact one another. In the next chapter I will discuss the political psychology of the intrapersonal as it is affected by the political psychology of the interpersonal. As a scientist I ask questions concerning the mechanisms by which the interpersonal becomes the intrapersonal, but as a moral philosopher my strong bias is toward democratic, humanistic, and open forms of interpersonal political interactions. I make no appeals for the democratic based on science since none exist. I do not believe that science will discover that democracy is more natural or that human nature assures its ultimate ascendancy over authoritarian systems.

My bias toward democratic forms of politics is moral and ethical as well as experiential. I have lived long enough in both types of systems to have concluded that the price I pay for living with democracy is far less than the price I pay for participating in an authoritarian political structure. Similarly, the rewards of democracy seem to me to be much greater than the rewards provided by the closed society. My work as a scientist involves trying to understand the processes that shape each type of political system and the individuals within them that we might in our collective wisdom choose to change our political structures and relationships from closed to open, authoritarian to democratic. I turn now to a discussion of the psychology of the individual as a function of the politics of the self.

CHAPTER 8

Politics of the Developing Self

INTRODUCTION

And God created man in His image, in the image of God He created him; male and female He created them.

—Genesis

If I am not for myself, then who will be, If I am only for myself then what am I, If not now, then when?

—Hillel

In this chapter I explore some of the intrapersonal and interpersonal ramifications of psychological development in authoritarian and democratic social structures. I write much of this in personal terms, in part because I seek to create descriptions that deal with literal experience not only abstract conceptualizations. I believe that my personal experiences provide a model of analysis that any reader might use for creating an understanding of their own or another's struggles to develop an identity such that they are part of their society and culture and simultaneously still an individual. I believe that such an arrangement within and between people reflects participation in a democratic, humanistic, and open set of human relationships.

I also write in personal terms because I wish to present my notion of the good life. In the next chapter I discuss my version of psychotherapy and suggest that therapy is and must always be directed toward some moral goal expressed as the manner in which people should live. Therapy is always directed by some version of the good life. While I would never impose my version of the good life on another human being I feel morally compelled to live out my version even when I see patients in a professional capacity. For me, the good life is one in which I treat others according to democratic/humanistic principles and demand that I am treated in a similar manner. Therefore, when I see patients I will do nothing, insofar as I am aware of it, to treat them otherwise and help them live what I would consider a bad or immoral life. What is interesting is that any patient who stayed in treatment with me and agreed with me that our relationship was successful either held the same expectations of the good life that I hold or developed them afterward.

My notion of the good life has evolved since my neophyte days as a therapist but the principle defining a successful relationship with patients remains the same. My notion of the good life continues to evolve even yet which is still another reason why writing in the first person makes sense at this juncture.

THE GOOD LIFE

When I was a child of perhaps seven or eight and receiving religious instruction in Hebrew School I was taught that I was created in God's own image. *If I was created in God's image, and if I take the story of Genesis seriously, then my primary goals in this life would involve being actively creative.* It amazes me now, as I enter my seventh decade on this Earth and a new millenium, how long it took me to understand this aspect of the religious lessons of my childhood. Even as a child I did not take the biblical tales of the Old Testament as literally true and perhaps that is one of the reasons why it took me so long to understand the philosophical wisdom contained within them. By disbelieving the stories I did not examine them carefully enough and, in effect, threw the baby out with the bathwater.

I have concluded that I need not conceive of God as an actual being or the Bible to be literally true but instead think of God as a symbol or idea. Genesis and the other stories in the Bible need not be seen as sacred and inviolable but, instead, can be understood to be myths. As is so often the case, myths contain much that is true and wise. What I find most astonishing and not a little upsetting is that by not trying to understand the wisdom of Genesis I did not ask as to the nature of creativity and failed to either make creativity the main goal of my life or make my life more fully creative. I neither focused on creativity as a scientific topic nor the moral one it must be if the idea of God and the Bible are concerned. I did not think of creativity as, in part, my own or any individual's political response to the interpersonal politics that helped shaped us.

I have also discovered that a developing awareness of the good life, in this case one based in creative activity, involves not only a study of biblical texts but of those texts that have survived the centuries and are collectively known as "the canon." While the canon continues to evolve and texts are always being added to it, it does seem to take time for those whose lives comprise history to sort through and discard the fads, trash, and works that fail to meet the highest standards of moral and intellectual excellence.

It seems true that totalitarian political structures eventually destroy themselves (and unfortunately much of everything else around them before they collapse) and become consigned to the trash heap of history. So, too, do the music, art, literature, and science that fail the test of truth and quality eventually get tossed on the same heap. Barbara Tuchman (1980) suggests that she cannot quite define quality but she seems to know it when she encounters it. History seems to operate in much the same way when it comes to those human products of creativity that enhance human existence and help life to flourish.

Over time, however, I made my understanding of creativity the central goal in my role as scientific psychologist. I also began to apply what I had learned to my roles as college professor and psychotherapist. It was then that I discovered that the writer Oscar Wilde was right when he suggested *that a life not lived as if it were art is mere existence and can be quite joyless.*

Until I identified with the ideas of creativity contained in Genesis and set them as the criteria of the good life most worth living, that is, took seriously the notion that for my life to be most meaningful I must create, it always felt as if something were missing. Not only did I feel the lack of something in my personal life that I could not quite define but my work as scientist, educator, and psychotherapist suffered as well. My interactions with my students and patients never turned out the way I hoped for and even when I succeeded in feeling personally successful and enjoying the praise of my colleagues in these endeavors I was not quite satisfied.

I learned to be a scientist and a psychologist and in so doing discovered that science represented the best way to understand the worlds in and around me. The scientific method has no peer when it comes to solving puzzles and unraveling mysteries. But what I never could quite articulate was that science can never establish the proper goals for scientific activity, nor could I state with any certainty just what was morally worth trying to understand or seek to achieve. Science contains the rules to achieve insight and mastery of problems but fails to contain within itself rules for the setting of worthy and moral life goals. Science can try to state ideal methods of studying a given problem but not those ideals whose pursuit makes life fully worth living. Moral and ethical goals derive from religion and moral philosophy and the texts of the canon accumulated over the millennia. There are many worthwhile goals to pursue and many ways to make life rich and purposeful. Only by selecting meaning-ful goals to study can science and, in this instance scientific psychology, be made meaningful.

CREATIVE LIVING

I offer the following definition of creativity: *Creativity exists when peo-ple find the means to express themselves concerning any aspect of human existence as only they can as individuals and when they are also able to communicate their visions with the potential to morally enrich themselves and humanity.* What is implied in such a definition? It suggests first that we human beings are para-doxically all the same but at the same moment all unique and different one from another. As we look around a crowded room we instantly recognize each face, including our own, as human and sharing in a multitude of similarities. In the same instant we see that each and every face, including our own, is unique unto itself. So, too, are the human brains we are born with and the so-cial and psychological experiences that follow our births simultaneously simi-lar and different. We have no choice in the matter: We are all a part of common humanity and all separate and different from each other.

What is further implied in my definition is that creativity is not a thing or a characteristic of human beings brought into existence by the use of a moral judgment. Creativity is a way of life; it reflects the political orientation of individuals to themselves and others. To be creative each person must find a way to live a kind of balancing act between being both part of the human community and simultaneously separate from it. A life lived as art must be a life lived within the human community but never fully of that community. To be fully embedded in shared human experience is to lack individual vision and therefore be devoid of creativity. It is to live someone else's life not one of one's own. To live as an individual divorced from humanity is to express vi-sions that might be unique but reflective of what will ultimately be judged to be madness or criminality but not creativity. I believe that to live creatively is to live fully and to live fully we must find a way to share the human experi-ence and be separate from it as well. To live without individuality is to live in safety and personal emptiness; to reject our fellow human beings is to live in rage, despair, and unending loneliness.

We live with our fellow human beings and struggle to make our lives within a specific culture and the various institutions such as schools, busi-nesses, churches, and, perhaps most important of all, families, which com-prise any given culture. These cultural institutions reflect and maintain the values, attitudes, morals, and means of survival and growth that define the lives of those who comprise the institutions and the culture they make up.

As children develop they are expected to learn the social roles and skills that are valued by the culture and the specific institutions that enfold them, as well as live according to the values and morals which define those roles and skills as those both proper and good. The institutions that comprise culture demand that developing persons share the dominant cultural values, develop the skills valued by the culture, and learn to ignore or give up those individual differences that are not sanctioned and approved of by the culture.

A culture approves only of individual differences that those who are the cultural authorities agree are good (or at least not harmful) for maintaining the life of the culture and its institutions. *Since all human beings are unique, all human beings eventually find themselves in conflict with their culture, its institutions, and the individuals who represent authority within those institutions.*

My definition of creativity, therefore, also implies that the source of creativity is inevitably conflicted and the delicate balance of living both as a unique individual and as a member of a society required for creativity will be reflected in the outcome of how interpersonal conflicts are resolved. Conflict is necessary for the existence of creativity. How developing individuals and the authorities who see to their socialization and induction into culture negotiate and resolve the inevitable conflicts that mark human growth will determine who will express themselves as individuals and accepted members of society and who will live as outcasts, criminals, and mental patients.

The mode of conflict resolution between members of a society will also help determine the manner in which individuals experience and resolve conflict within themselves as well. There are significant differences in any individual's ability to express their unique visions of life based on how they treat themselves and the facility they develop in dealing with the thoughts and emotions that define their own personal meaning of the world in and around them. I suggest that only individuals who have learned to treat themselves and their own consciousness with respect and the politics reflective of an open society will be capable of genuine creativity.

The process of socialization will, therefore, in part, determine who will experience the joy that attends creation, who will live in empty, numb silence lost to their own unique voices and whose painful screams will be incomprehensible to others. I suggest that it is the love, kindness, and respect between people, which may or may not exist, that will determine the manner in which conflicts will be resolved and therefore the outcome of development in relation to creativity. When love and respect fail, conflict is resolved through violence, or violence in the name of love. Violence destroys creativity or begets those creations that embody violence and destroy life itself.

THE POLITICS OF CREATIVITY AND
THE DEVELOPMENT OF THE GOOD LIFE

While as a child I could not put into words how social processes affected my life and the manner in which I would live it with or without creativity, I now realize that a constant conflict was going on concerning the interpersonal balancing act required to live creatively. I was given the name Laurence Simon. Sometimes it was acceptable for me to be Laurence but at others I was expected to be a Simon. I often accepted my role as a Simon but often wished to be a Laurence before I was a Simon. Laurence was a Simon but not all aspects of being a Simon matched up to the emerging needs, desires, and awareness and skill preferences that defined the self whose name was Laurence. To live creatively and express myself as a unique individual I had to be Laurence. To remain alive and be nurtured by my parents I had to remain a Simon.

I realize now that for whatever differences and conflicts I had with my parents I was loved. Being loved as an infant and child made me a very lucky individual indeed. (I was also lucky because I lived in a time and place where food was plentiful, life was relatively safe, the politics were relatively benign, and my parents had the wherewithal to nurture me as the object of their love. In what follows, I do not wish to imply that love is all that is necessary for children to be nurtured. Love provides the motive but not necessarily the means of caring for children.)

When individuals love one another they form a unique type of political arrangement. In the lexicon of psychology, love, especially the love of parent for child, is referred to as "attachment." Mary Ainsworth (1985, 1989) suggests that when a parent loves a child (or, for that matter, anybody loves anyone) they are unique and irreplaceable to that parent. Separations must be planned or else extreme emotional distress results. The reappearance of the loved one brings pleasure, comfort, and joy. Permanent loss is followed by grief and some of the most painful emotions human beings are capable of experiencing. Emotional bonds that include love create enduring relationships—ones not easily set aside or made hostage to the inevitable conflicts that occur between individuals. The loved individual is not told that the expression of their individuality will ever be punished by the loss of necessary relationships. Therefore, the loved child does not have to endure the terror of losing a parent or the parent's love merely because of individual self-expression.

Love creates and maintains a humanistic relationship, one in which individuals might learn to live in and maintain a democratic society based on the free expression of thought, emotion, and speech necessary for human creativity. Love creates a politics between individuals in which there is respect for the privacy of individuals, allowing them to create internal spaces from whose confines creativity springs. Love brings into existence one of the few types of situations where individuals can transcend self-interest and accept the expressed needs of others without threat or resentment. Anita Craig (1999) writes, "To be loved, and the life giving force of this, and to be held in esteem, and the elevating experience this entails . . . establishes our uniqueness. These are the ways in which 'all short, ugly, fat people' are changed into an infinite variety of particular someones, that is, separately valued individuals for significant others" (p. 212).

Analyst, such as D. W. Winnicott (1965), describe the kind of holding and facilitating environments that exist in the space between individuals that are loved. The parent accepts the fears and anger of the child as belonging to the child and not as either threats to their own selves requiring retaliation or as emanating from themselves, thereby confusing their emotions with those of their offspring. It is within this type of political action that children learn that they are separate beings from their parents. They learn as well that they need not censure, split off, project, or otherwise try to dispose of the thoughts and emotions that define the self, the meaning of the world to the self, and the self's desires and motives.

The spaces between individuals that are based in love tend to be spaces experienced as safe and therefore places to play. I define *play* as any activity done for its own sake, having intrinsic motivation, or to utilize a concept of Heinz Hartmann's (1958), as belonging to the conflict-free sphere of ego development. Play can be contrasted to work that is defined as activity that is performed to achieve a goal external to the activity itself. When individuals must act to survive, please others, or earn rewards arbitrary to the activities rewarded, they are working. Human beings must inevitably work, but the loved individual need not work to please parents or others with whom they share their lives. Loving parents tend to delight in the activities and especially the individuality of their child (unless they are perceived as dangerous to the child) and do not threaten or blackmail as a means of changing behavior.

Play is activity in which individuals comfortably and enjoyably explore a wide variety of means to ends as well as the objects and activities that are the goals or ends sought. Play therefore creates the conditions necessary for creative science and art, two activities that are quite similar when they represent play at its most creative. In play individuals not only lose themselves and become the activities that they enjoy but they also can engage in the kind of self-criticism and correction that exists when individuals have themselves as well.

We can describe all aspects of development through the dialectic of being and having. Assimilation and accommodation can be reconfigured as being and having. The self is defined by its activities. We can engage some activity and exist purely as the doing or become aware of our doing and exist as the self that observes the doing. When we are fully engaged in play we are our activities. With psychological development we develop a self that is defined by increasing numbers of perspectives. It is beyond the capacity of this volume to detail this aspect of development. However, the development of multiple selves and perspectives seems to be enhanced by a childhood marked by loving, democratic, humanistic, and open relationships that include genuine dialogue, respect for differing points of view, and plenty of time to play.

We begin by playing with blocks and hopefully progress to playing with ideas. In this way we can be our history or have it, the latter providing us choices as to which aspects of our history to live by in the future. We can be our relationships or have them, be our passions or have them. In each case the growth of new selves is founded on new perspectives and a greater number of choices and freedom with which to live our lives. I believe that the more of ourselves we have in terms of our thoughts and feelings about the world around and in us the more expressive and creative we can be. The more we learn to express ourselves, the better we develop the kind of skills that are marked by excellence and quality.

Loving parents not only provide a safe space for their children to play, and thereby develop and own the necessary skills of separation and individuation, but they also create demands for their children to develop standards of genuine morality and excellence. The loved individual is not treated as an object for the good of others but as ends in themselves. There is an inherent respect for the individuality of the loved one that includes the firm belief that the loved one is capable of making choices and hence deserves freedom. In the case of loved children, parents believe that their children are always to be given choices and that the development of newer skills means both an increase in freedoms and in expectations of increased responsibilities. In such political arrangements there is an implicit recognition that freedom without responsibilities is anarchy and responsibilities without freedom is oppression.

All children must be taught and this applies to the teaching of moral truths as well, a process referred to as "discipline." However, how the child is disciplined may well determine the type of moral reasoning used by the developing individual. Lawrence Kohlberg (1984) described three levels of moral reasoning along Piagetian lines of cognitive development. Younger children live by a form of hedonism: If the consequences of actions feel good they are good, if the consequences feel bad, then the act that produced them is bad.

Adults soon intervene to replace a moral philosophy based on hedonism with one that will increase the child's capacity to delay immediate gratification of desire and recognize long-term consequences of gratification that might prove dangerous or deadly to the child. Moreover, most adults wish to see children able to consider the social consequences of their actions as well as the gain to themselves. The child's recognition of authority and the acceptance of moral rules to govern behavior announce the child's entry into the second level of moral development, referred to as "conventional morality."

In conventional morality children unquestioningly accept the moral rules given them because of their belief in the inherent superiority of the authorities promulgating the rules. Acceptance of these rules confers goodness on the child in the eyes of authority; rejection of them defines disobedience and the child's descent into a state of wickedness, badness, or deficit.

Kohlberg suggests that children are capable of growing beyond conventional morality and living according to the rules of postconventional morality.

In this third level the older child and adolescent develop recognition that all human relationships are based on contracts and that the superior contract is one based on mutual honesty and respect. At this stage individuals increasingly live according to self-accepted moral principles as they recognize that responsibility is a function of the consequences that derive from their own actions.

I have suggested elsewhere (Simon, 1998) that Kohlberg's formulation of moral development (like Jean Piaget's from which it is derived) would be strengthened if seen within the political context of children's upbringing. I theorize that individuals do not necessarily move from stage to stage and if they do it is, in part, a function of the type of political structure in which they live. Individuals who live according to hedonism are a product of anarchy, those remaining in conventional morality are adapting to the demands of authoritarian/totalitarian political systems, and those who emerge into the postconventional stage were induced to do so by the demands of adapting to a democratic, open system of social interactions.

Loving parents and others following democratic political rules discipline their children by setting clear rules of behavior that they themselves follow and by giving their children choices with clearly defined consequences based on the child's choice of action. As children grow, authority renegotiates the contracts with which they are all bound, increasing the acceptable range of freedoms allowed the child upon children's demonstration of ability and willingness to accept the consequences of their actions. These negotiations are carried out in an atmosphere of respect for the children as human beings capable of making choices and inherently deserving of dignity and increased autonomy. In general, parents living in a democracy realize in one way or another that for their child to become a member of a democratic society they must be given the skill to live with the burden of knowing that the rules and laws governing social interaction can only be created by human beings conceived of as equals rather than being imposed by superior creatures from on high.

The moral education of loved children capable of owning and playing with their own ideas and emotions has as its goal the children's learning to control their behavior but not their thoughts, emotions, or conscious experience itself. Right and wrong is about what is actually done to the self and others, not what is thought or felt. The inner life of children is left rich and intact and children are *never* taught that the price of being a good person is the obliteration of ideas, emotions, drives, fantasies, dreams, and the skills to express any of these psychological activities.

Those who see their goal to be the moral education of children as human beings recognize the importance of empathy, compassion, sympathy, forgiveness, and redemption as part of the process. *There is respect for the child's struggle to learn and recognition that learning to solve problems invariably involves trial and error.* Therefore, children are not criticized for making mistakes, indeed the word *mistake* is not even used as the adults in children's lives provide support and encouragement as the children continue to explore various avenues to reach their goals. Parents hope that their children will seek to develop excellence, recognizing that excellence in human terms is a search for gradual lifelong improvement rather than an ever-frustrating search for perfection.

The ability of an individual to tolerate failure increases dramatically if there is an ability and willingness to see one's own learning process as one of trial and error and experimentation. Creation becomes joyful if it is, at least in part, play and individuals are tolerant and compassionate when they experience difficulty in their own adaptive processes. It is when I learned to be tolerant and accepting of my own "mistakes" and able to describe rather than judge my own efforts to solve problems that I began to write and express my own ideas and opinions related to psychology and psychiatry. Interestingly, but not surprisingly, I became more tolerant of the struggle to create in those I taught both as a professor and psychotherapist.

In general, children who develop within a humanistically organized political structure of relationships tend to see the world and themselves as constantly in flux and capable of transformation. There is a sense that while the self is being shaped by vast historical forces change is still possible and that the future is not determined only by the past but by the forces operating within the moment representing the present. Moreover, and perhaps most important, there is the sense that the self is an agent, a being possessed of decision-making capabilities that allow the self a measure of free will and a place in determining the future transformations of self and the world. Such individuals do not feel that their selves are an essence defined by moral judgments and determined solely by historical forces. There is a sense of self that has history, weight, substance, and narrative coherence, and these beliefs are accompanied by hope in the future, a belief in forgiveness and redemption, and the possibility of renewal and positive transformation.

As my childhood progressed I discovered that I was a Jew as well as a Laurence and a Simon. My religious teachers often demanded that I be a Jew first and a Laurence second. Here, too, was a source of conflict. I felt comfortable and proud to be Jewish but only as a Laurence Jew and then as a Simon Jew. I was told from my first consciousness that I was an American and that also sat well with me. But I have also wanted to be a Laurence American, and a Simon American and never give into those voices, often angry, strident, and promising punishment, that demanded that I be an American before a Laurence and a Simon. Similar conflicts arose as to my being a male and/or a Laurence, a student and/or a Laurence.

Later I had to struggle to remain as a Laurence and a psychologist, a Laurence and a professor, a Laurence and a psychotherapist. This volume is an expression of Laurence the psychologist rather than the psychologist who is Laurence. I became more fully aware of the difficulties of being Laurence who was white rather than a white person who was Laurence. Changes in my culture also deepened lifelong conflicts over the type of Laurence I was as a male. The struggles for identity go on and will continue until there is no more Laurence that seeks creative identity.

In many of these conflicts (including some with my parents) I experienced treatment as a thing rather than as a person consistent with responses based on love and democratic forms of discipline. Many of my social interactions were reflective of my discovery that I was often a member of closed authoritarian political structures and that my adaptation to these forms of social organization required vast differences than to my response to open social relationships. In general I was fortunate enough in my social development to be able to contrast my experiences in both closed and open political systems and therefore be able to develop enough skill to ultimately "own" some of the effects of having adapted to a closed system. As a result I have been able to slowly define and struggle to reach those goals that for me represent the good, creative life.

A central theme of my thesis is that whenever terror, shame, or guilt led me to be a Laurence that lived according to a god-thing narrative I lost, or failed to develop, my capacity to create and live a life of art. I judged myself rather than described myself. I believed that I knew my own essence and that my inner qualities were never as good or worthy as they should have been. I felt myself to be embedded in a history whose end was already written by forces beyond anything I might influence or alter.

During the years I was trapped in similar god-thing narratives I could not write. I could never hope to publish works that would be judged alongside the "great masterpieces" of Sigmund Freud, Karen Horney, B. F. Skinner, Abraham Maslow, Carl Rogers, and others in the pantheon of the gods that I worshiped. On the other hand, I could not bear the thought of the riffraff of society criticizing my efforts that changed hourly in my perception from lofty expressions of perfection to humiliating pieces of trash. I thought of myself as either the great professor or "stupid" and "retarded" if I could not achieve my aims in a single draft and would either destroy works in progress or put them away for years at a time unable to face the dread of working on them further.

Horney (1950) describes life in closed political systems and the dynamics that shaped my conflicts over creating my own works, although she frames her discussions in terms of neurosis and mental illness that obscure the social and personal politics involved. In hierarchical systems the more powerful tell the less powerful how they "should" behave, think, feel, and, in general, live their lives. In totalitarian societies authority extends the "tyranny of the shoulds" from overt behavior to the very processes that define human consciousness. One should not think, feel, or say, even to oneself, anything that angers the authority and which can be punished by rejection, withdrawal of love, ostracism, physical pain, or even death. Life feels very different when individuals only do as they should and not as they want and all of life is work and not play. It feels still different when individuals experience themselves as completely stuck because they do not even know what they want.

Under these circumstances individuals may well split off, repress, or otherwise deny whole aspects of the self, creating an intrapersonal condition in which individuals simultaneously become an authoritarian critic of their own thoughts, emotions, and desires. The rejected aspects of the self are treated as if they were the other, a thing, an it or some other defective inferior being. There can be little creative expression when individuals spend their time and energy criticizing and guarding themselves from aspects of their own selves. When psychologically divided in this way individuals can come to fear and loath themselves in much the same way as they would be feared and loathed by those authorities who demand total loyalty and obedience to their powers. The theme of the inner political life of individuals seeking dominance over aspects of their own self can become one of self-control through denial of pleasure; endless, harsh self-judgment; and even physical self-abuse and suicide.

The politics practiced intrapersonally mirror the interpersonal politics of closed societies. Not only must there be complete censorship both within and between individuals but the goals of development change as well. It is not excellence that is sought but an impossible-to-achieve type of perfection. Individuals seek to project to themselves and others an idealized self that often takes on godlike qualities. The human qualities split off and rejected as sinful, loathsome, or representing mental illness are replaced with moral labels of inherent superiority. Demands are made on the self and others that are unachievable except in fantasy, that are exhausting and ultimately doomed to bring about the very "weaknesses and deficits" the individuals seek to ban from themselves and society.

The fantastic strivings and search for perfection of self required by these political machinations can be achieved only with the use of preoperational logic. Preoperational thought permits individuals to use the kind of magical thinking needed to believe in self-perfection and the inherent perfection of others considered great and beyond human failing. Preoperational thought permits individuals to ignore the humanity in one's enemies. Preoperational thinking allows one to accept the essentialisms, historicisms, and fusion of descriptions and judgment necessary to maintain personal adaptations to closed societies based on god-thing narratives. Preoperations allow for the creation of sacred stories that remain immune from the kinds of evidence that might convince individuals to change their stories and thereby instead live by theories.

I have already discussed the price individual's pay for adaptations based on preoperational logic. One more consequence of using a child's form of logic requires explication and that is the individual's continued experience of being a perpetual child, especially when confronted with authority or with situational demands for formal operations. I will further develop the importance of this concept in my discussion of psychotherapy in the next chapter.

Horney describes the "viscious cycles" that emerge within the individual as failure to achieve perfection leads to ever more desperate attempts to do the impossible, avoid mistakes, and seek complete control over those emotions that represent weakness, sin, immorality, and mental illness. Moreover, there is a lack of seriation involved in the assessment of weakness and failure. There are, therefore, no small mistakes or weaknesses, only terrible failings that require terrible punishments. Trying to achieve perfection becomes so exhausting and time-consuming that the human processes involved in creative excellence appear as mountains to be climbed rather than playful attempts to experiment over time. The idea of showing off one's efforts to others, either the "gods" above whose efforts are perceived as always more perfect than one's own or the lowly creatures and things below whose opinions and criticisms are to be held in contempt, becomes a feared and odious exercise.

The gods never admit to mistakes and never say that they are sorry. Virtually every individual plays a dual role while participating in a hierarchy of gods and things. There is endless guilt and shame over personal failures to be perfectly good, perfectly independent, perfectly masterful, and in control. There is endless guilt and shame in playing the role of god or thing in the lives of others. Most individuals often get glimpses into the damage done to others when the psychological justifications of power, greed, and hubris that dehumanize others fail and the gods confront the fact that they have become monsters. There is always the possibility of deep and powerful reactions of shame overwhelming an individual that flatters, begs, and grovels a superior for some crumbs of that which might nurture the body or soul.

History demonstrates that no political system is immune from disruption and I believe that this is true of the intrapersonal and interpersonal systems I now sketch. Totalitarian systems are never far from anarchy. Shame breeds rage and a desire for revenge. The political systems I describe are, of necessity, filled with deceptions of self and others. People plot the downfall of the monsters above them even as they flatter and imitate them as gods. Time and energy consumed with deception, activity that is by definition hard work, can hardly be spent in the kind of play genuine creativity demands. Competition often exists in which individuals seek to wound or destroy and which tends to overwhelm cooperation and with it the emotions that promote sympathy, empathy, mercy, and forgiveness.

While believing that they are gods, individuals often see little reason to avoid self-indulgence. Innately superior beings might believe that they and their children deserve the best of everything and deserve it the moment that they desire it. Individuals experiencing deprivation of their human needs but unable to articulate or even recognize the emotions that represent their desires and problems might well experience unbearable "hungers" requiring immediate "feeding" and satisfaction. To the degree that individuals construct visions of themselves as gods and to the degree that individuals loath, split off, deny, and fail to understand the emotions that define their human needs is the degree to which they might seek immediate gratification of their needs and solutions for their problems. Unfortunately that might well be a majority of individuals within a given closed, totalitarian political structure.

Under circumstances in which children do not develop an ability to recognize and delay gratification of the emotions that define needs and problems and in which individuals feel as if they are helpless children then individuals tend to develop skills in begging, blackmailing, and otherwise manipulating others in doing necessary work for them. These are not the attitudes and skills that promote creative living.

Societies built on the notion of perfection and comprised of idealized leaders and defective followers litter human history. Virtually all tell the same story of harsh demands for obedience and virtual, if not actual, enslavement for those lower in the social hierarchy, finally destroying the necessary creativity and excellence that allows for societal renewal and leading to the eventual collapse and destruction of the society. Therapists are confronted with patients whose personal histories mirror those of the society that shapes their individual psychologies. A patient tells me that when he is morally debased by his mother ("she is a sharpshooter when it comes to attacking my soul") he "deconstructs himself" so that he no longer even exists. When he wakes up in some undetermined time in the future, he is inevitably in a mental hospital drugged and unfeeling.

There were times when instead of complying with authority's demands I completely rejected the roles and expectations of those individuals and institutions that defined, protected, and nurtured me. I experienced alienation, loneliness, and fear. Even if I had something unique to say it did not seem to be worth saying as there was no one willing to listen. I realize now that life could not continue if I did not give myself to society in order to have what I gave returned with all that my culture had to offer. At such times the loss of my creative identity seemed well worth the price.

At other times I lost myself in the face of demands from authority that benefited only authority. Giving in to threats and blackmail seemed, at the time, necessary but often not worth the price of my individuality. At such times I was filled with shame, despair, and even self-loathing even as I acted to reduce my fear of the consequences of authority's wrath. Harder to deal with were the adaptations I made to authority, which because of fear I convinced myself of the truth of their point of view making it mine and turning Laurence into the mirror image of a parent, teacher, or supervisor at my job.

It is one thing to willingly try and become like individuals with whom I identified and emulate authority that I loved and respected but quite another to convince myself to see through the eyes of another out of terror, shame, and guilt. Identification with loved figures helps create a voice with which to create; identifications based on fear lead to the loss of creativity. Whenever I find myself acting on or speaking about a subject that seems to emerge from my own passions and efforts, I feel myself to be authentic. Whenever I become aware that I have been pleasing a feared authority, I look back and realize that I have been acting and while acting felt as if I were sleepwalking through the important events of my life. It is still amazing to me to suddenly realize that I might have been living a life alienated from myself and others and acting the role of son, husband, father, professor, and psychotherapist. I am still transfixed by how joyful it feels to be restored to a self that feels genuine and authentic especially within these same roles.

Like all authority, I justified my demands for conformity and obedience from others by telling them it was for their own good that they comply, when much of the time it was for my own good. These conflicts, resolved as they were with my use of personal verbal attacks on the worth of others, blackmail, or threats of and overt physical violence were often motivated by fears of the same by those of authority in my life. (At other times I have attempted to silence the voice of others in a desperate attempt to have my own heard.) I have experienced long periods of life as part of a social institution in which all creativity was lost as I tried with futility to please authority by giving up my own voice and song by forbidding and squelching the poetry and music of others. Perhaps the most enduring lesson gained from these conflicts and the varieties of their resolutions was that destroying the individuality in others invariably meant losing my own; allowing my own identity to be lost in the face of hostile authority sowed the seeds of my own desires to invalidate others. The result was always anger, numbness, silence, alienation, a feeling of being stuck, and self-hatred rather than creativity, love, loyalty, and voluntary cooperation.

Another implication concerning my definition of creativity involves the ethical and moral concerns of the individual seeking to live creatively. I believe that unless the goals of a creative act involves the potential betterment and enrichment of the lives of others then we run the risk of defining Adolf Hitler, Joseph Stalin, and myriad other dictators and monstrous authorities that litter history as creative and artistic. Part of the burden of living creatively involves a constant self-questioning as to the emotions and goals that accompany the living of our lives. Do we create with love or with hate? Do we seek to enhance the freedom and dignity or instead enslave and degrade others with whom we interact? Do we truly love or mask violence in the name of love?

If we discover that we do violence to, hate, and enslave others do we seek to make restitution and beg forgiveness of those we have hurt? Do we attempt to realize our human potential or do we seek to rise above or sink below our human condition? Are we playing god with others or allowing ourselves to become things, puppets, or slaves by permitting others to play god with us? Do we follow rules claimed by authority to be moral only to find that we have been silenced, enslaved, and stripped of our dignity and pride? And if we experience such enslavement do we follow the dictates of Elie Wiesel and "speak truth to power"?

Finally, I do not imply that a creative life must involve the arts such as painting, music, and the like, nor do I imply that a person must become famous or a celebrity to live a life of art. People can live creatively in any job, social role, or aspect of life. The products of life can bear the signs of creativity, as can the means of achieving those products. There can be creative parenting, teaching, psychotherapy, studying and learning, athletics, cooking, housekeeping, professionalism, the performance of crafts, and so forth in both the products of these activities and the means and modes of their being carried out.

Creativity does not exist as an abstraction; rather, it is a judgment of how we live our lives in the specific situations with which we interact, the specific events that happen to us, and the manner in which we treat the people who live in our world. As I grew more conscious of my need to live more creatively I became more of the Laurence who could reflect on the meaning and purpose of his life. The development of such perspectives allowed me to question the origins of creativity and reflect on those social and historical forces that enhance and inhibit the emergence of a self capable of writing a creative life story. Moreover, as I became more able to examine life from this new psychological perspective I also became able to develop strategies to better deal with the inevitable conflicts that ensued as I felt forced to choose to live differently in each arena of my life. I found myself changing many of my important life roles including that of "clinical" and academic psychologist.

As a clinical psychologist I had been taught to diagnose and treat mental illnesses or disorders, the name given to various patterns of human behavior by psychiatrists and other clinical psychologists. I discovered instead that my patients were not literally mentally ill but were demonstrating individual differences in solving problems in living that society, their families, schools, other cultural institutions, or even they themselves neither accepted nor understood.

Being labeled "mentally ill" or "disordered," therefore, was a moral judgment rather than a medical or descriptive term. I learned that I had been taught to judge my patients rather than understand them. As such I was often acting as an agent for some cultural institution in getting patients to suppress individual differences that were often their most creative means of adapting to society (however I might believe these behaviors to be maladaptive and the source of my patient's intense misery). I realized that I was a member of a profession in which unwarranted and unproven assumptions governed both my behavior and those of my colleagues.

If I had loved and respected my patients more and had been less afraid of those who paid my salary and demanded conformity of me to empty psychological and demeaning clinical theories of mental illness, I would have begun sooner to work creatively with these people. I would also have begun my current vigorous opposition to the current direction of my field, which is inimical to any ideas I might have on creativity. My goals would be what they are now: helping others to satisfy their human needs by finding their own balance between pleasing others and socially conforming while maintaining the uniqueness of their own modes of 'being in the world.' I no longer work with sick, defective people but individuals different than me who might want to learn to express themselves in ways other than they currently do.

I no longer try to cure mental diseases but teach individuals how to understand and better deal with their own unique ways of seeing the world. I help them understand the psychology of those with whom they interact, and the rules that define the relationships between themselves and the significant others and institutions in their lives. I also try to help them find genuine psychiatric and psychological help rather than the harm they so often find instead.

It took me longer to understand how the typical school so often crushes and destroys the creativity of many of its students (and the teachers who work there). It took me even longer to understand how as a teacher I was all too often depriving my students of developing the skills that would allow them to reach the goals that have brought my own life some of its greatest joys. I have learned that it was only because of those few teachers who loved and respected me as a student, and demonstrated a creative involvement with their chosen fields, that I survived my education with any creative individual voice. I describe how I found my critical creative voice as an educator in my book *Psychology, Education, Gods, and Humanity* (Simon, 1998).

One of my students (and this might also be a patient) writes,

I never wrote a paper on a free topic. I feel great that I can write and express my thoughts and feelings. I do it from the bottom of my heart and don't have to force or contrive like I usually do in papers for other classes. I can write and write. The more I write the more things are coming to mind. I am planning to keep a diary because it's great going back, and rethink about it. It's like self-teaching. I regret that I didn't start writing a diary since I was a child, but I think it's never too late. Childhood never ends, there are so many things to learn!

My student has begun to discover and invent herself and the world around her. She has discovered the joy that attends an act of creation that she fully experiences as her own. She is not demonstrating an ability or thing within herself but choosing to express herself in what I hope will continue as a lifelong process. Her choice to express herself is based on her experience that it is safe for her to do so. I have struggled with her to get her to understand that much of her education has been geared to pleasing authority for good grades and avoiding the punishment of bad grades. I have tried to create an atmosphere in my classroom similar to that in my therapy office in which her education would be more than another test that would involve providing the teacher with a preselected right answer. She has begun to understand that life is more than right answers and that pleasing herself is at least as important as pleasing others. She has begun to comprehend that the morality that demands she do right by all other human beings includes herself, since she, too, is human. She finally understands that the various types of tests and the hostile comments of the many in her life who fear her self-expression judge her and therefore do not help her understand either herself or the subjects she studies. She now knows that she must be in control of her thoughts and not those of others and that unless she is critical of her own work there can be no genuine growth in her skills. She must have standards but these must, in the end, be her own. She no longer stands before me in confused dread when asked to write about how the psychology we study relates to her own experiences. She no longer asks "What do you want me to say?" or "How long should the paper be?" or "My other teachers just give short-answer tests, why do you make me work so hard?" She no longer sits in my class staring ahead without expression or looking bored, indifferent, or with barely concealed rage.

My student has also begun to understand that the freedom to think must be accompanied by a freedom to feel. Passion about life is as necessary as information about life and only by integrating her passions with what she knows can she have any true knowledge and wisdom. Her experience of creativity and herself as the one doing the creating is infused with emotional excitement. As she writes she becomes a whole human being fully connected to a world that feels very real and meaningful. We work together. We thank each other. We create ideas together. We create each other with love, mutual respect, and joy. We create ourselves as we most wish ourselves to be.

CHAPTER 9

Psycho"therapy" and the Creative Citizen

INTRODUCTION

Psycho"therapy" is the word I now use to denote the professional activity I used to refer to with the word psychotherapy. The new spelling makes clear my intention to totally free myself, those with whom I work, and any professional colleagues choosing to join with me, of the lies and pretensions of psychiatry and the medical model of mental illness and disorders. It demonstrates my desire to avoid calling myself a "clinical" psychologist or any other type of imitation doctor of "sick" minds. It also makes clear my commitment to base my work in a human science and a democratic/humanistic form of interpersonal politics. I would much prefer to call what I do "psychoeducation" or "personal education" and those who seek my professional expertise as "students" but this would sow much confusion as these words have other widely accepted meanings. Psycho"therapy" allows me to retain a familiar word but tells my reader that I perform metaphorical treatment with individuals suffering metaphorical illnesses.

This chapter seeks to outline and update arguments developed earlier concerning my vision of psycho"therapy" (Simon, 2000a). For the sake of clarity of style I will dispense with the quotation marks around the word therapy but will differentiate between my concept of the process and those based on the medical model or other types of god-thing narratives. When I first outlined my visions of psychotherapy I had reached a point in my career where I could no longer function within the field and remain true to myself as scientist, moral philosopher, or human being. The simultaneous rise of managed care and biopsychiatry were daily increasing the harm done to patients in the name of helping them and I felt helpless to do anything about it.

I was not alone in my unhappiness with the changes taking place in a field I loved despite my long-standing criticisms of it. Many shared my alarm over the dramatically increased use of both toxic drugs to control unwanted behavior and the torture of patients in the name of forced treatment. There were others who shared my growing upset over the diagnosing and drugging of millions of children rather than focusing on overworked confused parents; underpaid, undersupervised, and undersupported teachers; and growing, massive social dislocation and alienation.

Many colleagues complained about the replacement of psychodynamic and social explanations of behavior (as inadequate and reductionistic as these were) with the extreme reductionisms, essentialisms, and historicisms of simpleminded neurological theories held as absolute truths and spouted as if they were a catechism. Many despaired with me over the deprofessionalization of therapeutic work to be little more than "case management" that saw to it that patients complied with demands that they take their drugs. There was, of course, a universal outcry against the loss of incomes for those working within the changing field of mental health which was dominated by pseudomedicine and big business.

There are two points I make at this juncture. The first is that while many colleagues, those I knew personally and those that remained strangers, shared my concerns, very few openly spoke up and fought to even debate the bad science and dubious morality that was increasingly becoming the norm governing the work we were doing. The second point concerns the fact that when I wrote *Psycho"therapy"* I focused solely on the politics within my field. At present, I have come to the conclusion that what was happening to patients and professionals alike as my field descended toward anarchy and totalitarianism was reflective of the politics of my entire society. In fact, our continuing failure to stand up and live by the rules of genuine science and humanistic morality and politics is one of the powerful determinants of the loss of Enlightenment values and the possible demise of Western democracy.

I need not dwell on why my colleagues did little more than complain about the terrible transformations taking place in our professional lives. Those near the bottom of the power structure often feel they must hold tightly to whatever small benefits they derive from controlling those further below them while ignoring the greater benefits derived from their efforts by those higher in the social hierarchy. Many of my colleagues made clear that to give up convincing patients that they were hopelessly sick would be open rebellion to authority above. It could also convince patients that not only did they not need their therapists but their therapists and the whole mental health structure were anything but their benefactors. I soon discovered that I was labeled "a troublemaker," that I had an "authority problem," and, ultimately, that I was "seriously mentally ill."

What did fascinate me was the fact that those who complained the most about their small salaries, the poor quality of their patients, and the cruelty and stupidity of their psychiatric superiors were the angriest with me for my "rebelliousness" and "disobedience" to received truth. I assume that it was these individuals who felt the guiltiest, the most ashamed, and the most helpless and hopeless about continuing in their present life course. They were also the most terrified about engaging in a struggle to change what made them most unhappy as professionals. But these are often the dynamics of life in a closed, authoritarian political system.

After leaving the clinic where I had worked for a quarter of a century and had attained the position of chief psychologist, I grew increasingly disaffected and alienated from my field. An attempt to maintain my private practice without diagnosing any patients and filling out insurance forms soon left me with few patients and even more distant from my field. Without a full-time, tenured professorship I would have had little or no income and I would have been totally isolated from other psychologists as well as professionals. However, I watched my field continue to spiral downward and listened as my colleagues helplessly complained and gnashed their teeth over a victimization of which they believed they were perfectly innocent. When the American Psychological Association announced it would seek prescription privileges for psychologists, I believed psychology and psychotherapy had perhaps reached their nadir. (As of this writing the New Mexico State Legislature has passed and the governor signed a bill giving psychologists prescription privileges. Needless to say I believe this is a betrayal of all that psychology should stand for and a disaster for the field and society at large.)

I write this feeling deeply uneasy about the future of psychotherapy and of the society that has nurtured me and to which I feel committed. Yet, I also feel curiously hopeful. I discovered and became deeply involved with the International Center for the Study of Psychiatry and Psychology (ISCPP), a robust and growing group of psychiatrists, psychologists, clinical social workers, teachers, and allied professionals who see the world through eyes similar to my own. ICSSP maintains relationships with the growing number of grassroots organizations comprised of psychiatric survivors and others politically active in restoring democracy and genuine science to the mental health enterprise.

On some days the alliance of big business, power politics, and biopsychiatry still appear to me to be monolithic and invincible. At other times, however, I sense that the intellectual and moral rot at the heart of this grouping are quickly bringing it to its rightful place on the garbage heap of history. I no longer feel either isolated or impotent but rather sense that I might live long enough to see history happen and know that I played some small but positive role in it.

I believe that there is a genuine place for psychotherapy in a highly complex democratic society in which life no longer revolves around small tight-knit families, communities, or tribes. Like millions of others I have adapted my life to a cosmopolitan, technological society in which parents and small communities are no longer able to provide all of the education and skill development that their children require to live in such a society. The "expert" is here to stay. The key issue involves making sure that the experts recognize that their proper political and moral role is to help families and communities maintain themselves as democratic and humanistic institutions. It is not the role of experts to help destroy the integrity of families and communities and mindlessly turn our society into a totalitarian nightmare of helpless drug addicts and lost, alienated individuals. I turn to a brief description of the science and political morality of psycho"therapy", making clear that I speak only for myself, expressing opinions that might well be mine alone.

THE SCIENCE AND POLITICS OF PSYCHO"THERAPY"

I begin this brief discussion not with science but with my view of the morals and politics that must provide the ground for the practice of psychotherapy, even though I demand that psychotherapy be based in science. I have argued throughout this book that human beings do ground their personal roles as scientists in their roles as moral philosophers. I have further opined that we often conflate our moral judgments with our descriptions of ourselves as human beings. As a result we come to use our moral judgments as explanations for our behavior rather than relying on descriptions of our motives expressed in terms of our thoughts and feelings about the situations and events to which we seek to adapt.

It is my contention that the confusion of judgment and description is greatest in totalitarian, closed societies where an endless series of moral judgments helps maintain a rigid social hierarchy. Those greater in power wrap themselves in a mantle of moral purity and perfection justifying the political actions used to demand obedience and punish rebellion in those with less power conceived of as beings that are basically defective and morally corrupt. I have argued that psychiatry operates in a manner consistent with a totalitarian society in which clinicians pretend to describe their patients with medical diagnoses that are in reality harsh, dehumanizing moral judgments. In this way the clinicians play God as they help control a large and growing segment of the population unwilling and/or unable to comply with the moral demands of society by treating them as things, objects, wild animals, and the outcast other.

I submit that we can only understand how the psychiatric profession could, over its entire history, conceive of terror, unbearable pain, and damaged brains as both scientifically sound and beneficial medical treatments unless we recognize the underlying morality and politics of the mental health field. *Torture and atrocity can only be justified if we look at the patients through the eyes of institutional psychiatry. From the perception of the morally pure professionals the patients were so morally damaged as to actually deserve the forced treatment and abuse heaped on them. I conclude that we can separate ourselves from institutional psychiatry and let this evil die only if we accept that our work with patients is an inherently moral activity and dedicate ourselves to seeing to it that its morality comply to humanistic and democratic political procedures.*

I also suggest that we will begin to develop a genuine science of human behavior and psychotherapy including an adequate understanding of what Michael Mahoney (1991) refers to as "human change processes" only when we deconstruct the underlying, unexamined, and invisible moral visions now guiding psychology and psychiatry. The power of science and its rise to prominence in human affairs was based in its adherence to two principles. The first was its rejection of preoperational thought as its cognitive mode understanding the world and with it the removal of magic, supernatural forces, and concrete thinking in the human worldview. Preoperational thinking was replaced by formal operations permitting abstract theories and the recognition that the universe and everything in it is a mechanism capable of being understood in impersonal terms.

The second principle relates to the first and that is science's insistence that the universe be described, explained, predicted, and controlled but not evaluated or judged. I suggest that these two principles are constantly being ignored when it comes to our understanding of human behavior. Psychology's insistence in adopting the methods of the physical science was part of the rejection of genuine science and a regression to god-thing narrative that permitted psychologists to look down on their subject matter as mechanical objects, wild animals, and the like. I need not repeat any of my arguments concerning institutional psychiatry's abandonment of anything resembling science for its persistent stance as a debased, secular religion.

I have already outlined my own theory of human behavior in which I try to conform to the principles of science by describing human beings in terms of the developmental changes that possibly take place in human consciousness as we struggle to adapt to the physical and social world in and around us. I have tried to create a picture of human beings that places us within the animal kingdom and yet retain those characteristics that make us special in all the world (and possibly in the universe as well). I have tried to avoid any vestige of god-thing narrative while recognizing our human capacity to make choices, hold ourselves morally responsible, and endlessly create and re-create ourselves and the worlds that enfold us. I have tried to outline a theory, rather than a sacred story, that is free from essentialisms, historicisms, and other features that exist when a theory is embedded in and seeks to justify a closed, authoritarian social structure.

I certainly recognize the gross inadequacies in my theory. It has little power to explain or predict human behavior however correct I believe its respect for and focus on human experience and consciousness to be. It is my firm conviction that when a patient enters my office she/he represents the end product of, up until that moment, human evolution, her/his culture and its history as embodied in its practices and the entire individual history of the patient. I believe these individuals are to be understood in terms of their personal consciousness. Their consciousness has, in part, been shaped by the totality of the interaction of every gene they have inherited with every event that has ever happened to them as they experienced it. I believe that their consciousness is also a function of the sequence of each and every event that these individuals experienced as well as every decision they have ever made. I further suggest that many decisions made by the individual operate according to the rules inherent in human consciousness that are not reducible to biology or culture. Such rules have not yet been the serious focus of scientific inquiry.

The inadequacies of my theory are therefore, in part, a function of the sheer complexity inherent in the development of human consciousness as millions of possible variables interact in such ways as to obscure causes and effects and present us with a puzzle that might forever lie beyond our capacity to solve. I recognize that when a patient enters my office (or a student my classroom) I will have to operate in the face of enormous, unending, and anxiety-provoking ambiguity. In the face of such ambiguity there is little question that I will operate more like an artist in making decisions even as I refuse to give up on my role as scientist. The struggle to understand my patients should not be reduced to either the creation of an aesthetically pleasing narrative, no matter how complex, or to a simple set of variables interacting in linear causal fashion.

Science, suggests Gregory Bateson (1979), is a search for the pattern of things and, at this stage in psychology's development, a perfectly acceptable goal for human beings working with human beings while both are embedded in the same complex set of forces. If my role as scientist is a humble one and my work with my patients and students that of an artist, then I must be ever careful to examine the political and moral nature of my interactions with those seeking me in a professional capacity. My work as a scientist and an artist must be examined in terms of those coconstructed transferences that deviate from democratic and humanistic politics and take on the qualities of totalitarianism and god-thing narratives.

I might not know what I need to about the human condition but I need not know the rules governing human consciousness to know what is right and wrong as I deal with another human being. If I can hold on to what I believe is politically and morally right and wrong I can evaluate both my therapeutic efforts with my patients and the theories I use to explain our mutual actions for signs that I have left the realm of the democratic for that of the authoritarian. At this point in time I feel little anxiety that my science will be corrupted by my values if I seek to create a theory of human behavior that explains how best to convince people to live according to democratic and humanistic values while I ignore the vast body of accumulated evidence that boldly states that human beings are creatures incapable of choice, freedom, and life in a free society. If it is ever proven that human beings are nought but passive robots I will have to revise my thinking. However, I feel confident that the prejudices of my field will never be able to close the door on my belief that human beings are capable of living creatively while maintaining an open society.

ASSUMPTIONS INVOLVED IN DOING PSYCHO"THERAPY"

Psychotherapy consists of an encounter between two human beings in which one seeks out the assistance of the other. I limit this brief discussion to those encounters in which I am sought out by individuals who are desperate about some aspect of their life and whose concerns relate to their most important social relationships or the lack of them. I am not concerned here with individuals who seek, and could benefit from, bits of information or advice but those experiencing genuine crises of the soul. I pay attention to those suffering from disabling anxiety, guilt, shame, nausea in the face of nothingness, and other painful emotions.

I write about those who worry about loves that are dying and who fear for the future of their children and, even as they watch disaster happen, are unable to act. I am focusing on those who understand on some level that a meaningful life is slipping away from them and cannot bear the life they are living but feel too terrified and stuck to do anything effective about it. The therapy that fascinates me is concerned with those suffering in both their intrapersonal and their interpersonal life and are unable to change that suffering because of their current solutions to both sets of interrelated problems.

I keep in mind that the individuals who enter my office are not sick (unless an undiagnosed medical condition contributes to their suffering) but are in crisis of living. Each individual, in one way or another, can no longer live with their political–moral adaptation to the others in their lives and with themselves. A crisis involves emotional pain and, as long as it goes unresolved, preempts many, if not all other, aspects of daily living. It is true that the individuals suffering a life crisis may have difficulties in eating, sleeping, working, and loving. But a crisis is always an opportunity for change and I keep in mind as I meet new individuals that the very decision to seek treatment means that my prospective patients are motivated to find new ways of living. While most cannot see past the immediacy of their pained lives, and most cannot say what it is they seek beyond lessened discomfort, I keep faith that a great opportunity for growth is made manifest.

I try, but rarely succeed, putting away all of my prejudices and theoretical preconceptions when meeting another human being for the first time. (I understand in advance that I can never know another independent of the effect I have on them as we interact.) To the degree that I succeed and experience the other as a human being, as a person motivated by a self whose core is to be treated as a precious soul, I feel anxious, awestruck, exhilarated, and weighed down by the responsibility I might be undertaking if I become involved in this person's life. I know nothing about these people and never will be able to fully fathom them. I believe what my religion teaches me: Every human being is a world entire unto itself. My struggle to avoid prejudices and preconceptions when greeting new patients (or students) does not mean that I begin these encounters free from a variety of complex, interrelated assumptions. I must clarify these assumptions before discussing the specifics of treatment because they determine much of the nature of the therapy I will engage in and if there is to be a therapy at all.

I make clear that when I do therapy I am not practicing medicine and therefore not bound by the morality of medicine that states that I must treat anyone who needs my help regardless of my feelings for them. Ultimately, I work *with* patients not *on* them and believe that our work together must conform to humanistic moral and democratic political values. While the patient must direct the specifics of any therapy, the ethics, morals, and politics to which I subscribe must bound the therapy itself. I have never turned a patient away but my courteous, firm refusal to practice authoritarian politics or agree to help individuals achieve goals that are morally repugnant to me have led many patients to conclude I was not the person to help them.

I do not assume that my patients either know or want to share my values but that they will have no choice in the matter if we are to work together. A patient who cannot tolerate the politics of democracy or who is seeking to be either a better god or a happier thing will soon become disappointed in our relationship. While I always hope to have time to help the patient become acclimated to a democratic, open relationship I know in advance that this might not be the case. A person committed to improving their skills as dictator, reducing their guilt as a killer of human souls (if not persons), or becoming better at remaining a numb object beyond human pain will soon choose another venue for help.

I believe that there are many individuals whose life goals are inimical to my own. I share little of the faith evinced by many of my colleagues that all human beings have by nature a "true self" that seeks love, dignity, and a balance between independence and social harmony. Fortunately, most of the individuals who seek me out do discover that the misery in their lives is, in some measure, the result of their active participation in politically closed relationships as either false god or thing.

My first assumption concerning therapy is that my patients and I will create a relationship that is defined by a process that has a content and is directed toward a variety of goals. The specific process of therapy will be a dialogue, the content of which will, in large part, be provided by the life narrative supplied by the patient. The goals of therapy will involve changes in both the construction and the function of the life narrative of the patient and the intrapersonal and interpersonal relationships reflected in the content of the narrative.

It has been my experience that patient's narratives express their developmental mode of experience and the manner in which they function as scientists and moral philosophers. Further, it has been my experience that the goals of therapy, in one way or another, help patients change their life narratives and with them the intrapersonal and interpersonal politics with which they live their lives. Specifically, if therapy is successful, then the particular life lived by any given patient changes from one based on totalitarian politics to one built on democratic and humanistic principles.

The changes in intrapersonal and interpersonal politics are further marked by a scientific worldview utilizing formal operations rather than preoperations, theories rather than sacred stories and the disappearance of essentialisms and historicisms. The moral philosophy of patients will reflect the seeking of moral improvement rather than perfection and all that follows when human beings deal with another or themselves as "I" and "thou" rather than as gods dealing with things, despised others, and an "it." Perhaps most of all the changes helped brought about by our relationship will lead to a living that feels real and authentic rather than one experienced as an act or false performance.

My second assumption is that the relationship my patients and I are creating exists within a matrix of other relationships that involve a variety of other social institutions. I assume that my patient and I are citizens of our community and society at large as well as patient and therapist. I take it as truth that whatever my patients are seeking to achieve must in some way be worked out both as individuals and as citizens in relation to a society without which a meaningful life is impossible. Therefore, therapy is unavoidably civics.

If therapy is indeed a form of civics, then as therapist I cannot help evaluating my work in terms of the freedoms and responsibilities of myself, my patients, the others with whom the patients share personal lives, and the larger society in which we share citizenship. I agree with Daniel Robinson (1997) when he writes, "Those who would help others find a place for themselves within the larger moral order of things must have a secure location themselves" (p. 680). This means that at times I might well have to stand with society and refuse to ally myself with those freedoms patients might define as their goals for treatment. At others times I might have to stand with my patients against the goals of a family, school system, religious institution, or the society at large that might be totalitarian and therefore seeks to destroy my patients' abilities to achieve a richer, more meaningful, and creative existence.

The changes patients initiate in their own lives reverberate throughout all of their relationships and often threaten the stability of all those comprising a given societal institution. The success or failure of any given therapy often depends on how changes in the patient are viewed by others in the patient's life and how the therapist negotiates the ensuing political responses. It is not easy given the values of therapy and the need to earn a living to oppose one's patients. It is always dangerous, in one way or another, for patients and therapists to oppose one's society. The danger is greatest to the degree that therapy succeeds in undermining closed political structures. The collective of changes initiated by patients because of therapy might be great enough to change society itself, either for better or worse, depending on the politics of patients and their therapists.

I insist that our therapeutic relationship be humanistic and reflective of democratic politics. I believe that our work together must reflect free speech, genuine privacy, and confidentiality. *The ideal psychotherapy is a politically safe psychotherapy*. It creates a situation in which both my patients and I feel safe to say to each other what we both feel needs to be said free of the type of moral judgments, personal attacks, and blackmail that marks relationships in totalitarian, closed relationships. I try to be neither god nor thing with my patients and through example convince them to take the same stance.

The early steps in initiating a genuine therapeutic relationship occur after the normal social introductions and civil niceties that should begin every relationship. There are three interrelated steps that begin any treatment: establishing the goals of therapy, establishing a contract that includes, among other things, the fees, and assessing the reasons the patient is seeking treatment in the first place. I begin by discussing fees. I have not spent much time in this book on the critical role played by economics in creating and maintaining closed and open societies but therapy cannot begin until someone agrees to pay for it. The issue of money in psychotherapy is a vast and complex one and always involves transferential issues.

Governmental subsidies and third-party insurers have dramatically changed the therapist–patient relationship and vastly expanded the opportunities for millions to seek mental health services. My experience has shown me that patients who do not have to pay for therapy often see it as much less valuable than those who do. The same experience tells me that patients who pay are seen by their therapists as more valuable than those who do not. Moreover, if the patient does not hire the therapist, it makes it more likely that the goals of therapy might well tip toward the desires of those footing the bill rather than those who are supposed to receive its benefits. I have suggested earlier that this is a topic rarely discussed among therapists as it would create real guilt in relation to the patient and real fear as to what and who maintains the bulk of the field.

There is often genuine conflict over the setting of fees in private practice as therapists struggle to make their services affordable for more than the upper-middle classes while trying to remain a member of that same socioeconomic grouping. Money has much to say about personal status and importance in our culture and there is little that therapists can and perhaps should do about it. I have never felt that society recognized my value in economic terms as a professional who tended to deal with the poor in both my roles as clinic psychotherapist and college professor. To this day I have still not worked out my conflicts over the fees I should/want to set in my private practice.

My difficulty in setting fees seems to derive, in part, from my ambivalence concerning the basic value of psychotherapy. My ambivalence extends to money itself. I believe that poverty can cripple any individual's struggle to create a good life based on individual creativity by convincing them they are a "thing" of no value. So, too, can creativity be stifled in the search for money and economic success in which individuals become "godlike" in their appraisals of self. I have not outgrown my working-class roots and the commitments I made, however unconsciously, to work with the poor and use my skills to help others escape from the ugliness of poverty and near poverty even as I seek greater material comforts and status from the work I do as a therapist.

Some time ago a colleague, a successful analyst, suggested to me that all of my difficulties in setting high enough fees comes down to how I feel about myself as a person. All of my other arguments were rationalizations and defenses. Perhaps; but I countered with How can you be sure that the argument that self-esteem is measured by how much is charged in treatment isn't a rationalization for setting high fees? After three decades of therapeutic work it remains difficult for me to set fees that I consider appropriate. However, to the degree that I can avoid the desire to give in to a god-thing narrative and be a saint who is morally pure and above mere money, the difficulty of setting fees lessens.

The beginning phase of treatment also involves a dual assessment as to why the person has sought me out: what the goals are they wish to pursue and if they are here of their own free will. I will not see any patient who enters my office under coercion or blackmail. While I might try to motivate such individuals to find reasons to stay and work on their own accord, I will refuse to initiate a therapeutic relationship unless I am convinced that these individuals seek treatment for themselves alone. I will not work with individuals placating parents or following their attorney's advice to mitigate criminal indictments or long sentences, or judges seeking alternatives to sentencing or releasing a felon.

I find it important to define and explicate, if necessary, the specific role I play with patients if I am to maintain my democratic role and properly assess the psychological effects therapy is having in helping patients achieve the goals important to them. First in this assessment is that the therapeutic relationship is a means to an end and never and end in and of itself. I believe that my role as parent, teacher, and psychotherapist should last only as long as it takes for those with whom I am involved to no longer require my services. While I hope to maintain good relationships with my children over our lifetimes, I would consider my work as father to have failed if they had eventually not developed the skills to parent themselves and, as they have chosen, parent the next generation. I consider myself to have failed with students if at the end of a semester they are no closer to being their own teachers and as therapist if, over time, my patients are no closer to being their own therapists.

During the therapeutic dialogue I will try to avoid being a detective and ascertain whether or not my patients are telling me the truth about their lives. The patients can lie, posture, or deceive me all they want. If they succeed, they will fail to benefit from the encounter I am proposing to them and in all likelihood will find me the wrong person with whom to work. I am not concerned with the accuracy of their reality testing (that is, it conforms to mine or to society's) either of the past or present but of their perception of reality. If my patient's reality has been reconstructed along deceptive lines then, it is my job to create conditions that might induce them to deconstruct and reconstruct their modes of experience along different, less deceptive lines.

I am also resolved not to be my patient's social advocate, good friend, or protector or play any other role that would take me out of my office to engage others on their behalf. I do not write letters on their behalf to social agencies attesting to the fact that they cannot work because of mental illness and therefore deserve disability payments. I simply do not ever know enough about a person to determine when they cannot or will not work. I will not under any circumstances be their expert witness in court, as I recognize how little of the truth of their lives I might know through our dialogue. Our relationship stays in the office and remains between us. I certainly consider a patient's desire to discuss the development of skills that will allow them to achieve their own chosen goals as a valid topic of treatment.

I will avoid, with equal diligence, playing the role of a cleric who either morally condemns or hears confessions leading to forgiveness, absolution, and entry into heaven. Patients almost always choose to work on issues related to their moral–political lives; and if as a result of our dialogue they conclude that they need forgiveness from others or God, I feel it is their responsibility to seek it from those sources. Of course, it is not unusual for such discussion to result in a reduction of preoperational thinking and with it the discovery that the guilt the patient was carrying around was a function of childhood beliefs in magical powers, egocentricity, and the inability to discriminate between his responsibilities and those of others. If such a discovery is achieved, then there is little or no guilt left to assuage.

Most of all I will avoid playing the role of substitute parent. It may be true that patients might be seeking a good parent as substitute for a bad or lost one, might be trying to save a symbolic parent because of a failed attempt in childhood, or might seek revenge or to challenge a dominating or cruel parent. While it is necessary to deal with an individual's narratives and fantasies about parents (and other important childhood figures), my belief is that we get one set of parents and no matter how that relationship worked itself out it cannot be relived or reconstituted later in life. The dynamics and expectations that derive from parent–child relationships make excellent topics for psychotherapy, especially when therapy permits individuals to experience a democratic/humanistic relationship for the first time in their lives. However, I think it futile and destructive for therapists to set themselves the task of literally attempting to correct any earlier relationships, especially those of parent and child.

The last necessary step in beginning treatment involves the setting of therapeutic goals. In one way or another this involves helping patients begin to articulate what for them represents the "good life." The goals of therapy are constantly being reassessed and continually change if patients continue to change their cognitive–affective modes of experience, life narrative, and interpersonal politics. Early goals might be based on patient belief that the best that they can accomplish is to simply make life less awful by finding ways to reduce, escape, or avoid the anxiety, shame, guilt, and constant painful interpersonal combat that marks their existences. Later goals might be made in the light of attitudes and beliefs that life can be directed to include relationships based on love, dignity, and genuine creative self-expression.

As long as patient goals conform to life in a democratic/humanistic social system, it is the patient who chooses the directions toward which treatment is to be directed. I agree with Isaiah Berlin (1969) that the good society is a pluralistic one that supports a multiplicity of perspectives and forms of excellence in individual self-expression. Diversity has been shown to define robust existence on biological, psychological, and social levels and, ultimately, a psychotherapy that supports the development of diverse expressions of individual excellence best serves both individuals and the societies with whom they are dualities.

As we begin to work together I assume that my role will be that of a teacher of sorts and that my patients and I will function according to democratic/humanistic rules of what I now believe to be good education. I have already made clear my indebtedness to Jean Piaget in this regard and now add some of the notions of Lev Vygotsky (1978). Vygotsky conceives of education as an inherently social process. The teacher, mentor, guide, or whatever term we give to authority evaluates the learning process of their students in face-to-face encounters. The teacher attempts to understand the mode of student learning in terms of its level of development as well as the emotions that define motivation to learn and the student's experience of difficulty at any given stage of the learning process.

Vygotsky recognized that when students try to learn alone their level of attainment is lower than when they are involved with individuals that ask questions, direct the student's attention, and otherwise help create a scaffold on which development takes place. The gap between individual and dyadic achievement is known as the "zone of proximal development." It is my contention that it is most useful to view the therapeutic encounter and the dialogue that comprises it as a series of ongoing, shifting zones of proximal development that continues until patients attain the goals representing what for them is the good life.

I suggest that the therapeutic encounter represents an ideal learning environment in which the teacher is in intimate contact with the student's struggles to achieve their goals. The therapist can monitor intellectual and emotional changes and dynamics as well as the nature of the politics being practiced in the therapeutic zone. In this way the therapist is a teacher who knows when to introduce new ideas to the patient that can be assimilated without undue intellectual confusion or emotional anxiety and distress. The therapist simultaneously creates what many psychoanalysts refer to as a "holding and facilitating environment."

It is difficult to describe in any detail the actual nature of the therapeutic dialogue that comprises my relationships with patients. I do note several ongoing activities that comprise the dialogue. The first is the usual Socratic questioning that is common to many forms of therapy that derive from psychoanalysis. The second involves my belief that growth and change in the processes and procedures of living requires growth and change in the content of individual knowledge. There is a bidirectional relationship between what we know and how we know it. I believe therapy should help increase what individuals know about themselves and the world as well as how they know what they know.

Part of what a person knows should be about how they know as well as the historical nature of both what and how they know as they do. I either direct questions or, when appropriate, provide direct information to patients concerning many of the topics that comprise this book. I think it necessary that therapy contain a curriculum of topics that include the following: the difference between judgments and descriptions, the difference between moral and medical judgments, the difference between preoperational and operational thinking, and the difference between closed and open societies and relationships. I am not suggesting that these topics are ever taught didactically but are instead woven into the fabric of our dialogue and integrated into patient's growing emotional understanding of themselves and their personal history. In this context I consider it a therapeutic triumph if patients continue their formal education or seek to complete their degrees.

The third activity involves changing the script that exists between patients and those with whom they interact, including and especially themselves. If we utilize the metaphor of narratives to describe the manner around which individual personality is organized, then it makes sense to understand the moral and political dialogues between individuals as being comprised of scripts. Helping individuals change the intrapersonal and interpersonal scripts from "I-It" to "I-Thou" involves more than discussing past and present relationships. I believe it involves actual ongoing role playing within the safety of the therapeutic relationship, which itself provides an opportunity for individuals to experience profound changes in the scripts that define their relationships.

It is in the safety of the therapeutic relationship that patients begin to develop selves that own their history and evaluate their moral lives in terms of descriptions rather than punitive and unbearable moral judgments. I feel that therapeutic progress and growth takes place when patients comprehend the difference between understandings of self based on description rather than judgment at the same time that they experience being understood and affirmed as individuals rather than judged in the eyes of the other. My notion of therapy as a political process is defined by the free flow of ideas between individuals who experience each other as moral equals.

My notion that my patients and I are moral equals is necessary for our relationships to be democratic and humanistic. However, while I seek to avoid being authoritarian I still hold that I must be authoritative with my patients if I am to be of any real use to them. If I do not understand and live by the curriculum I wish them to learn, then I have little to offer them, intellectually, morally, or politically. My expertise does not make me an inherently superior being to my patients or students but my patients still seek and deserve therapists (as well as parents and teachers) who can function as experts, guides, and catalysts of moral and intellectual development.

The privacy and freedom to express thoughts creates a situation in which individuals can play with their thoughts and feelings. They can better deal with those contained in the historical narrative that defines much of the self as well as those that relate to their current life. The freedom to play with their thoughts, emotions, and personal narrative allows individuals to simultaneously develop selves defined by intellectual skills that own their psychological processes rather then to simply be them. It also permits the development of social skills that can lead to profound change in the political lives of the patients.

I conceive of success with my patients as a developmental set of issues with moral–political consequences. If I am successful, my patients will experience themselves and their world through a maturer mode of consciousness, which includes more effective social–political skills. I tend to direct the focus of our dialogue from the past to the present, making my patients aware that the past is not necessarily important for its own sake but for an increased understanding of the present. It is in the context of the past that current modes of understanding and social interaction can be best understood and changes instituted that can dramatically alter the future.

Part of increased maturity involves the development of formal operations that make possible the kind of self-examination that psychoanalysts refer to as "insight." Formal operations permit individuals to examine human thinking, their own as well as others, for evidence of egocentrism, magical thinking, lack of seriation, and the like. Individuals whose interpretive modes are comprised mainly of preoperations and have little or no access to the formal operations necessary for evaluating their own thought processes are often quite difficult to work with in terms of a dialogue. In these circumstances the work of therapy must be directed toward processes that help patients develop formal operations. It is beyond the scope of this chapter to deal with this issue as it relates to adults but I will briefly discuss the way it effects my work with children.

The development of formal operations (or any later developmental stage that I would judge as more mature) does not mean that earlier stages are replaced, as is often the interpretation of some who are concerned with cognitive development. I believe that newer achievements overlay the earlier ones and permit the emergence of selves that can own and use the earlier stages adaptively. I believe creativity often begins with hunches and imaginative productions utilizing preoperational thought. Formal operations are best utilized to logically structure hunches into theory and draw hypotheses from them. They are not necessarily best at encouraging the free flow of imagination.

It is difficult to catalog all of the profound changes that might take place in people's lives as a function of modes of experience utilizing formal operations in so short a space. Formal operations change individual's perception of time from one in which the present contains the past and future to one in which the individual lives in and is connected to the present but who understands the past as the context of the present and prologue to the future. Despair is often a function of living in an oppressive "now" with no hope of a better future. If an individual lives without the profound experience of a future, better yet a multiplicity of possible futures, there can be little motivation or urgency to change. Therapists who complain about their patient's low level of motivation and passivity often overlook the cognitive aspect of patient's resistance to change.

I have earlier suggested (Simon, 1986) that formal operations permit the development of a future principle (to be added to the analytic concepts of pleasure and reality principles) and with it the emergence of existential anxieties and concerns. I later agreed with Sydney Hook (1987) that it is equally necessary for individuals to possess a historical principal, especially if we are to live in a democratic society. I now suggest that it is impossible to live according to a future principle without a narrative governed by a literary sense of history.

The ability to understand "mind" in terms of thoughts and feelings as well as an individual's capacity to decenter from their own mental state creates the conditions for true empathy. Empathy is related to the emergence of stage three, postconventional morality, in which individuals are able to understand, in terms of thought and emotion, right and wrong as a function of the consequences of their own actions to themselves and others. I argue that democratic politics flourishes when individuals understand the moral necessities of basing their relationships on fair and equitable contracts with others rather than the word of morally superior beings. Individuals best develop empathy when they experience themselves in intersubjective relationships that affirm, value, and allow for feelings of being understood and treated fairly and with respect.

With increased cognitive development patients will be able to critique their own thinking as well as the logic used by others. They will critically examine the assumptions with which they live their lives according to rules of evidence rather than prejudice or appeals to authority. The ability to think critically allows individuals to develop the kind of self-control that render dictators unemployed. It certainly adds to the individual's sense that they are the political equal of others and, hence, a unique soul with their own voice, one of the important psychological elements in living a creative life.

However, cognitive development alone can mean little unless individuals can experience the affects that represent needs and problems and hence motivate behavior. Creativity cannot exist without curiosity, felt interest in the world in which we live as well as ourselves, and, perhaps most important, a genuine passion to explore, play, and learn. A successful therapy is marked by the emergence of new vocational choices, hobbies, and activities and all of the related skills that are created as individuals pursue creative interests. The ability to own emotions, particularly those connected to painful and terrifying historical events, permits individuals to begin to create a historical context for their lives. They understand as well that the events of the past happened to a younger, far-less-skilled person than the one now recalling them as well as the fact that emotions represent the events that aroused them, they are not the events themselves.

Patients come to experience their emotions as "mine" rather than as belonging to the "not me." They will no longer feel terrified of emotions such as fear or anger and worry that if they permit themselves to feel they will not be swept away or "go crazy." It is a powerful experience to watch as individuals realize that they will find sanity in the acceptance of strong affect rather than the madness they have assumed was there. As a result individuals feel more genuinely connected to themselves and those with whom they interact. They have not developed a real self but one that feels more real. It is interesting that with greater maturity individuals will report that they no longer feel literally like frightened, angry children and now seem to appreciate what being an adult is psychologically all about.

Many patients have long since gone numb in attempting to escape from painful emotions. Discussions related to their life narratives in the safety of the therapeutic relationship begin to reconnect patients to the painful emotions aroused in earlier difficult situations. Emotions embedded in earlier, especially preoperationally organized, memories do not allow for a separation of cognitive and affective elements. Therefore, remembering and discussing in detail the events of the past is experienced as difficult, as living through these events all over again. Evaluating the past in the light of the present, particularly through the lens of formal operations, permits individuals to separate thought from affect, present memories from actual past experiences.

The development of formal operations will not in and of itself allow patients to feel the terror, shame, guilt, and oblivion they seek to avoid. In fact, many therapists have discovered that logic alone can be used as a tool to avoid feeling. There are patients who develop what appear to be profound insights but in fact speak of their own lives as if they were someone else's. In recent years I have used meditation, deep breathing, and relaxation techniques to help patients experience strong affect in a mode that allows experience without panic. More important, I have found that my own attitude toward the expression of strong emotions, as they are expressed, is critical in determining whether a patient flees or accepts their own emotional expression. As long as I do not get upset in the face of the patient's strong affect (and especially avoid diagnosing them as mentally ill for feeling), my patients more easily come to own their own memories including the affects that now allow them to reconnect to their own personal history in a meaningful way.

One of the developmental goals of treatment involves a patient's recognition that the best way to approach moral issues is through discussion of the descriptives being judged. Who did what to whom and why? allows a better entry into moral issues than Who is at fault and to blame? Accusation and condemnation usually lead to guilty, shameful confessions, and/or strong denials of wrongdoing. An understanding of motives and description of the consequences of one's actions often allows individuals greater freedom to assess the morality of their behavior. It is important in this regard to avoid allowing explanations of behavior to mitigate the moral implications of that behavior. While it is true that moral judgments prevent us from understanding behavior, it is often equally true that to explain all is to forgive all. Finally, I believe that only behavior is to be morally judged, not the motives, thoughts, emotions, or narratives associated with overt behavior.

Another important goal involves the patient's understanding that conflicts are best understood as existing between individuals and not as a consequence of what is wrong inside of them. While part of such understanding involves discriminating between judgments and descriptions, another aspect involves recognition that we exist as dualities, that is, as individuals and as relationships. This insight is often very helpful to parents and others who feel suddenly empowered to help their children as they realize that their children's behavior is a function of context and relationships rather than their "badness," "brattiness," and so forth.

I close this section by suggesting that there are an infinite number of topics available for discussion related to changes in an individual's cognitive–affective mode of experience. I have tried to provide the flavor of my therapeutic efforts and the general goals I believe important to success. I have also not in any way exhausted the number of goals that might be sought by any individual patients. Clearly, my goals for therapy represent my own view of the good life and in no way exhaust the many other goals that patients might consider necessary for their own lives to be rich and meaningful.

For example, I see little role in my own life for participation in organized religion. My subjective experience of myself and the universe, the fact that I am a conscious being who for the briefest moment in geological time shares consciousness with other similar beings, leaves me breathless and in awe. Yet I reject that such an awareness as well as my love for music and poetry makes me literally a "spiritual" person. I fully accept that most of those with whom I share my life on this planet reject my position on religion. While they might come to agree that a creative, humanistic life lived with others in democracy is best, they also demand that their lives be embedded in a religion that provides spiritual sustenance. However, I have found that if my patients and I develop a humanistic relationship that transcends the differences in our religious outlook then religious differences matter little in our work together.

OTHER TOPICS RELATED TO DOING THERAPY

The first of these additional topics involves our field's predilection for working with individuals. Groups of individuals can suffer the same diseases but the group itself cannot literally be sick. It is the politics of group life that is often the source of the intrapersonal and interpersonal life crises affecting the individuals that seek my help. If the politics of a groups' life make life emotionally unbearable for its members and if group life is unbearable for one member it is often unendurable for all, then it makes sense for as many of the unhappy members of the group to work together to change the script and politics that mark their communal life.

I believe that therapy works best when individuals who live and adapt together work with one another to change the scripts comprising their group narrative and the politics that express those narratives. I believe that this is most true where children are concerned. Unless a child is orphaned and a ward of the state I no longer see children without the adults who are responsible for their behavior. I have earlier suggested that I will not do anything to further disrupt the family life of my patients. To do so further aids society as it blindly, but methodically, replaces the parents who might love their children and must have responsibility for them with professional experts who clearly do not love them and are in no position to take any real responsibility for them.

Therefore, I see it as morally and scientifically correct to assume that it is my job to help parents become the real "therapeutic" agents in their children's lives. When parent's understand that the problems with their children are between family members (often stemming from what lies between the parents), when they can feel comfortable communicating and setting proper moral limits with their offspring, and when they can treat their youngsters as human beings with a psychology different than themselves rather than as defective adults, then those children will often not need my help. I challenge my colleagues who play with children while the children's parents sit in the waiting room to first investigate why the parents are not playing with their children and require a professional to do it for them. I challenge my colleagues to logically demonstrate why they refer to play as "therapy," and however important and necessary play is for human growth and happiness, why one needs professional expertise to engage children in play.

My success in helping children greatly increased when I began to take seriously that unless the parents were part of the solution I could do little except act as the parent's agent and aid in the child's adjustment to the familial script. My goals in working with children are often to aid them in their adjustment, often helping them recognize that the manner of their rebellion can only lead to their own destruction. A compromise with a bad situation is often better for all concerned than a full-blown rejection of the very situations and people upon which life depends. However, there are many times when my assessment of a child's family life reveals a closed political system that demands of each of its members that they deconstruct whatever vestiges of individuality and humanity they might possess and become a willing pawn of the family's power structure. Under these circumstances I often end up working with the adults in the family. If I am successful in helping the child's parents unravel the totalitarian power structure (that might involve three or more generations) that marks their family life and if they establish a more humanistic home life, then I might well hear from these adults that there is no longer any problems to be dealt with directly involving the children.

One of my great sources of frustration in working with children involves the politics with which these children often have to contend while in school and my inability to influence these in any substantive manner. My pique is particularly aroused by the role played by a growing number of school psychologists, increasingly trained as "clinicians." These individuals, who often decry the authoritarian nature of the school systems that employ them, nonetheless "diagnose" and "treat" those children who fail to adjust to school demands. Many of these professionals will agree with my assessment that the schools in question act as a kind of educational processing plant with students treated as link sausages, expected to learn the same material, in the same way, and at the same speed.

Instead of joining with their colleagues who seek to humanize the schools by helping teachers set high standards and support individual creativity for themselves and their students, these psychologists use their positions to justify condemning children who deviate from the schools academic–political agenda with the pseudoscientific language of psychiatry. They form groups of psychologists and refer these "sick" children one to another for psychotherapy (often individual) and most upsettingly play an important role in seeing to it that these children are drugged into compliance by pediatricians and child psychiatrists. This is a topic that requires its own volume on the ways in which the schools and the school psychologists represent an authoritarian environment undermining American democracy and the type of psychotherapy that supports an open, humanistic society. The turning of schools into mental health facilities and the merciless indoctrination of young children as defective beings who become lifelong members of the mental health system represent a dangerous trend indeed.

I close this section with a brief discussion of therapeutic termination. Patients often decide to leave therapy for a wide variety of reasons before their therapists believe they should. I am often confronted by individuals with whom I have been successfully working who decide it is time to leave our relationship. While there are many reasons the patient has decided to terminate, there is an equally long list of reasons I might disagree or be frankly unhappy with their decision. The patient's announcement of termination is the therapist's cue to examine the nature of their transference to the patient. It is time for the therapist to ask whether their upset is due to economic loss, hurt pride, fear of failure, loss of control of the patient, or any other unmet personal adaptive need.

I believe it is certainly appropriate to question a patient's motives to leave treatment before the patient has achieved the goals set by patient and therapist. Such a discussion can help the patient understand the crisis that might be involved in their decision and work through a process that can leave them in a stronger position than they might otherwise be in. It certainly helps the therapist understand where corrections might be necessary in their work and how they might be instigating the patient's flight from treatment. But, if a patient does not wish to discuss their decision and if after discussion they are still committed to leaving, I will always respect, affirm, and support their choice.

I have never followed the advice of various therapy supervisors who suggested I tell patients that they are being "resistant"; that they are "acting out"; that it is their mental illness motivating their choices; and that "if you leave I cannot be responsible for what might happen to you." I am not responsible for my patients' lives and if I believe in democracy I must respect my patients' decisions if I am duty bound to make clear my disagreement with them. I generally ask my patients after each and every session if they wish to return for another and just what their motivation is to do so.

THERAPY: SUCCESSFUL AND UNSUCCESSFUL

I close this chapter and this book with a very few words about successful and unsuccessful treatment. I approach this topic differently than those researchers who try to measure the success or failure of therapy from the perspective of the natural sciences and the medical model and with the tools of mainstream psychology. I also completely disagree with those therapists who claim that the effects of treatment cannot be adequately gauged by science, our good intentions should not be questioned, and the fact that millions are involved in therapy is proof enough of its value. I do not say to either the public or my patients "trust me." After thirty-five years in the field and sixty-two years on Earth I believe in trusting only those who show the goods and earn my trust. I feel as a therapist I must also earn trust and neither ask for nor require it.

I think it important that if I take people's money and engage their time I provide a service that gives them at least some of what they seek, especially in reducing misery and suffering while increasing happiness and the general quality of their lives. I, therefore, agree with the field's goal of attempting to justify the safety and efficacy of the therapeutic enterprise but not with its methods or underlying assumptions involved in achieving its goals. A vast amount of research has been done that seems to have reached two conclusions. The first is that therapy seems to lead to a reduction in symptoms and/or generally meets with patients' approval as having been a valuable or worthwhile experience. The second conclusion reached is that all forms of therapy, based on any theoretical orientation and carried out by any type of therapist with any kind of degree or no degrees at all, seem to have the same rates of success and meet with the same level of patient approval.

The problem with all of this research is that it begins with the false assumption that the individuals who seek treatment are sick and success can be measured in terms of cure. The research also treats therapy as the independent variable and some measure of behavioral change as the dependent or outcome variable bypassing both the experiences of the patients that can and cannot be articulated. Moreover, like the diagnosing of patients, these experimental procedures fail to take seriously that lives are lived over time and that it is in the moments, days, and years after diagnosis that the effects of therapy might become manifest.

The whole process of diagnosis and measurement of cure fails to recognize the emergent qualities of human consciousness as people interact with the events that life never stops bringing to us. Finally, this research never seems to take into account the social context of the research itself. There is an inherent imbalance of status and power that exists when researchers with their Ph.D.s and M.D.s, committed to proving the worth of their field, engage former mental patients who might have suffered as a function of their place low in the social hierarchy of the mental health system. I therefore detail, in personal terms, my success and failure as a therapist.

I rarely, if ever, knew what happened to my patients after we parted. I cannot know what long-lasting effects our work together might have had. Most of the patients who entered my office came only one time; I do not know what they experienced but I hardly place these single visits in the category of success. In retrospect I realize that much of my work in clinics and hospitals involved participating with patients as they maintained their lifelong status as mental patients. My colleagues, particularly the psychiatrists, saw these relationships as successful because the patients stayed in treatment, took their drugs, and stayed out of hospitals.

I no longer see these cases as successful. My patients and I acted our roles and never really engaged each other as neither of us would risk the consequences that genuine life change would inevitably bring. Like so many human relationships that lack a genuine core or commitment we played at being patient and doctor, allowed the time to pass, and never filled in the growing abyss between us with the truths that lived in our minds and hearts. It took me many years to understand the existential nausea I so often felt when leaving the clinic after another day of earning my living by pretending with my patients that something that felt real and vital existed between us.

However, every once in a while, in either the clinic, my private practice, or a classroom (most of my interactions are with students who play at that role while I pretend to teach), something wonderful began to develop between me and those with whom I worked. In spite of the authoritarian/totalitarian politics surrounding us we constructed a relationship based on trust, honesty (always relative), respect, and a commitment to genuine, intelligent communication. Inevitably, my patients and I came to love each other in that special way that can exist between professional and client and which was described long ago by Erich Fromm (2000) whose works are now largely forgotten because biopsychiatry and pseudoscience dominate our field.

As our work continued my patients began to understand the political sources of the feelings of being defective and self-hatred that motivated their totalitarian treatment of self and realized that they were victims of the political oppression of others. Continued development permitted them to recognize that despite what they had endured at the hands of others their lives might still be their own if they accepted their own humanity as well as that of others, including those who had played God in their lives convincing them that they were "things" and objects of disgust. Therapy was well ended as these individuals accepted their roles as citizens, inherently the equal of others and capable of creating and expressing their own unique visions of the world in and around them.

Nothing will convince me that these relationships did not transform my patients and students as much as they did me. It was during these special interactions that my insight into human behavior increased; my ability to empathize and accept human suffering grew; and my perception of human beings as neither gods nor things grew more acute. It was in my therapeutic relationships, as much as in any others, that the full meaning and value of democratic and humanistic politics became clear to me. It was as I practiced psycho"therapy" that I not only did what was right and best for my patients but for myself as well. It was during these therapeutic relationships and my ability to write about them that my life felt real and creative as both a private individual and a citizen. At this moment in time I can think of no better way to live my life and feel myself very lucky to have lived as I have.

References

Ainsworth, Mary. 1985. "Attachment across the Life Span." *Bulletin of the American Academy of Medicine* 61:792–811.

———. 1989. "Attachment beyond Infancy." *American Psychologist* 44:709–711.

Armstrong, Karen. 1994. *A History of God: The 4000 Year Quest for Judaism, Christianity, and Islam.* New York: Random House.

Aron, Lewis. 1999. "Clinical Choices and the Relational Matrix." *Psychoanalytic Dialogues* 9:1–30.

Asaad, Ghazi. 1990. *Hallucinations in Clinical Psychiatry: A Guide for Mental Health Professionals.* New York: Bruner/Mazel.

Barkow, Jerome, Leda Cosmides, and John Tooby. 1992. *The Adapted Mind: Evolutionary Psychology and the Generation of Culture.* New York: Oxford University Press.

Bateson, Gregory. 1978. "The Birth of a Matrix or Double Bind and Epistemology." In *Beyond the Double Bind.* Edited by Milton Berger. New York: Bruner Mazel.

———. 1979. *Mind and Nature: A Necessary Unity.* New York: Dutton.

Becker, Ernst. 1973. *The Denial of Death.* New York: Free Press.

———. 1975. *Escape from Evil.* New York: Free Press.

Beit-Hallahmi, Benjamin. 1974. "Salvation and Its Vicissitudes: Clinical Psychology and Political Values." *American Psychologist* 29:124–130.

Benjamin, Jessica. 1988. *The Bonds of Love.* New York: Pantheon.

———. 1998. *The Shadow of the Other.* New York: Routledge.

Berlin, Isaiah. 1969. *Four Essays on Liberty.* London: Oxford University Press.

Bernstein, Douglas A., and Peggy W. Nash. 1999. *Essentials of Psychology.* New York: Houghton Mifflin.

Bickhard, Mark. 2001. "The Tragedy of Operationalism." *Theory and Psychology* 11:35–44.

Billig, Michael. 1994. "Repopulating the Depopulated Pages of Social Psychology." *Theory and Psychology* 4:307–336.

Bowlby, John. 1969. *Attachment and Loss.* Vol. 1, *Attachment.* New York: Basic Books.

———. 1973. *Attachment and Loss.* Vol. 2, *Separation: Anxiety and Anger.* New York: Basic Books.

———. 1979. *The Making and Breaking of Affectional Bonds.* London: Tavistock.

———. 1980. *Attachment and Loss.* Vol. 3, *Losses: Sadness and Depression.* London: Hogarth.

———. 1988. *A Secure Base.* New York: Pantheon.

Breggin, Peter. 1997. *Brain-Disabling Treatments in Psychiatry.* New York: Springer.

———. 1999a. "Psychostimulants in the Treatment of Children Diagnosed with ADHD: Part I—Acute Risks and Psychological Effects." *Ethical Human Sciences and Service* 1:13–34.

———. 1999b. "Psychostimulants in the Treatment of Children Diagnosed with ADHD: Part II—Adverse Effects on Brain and Behavior." *Ethical Human Sciences and Service* 1:213–242.

———. 2000. "The Psychiatric Drugging of Toddlers." *Ethical Human Sciences and Services* 2:85–87.

Breggin, Peter, and David Cohen. 2000. *Your Drug May Be Your Problem: How and Why to Stop Taking Psychiatric Medication.* Reading, MA: Perseus.

Bridgman, R. W. 1927. *The Logic of Modern Physics.* New York: Macmillan.

Bronowski, Jacob. 1963. *The Common Sense of Science.* Cambridge: Harvard University Press.

Brown, Laura S. 1994. *Subversive Dialogues: Theory in Feminist Therapy.* New York: Basic Books.

———. 1997. "The Practice of Subversion: Psychotherapy as Tikkun Olam." *American Psychologist* 52:449–462.

Bruner, Jerome. 1992. *Acts of Meaning.* Cambridge: Harvard University Press.

Buber, Martin. 1972. *Between Man and Man.* Boston: Macmillan.

———. 1976. *I and Thou.* Translated by S. G. Smith. New York: Simon and Schuster.

Burgess, Anthony. 1978. *1985.* Boston: Little, Brown.

Buss, David. 1994. *Evolution of Desire: Strategies of Human Mating.* New York: Basic Books.

Caplan, Paula J. 1996. *They Say You're Crazy: How the World's Most Powerful Psychiatrists Decide Who's Normal.* Reading, MA: Perseus.

Carnap, Rudolf. 1966. *Philosophical Foundations of Physics: An Introduction to the Philosophy of Science.* Edited by Martin Gardner. New York: Basic Books.

Chein, Isidor. 1972. *The Science of Behavior and the Image of Man.* New York: Basic Books.

Chodorow, Nancy. 1978. *The Reproduction of Mothering: Psychoanalysis and the Sociology of Gender.* Berkeley and Los Angeles: University of California Press.

Chrzanowski, Leye Jeanette. 2001. "My Turn: ECT Editorial Casts Shadow on Author and JAMA's Credibility." *Disability News Service,* 31 March.

Cloud, Dana. 1998. *Control and Consolation in American Culture and Politics: Rhetorics of Therapy.* Thousand Oaks, CA: Sage.

Cohen, David, 2000. "A Critical Review of Studies of the Drug Treatment of Schizophrenia." Paper presented at the Mind-Aid Conference, 30–31 May, New York City.

Cohen, I. Bernard. 1985. *Revolution in Science.* Cambrdge: Harvard University Press.

Colbert, Ty. 1996. *Broken Brains or Wounded Hearts: What Causes Mental Illness.* Santa Ana, CA: Kevco Publishing.

Conrad, Joseph. 1988. *Heart of Darkness.* New York: Norton.

Coon, Dennis. 2000. *Essentials of Psychology: Exploration and Application.* 8th ed. Belmont, CA: Wadsworth Learning.

Cortina, Mauricio. 1999. "Causality, Adaptation, and Meaning: A Perspective from Attachment Theory and Research." *Psychoanalytic Dialogues* 9:557–596.

Craig, Anita. 1999. "What Is It That One Knows When One Knows 'Psychology'?" *Theory and Psychology* 9:197–227.

Crews, Frederick. 1996. "Forward to 1896?" *Psychoanalytic Dialogues* 6:223–250.

———. 1997. *The Memory Wars: Freud's Legacy in Dispute.* New York: Review of Books.

Cushman, Philip. 1995. *Constructing the Self, Constructing America.* New York: Addison-Wesley.

Damasio, Antonio. 1994. *DesCartes' Error: Emotions, Reason, and the Human Mind.* New York: Grosset and Dunlap.

———. 1999. *The Feeling of What Happens: Body and Emotion in the Making of Consciousness.* New York: Harcourt Brace.

Danziger, Kurt. 1994. *Constructing the Subject: Historical Origins of Psychological Research.* New York: Cambridge University Press.

———. 1997. *Naming the Mind: How Psychology Found Its Language.* London: Sage.

Dawes, Robyn. 1994. *House of Cards: Psychology and Psychotherapy Built on Myth.* New York: Free Press.

Degler, Carl. 1991. *In Search of Human Nature: The Decline and Revival of Darwinism in American Social Thought.* New York: Oxford University Press.

Dineen, Tana. 2000. *Manufacturing Victims: What Psychology is Doing to People.* 3d ed. Montreal: Robert Davies Multimedia Publishing.

Doestoevsky, Fyodor. 1995. *The Brothers Karamazov.* Translated by Constance Garnett. New York: Random House.

Eisner, Donald. 2000. *The Death of Psychotherapy: From Freud to Alien Abductions.* Westport, CT: Praeger.

Fader, Ruth. 1996. *The Human Radiation Experiments.* New York: Oxford University Press.

Farber, Seth. 1996. "Testimony Submitted to the Assembly Standing Committee on Mental Health, Mental Retardation, and Developmental Disability." Unpublished manuscript.

———. 1998. *Eternal Day: The Christian Alternative to Secularism and Modern Psychology.* Salisbury, MA: Regina Orthodox Press.

Flavell, Jean. 1968. *The Developmental Psychology of Jean Piaget.* New York: Van Nostrand.

Foucault, Michel. 1977. *Madness and Civilization.* New York: Pantheon.

Frijda, Nico. 1986. *The Emotions.* Cambridge: Cambridge University Press.

Fromm, Erich. 1950. *Psychoanalysis and Religion.* New Haven, CT: Yale University Press.

———. 1980. *The Greatness and Limitations of Freud's Thought.* New York: Harper and Row.

————. 2000. *The Art of Loving.* New York: HarperCollins.

Frosh, Stephen. 1999. *The Politics of Psychoanalysis: An Introduction to Freudian and Post-Freudian Theory.* 2d ed. New York: New York University Press.

Garland, Janet, and Elizabeth Baerg. 2001. "Amotivational Syndrome Linked with SSRI Use in Youth for the First Time." *Brown University Child and Adolescent Psychopharm* 3:6–8.

Gay, Peter. 1988. *Freud: A Life for Our Time.* New York: Norton.

Giddens, Anthony. 1984. *The Constitution of Society.* Berkeley and Los Angeles: University of California Press.

————. 2000. *Runaway World: How Globilization is Reshaping Our Lives.* New York: Routledge.

Giorgi, A. 1970. *Psychology of a Human Science.* New York: Harper and Row.

————. 1994. "The Idea of Human Science." In *The Humanistic Movement: Recovering the Person in Psychology.* Edited by F. W. Wertz. New York: Gardner.

Glenmullen, Joseph. 2001. *Prozac Backlash: Overcoming the Dangers of Prozac, Zoloft, Paxil, and Other Antidepressants with Safe, Effective Alternatives.* New York: Simon and Schuster.

Glynn, Patrick. 1994. "Toward a Politics of Forgiveness." *American Enterprise* 5:50–53.

Goode, Erica. 2001. "Most Ills Are a Matter of More Than One Gene." *New York Times,* 27 June.

Gosden, Richard. 2001. *Punishing the Patient: How Psychiatrists Misunderstand and Mistreat Schizophrenics.* Victoria, Australia: Scribe Publications.

Grace, Randolph. 2001. "On the Failure of Operationism." *Theory and Psychology* 11:5–34.

Griffin, Susan. 1995. *The Eros of Everyday Life: Essays on Ecology, Gender, and Society.* New York: Doubleday.

Grunbaum, Adolf. 1984. *The Foundations of Psychoanalysis.* Berkeley and Los Angeles: University of California Press.

Hacking, Ian. 1995. *Rewriting the Soul: Multiple Personalities and the Science of Memory.* Princeton, NJ: Princeton University Press.

Hayley, Jay. 1976. *Problem-Solving Therapy.* San Francisco: Jossey-Bass.

Hartmann, Heinz. 1958. "Ego Psychology and the Problem of Adaptation." Translated by David Rappaport. *Journal of the American Psychoanalytic Association: Monograph 1.* New York: International Universities Press.

Held, Barbara. 1995. *Back to Reality: A Critique of Postmodern Theory in Psychotherapy.* New York: Norton.

Helme, William. 1992. "Reformulating Psychology as a Human Science." *Theoretical and Philosophical Psychology* 12:119–136.

Hoffer, Eric. 1963. *The Ordeal of Change.* New York: Harper and Row.

Hook, Sydney. 1987. *Out of Step: An Unquiet Life in the 20th Century.* New York: Harper and Row.

Hornblum, Allen. 1999. *Acres of Skin: Human Experiments at Holmesburg Prison.* New York: Routledge.

Horney, Karen. 1950. *Neurosis and Human Growth.* New York: Norton.

Izard, Carroll. 1977. *Human Emotions.* New York: Plenum.

————. 1979. *Emotions in Personality and Psychopathology.* New York: Plenum.

Jacoby, Russell. 1986. *The Repression of Psychoanalysis: Otto Fenichel and the Political Freudians*. Chicago: University of Chicago Press.

Joseph, Jay. 1999a. "A Critique of the Finnish Adoptive Family Study of Schizophrenia." *Journal of Mind and Behavior* 20:133–154.

———. 1999b. "The Genetic Theory of Schizophrenia: A Critical Overview." *Ethical Human Sciences and Services* 1:119–146.

———. 2000. "A Critique of the Spectrum Concept Used in the Danish–American Schizophrenia Adoption Studies." *Ethical Human Sciences and Services* 2:135–160.

Jules, Jane, and Howard Jones. 1992. *Bad Blood: The Tuskegee Syphilis Experiment*. New York: Simon and Schuster.

Kagan, Jerome. 1984. *The Nature of the Child*. New York: Basic Books.

———. 1994. *Galen's Prophecy: Temperament in Human Nature*. New York: Basic Books.

Karon, Bertram, and Annmarie Widener. 1999. "The Tragedy of Schizophrenia: Its Myth of Incurability." *Ethical Human Sciences and Services* 1:195–213.

Kegan, Robert. 1982. *The Evolving Self*. Cambridge: Harvard University Press.

———. 1994. *In Over Our Heads: The Mental Demands of Modern Life*. Cambridge: Harvard University Press.

Kelly, George. 1955. *The Psychology of Personal Constructs in Theory of Personality*. New York: Norton.

Kirk, Stuart and Herbert Kutchins. 1992. *The Selling of the DSM: The Rhetoric of Science in Psychiatry*. New York: Aldine de Gruyten.

Kleese, Deborah. 2001. "Nature and Nurture in Psychology." *Journal of Theoretical and Philosophical Psychology* 21:61–79.

Koch, Sigmund. 1992 "Psychology's Bridgman and Bridgman's Bridgman: An Essay in Reconstruction." *Theory and Psychology* 2:261–290.

———. 1999. *Psychology in Human Context: Essays in Dissidence and Reconstruction*. Chicago: University of Chicago Press.

Kohlberg, Lawrence. 1984. *The Philosophy of Moral Development*. Vol. 2. San Francisco: Harper and Row.

Kotre, John. 1995. *White Gloves: How We Create Ourselves through Memory*. New York: Free Press.

Kuhn, Thomas. 1970. *The Structure of Scientific Revolution*. 2d rev. ed. Chicago: University of Chicago Press.

Kutchens, Herbert and Stuart Kirk. 1997. *Making Us Crazy: DSM: The Psychiatric Bible and the Creation of Mental Disorders*. New York: Free Press.

Laing, R. D. 1967. *The Politics of Experience*. New York: Pantheon.

———. 1969. *The Divided Self*. New York: Pantheon.

———. 1982. *The Voice of Experience*. New York: Pantheon.

Lasch, Christopher. 1976. *The Culture of Narcissism*. New York: Norton.

Lazarus, Richard. 1991. *Emotions and Adaptation*. New York: Oxford University Press.

Leahy, Thomas. 1980. "The Myth of Operationism." *Journal of Mind and Behavior* 1:127–143.

Lehrman, Nathaniel. 2001. "Editorial Submitted to the Atlantic Monthly." Unpublished manuscript.

Lerman, Hannah. 1986. *A Mote in Freud's Eye.* New York: Springer.

Levinas, Emmanuel. 1969. *Totality and Infinity.* Translated by A. Lingis. Pittsburgh, PA: Duquesnes University Press.

Lifton, Robert. 2000. *Nazi Doctors: Medical Killing and the Psychology of Genocide.* Reading, MA: Perseus.

Loftus, Elizabeth, and Kenneth Ketchum. 1994. *The Myth of Repressed Memories.* New York: St. Martin's.

London, Perry. 1986. *The Modes and Morals of Psychotherapy.* New York: Hemisphere.

Luhrmann, T. M. 2000. *Of Two Minds: The Growing Disorder in American Psychiatry.* New York: Knopf.

Mahoney, Michael. 1991. *Human Change Processes: The Scientific Foundations of Psychotherapy.* New York: Basic Books.

Marin, Peter. 1981. "Living in Moral Pain." *Psychology Today,* November.

Martin, Jack, and Jeff Sugarman. 1999. *The Psychology of Human Possibility and Constraint.* Albany: State University of New York Press.

Maslow, Abraham. 1968. *Toward a Psychology of Being.* 2d ed. Princeton, NJ: Van Nostrand.

Masson, Jeffrey Mousaiff. 1984. *The Assault on Truth: Freud's Suppression of the Seduction Theory.* New York: Penguin.

———. 1988. *Against Therapy: Emotional Tyranny and the Myth of Emotional Healing.* New York: Atheneum.

McHugh, Paul. 1992. "Psychiatric Misadventures." *American Scholar* 61:497–510.

McKnight, John. 1995. *The Careless Society: Community and Its Counterfeits.* New York: Basic Books.

Meng, Heinrich, and Ernst L. Freud, eds. 1963. *Psychoanalysis and Faith: The Letters of Sigmund Freud and Oscar Pfister.* Translated by Eric Mosbacher. New York: Basic Books.

Miller, Gregory. 1969. "Psychology as a Means of Promoting Human Welfare." *American Psychologist* 24:1063–1075.

Mills, C. Wright. 1957. *The Power Elite.* New York: Oxford University Press.

———. 1959. *The Sociological Imagination.* New York: Oxford University Press.

Mitchell, Stephen A. 2000. *Relationality: From Attachment to Subjectivity.* Hillsdale, NJ: Analytic Press.

Morris, Charles G., and Albert A. Maisto. 1999. *Understanding Psychology.* 4th ed. Upper Saddle River, NJ: Prentice-Hall.

Mosher, Loren, A. Z. Menn, and S. M. Matthews. 1975. "Soteria: Evaluation of a Home-Based Treatment for Schizophrenia." *American Journal of Orthopsychiatry* 45:455–467.

Nozick, Robert. 1974. *Anarchy, State, Utopia.* New York: Basic Books.

Nussbaum, Martha. 2001. *Upheavals of Thought: The Intelligence of Emotions.* Cambridge: Cambridge University Press.

Ogden, Thomas. 1994. *Subjects of Analysis.* Northvale, NJ: Aronson.

O'Meara, Patricia Kelley. 2000. "New Research Indicts Ritalin." *Insight Magazine,* 16 October.

Orange, Donna. 1995. *Emotional Understanding: Studies in Psychoanalytic Epistomology.* New York: Guilford.

Ortega y Gasset, Jose. 1957. *The Revolt of the Masses.* New York: Norton.

Orwell, George. 1949. *1984*. New York: New American Library.

Patterson, Thomas E. 2001. *The American Democracy*, 5th ed. New York: McGraw-Hill.

Piaget, Jean. 1950. *The Psychology of Intelligence*. Translated by M. Piercy and D. E. Berlyne. London: Routledge and Kegan Paul.

———. 1952. *The Origins of Intelligence in Children*. New York: International Universities Press.

———. 1954. *The Construction of Reality in the Child*. Translated by M. Cook. New York: Basic Books.

———. 1959. *Biology and Knowledge*. Chicago: University of Chicago Press.

———. 1973. *The Child and Reality*. New York: Grossman.

———. 1975. *The Development of Thought*. New York: Viking.

———. 1981. *Intelligence and Affectivity*. Palo Alto, CA: Annual Reviews.

Pinker Steven. 1994. *The Language Instinct: How the Mind Creates Language*. New York: HarperPerennial.

———. 1997. *How the Mind Works*. New York: Norton.

Plotkin, Henry. 1998. *Evolution in Mind: An Introduction to Evolutionary Psychology*. Cambridge: Harvard University Press.

Plutchik, Robert. 1980. *Emotions: A Psycho-Evolutionary Approach*. New York: Harper and Row.

Polanyi, Michael. 1967. *The Tacit Dimension*. New York: Anchor Books.

Popper, Karl. 1961. *The Logic of Modern Discovery*. New York: Science Editions.

———. 1966. *The Open Society and Its Enemies*. Vols. 1 and 2. Princeton, NJ: Princeton University Press.

Praeda, A. R., C. Mazure, and M. Bowers 2001. "Anti-depressant Associated Mania and Psychosis Is Resulting in Psychiatric Admissions." *Journal of Clinical Psychiatry* 62:30–33.

Rawls, John. 1971. *A Theory of Justice*. Cambridge: Harvard University Press.

Reiff, Philip. 1966. *The Triumph of the Therapeutic: Uses of Faith after Freud*. New York: Harper and Row.

Ricoeur, Paul. 1970. *Freud and Philosophy: An Essay on Interpretation*. Translated by Denis Savage. New Haven, CT: Yale University Press.

Robins, Richard W., Samuel D. Gosling, and Kenneth H. Craik. 1999. "An Empirical Analysis of Trends in Psychology." *American Psychologist* 54:117–128.

Robinson, Daniel. 1997. "Therapy as Theory and as Civics." *Theory and Psychology* 7:675–681.

———. 2000. "Paradigms and 'The Myth of Framework.'" *Theory and Psychology* 10:39–47.

———. 2001. "Sigmund Koch—Philosophically Speaking." *American Psychologist* 56:420–424.

Rogers, Carl. 1961. *On Becoming a Person: A Therapist's View of Psychotherapy*. Boston: Houghton Mifflin.

Rogers, Lois, and Rosie Waterhouse. 2001. "Prozac Makers Told to Warn of Side-Effects." *Sunday Times* (London), 8 July.

Rorty, Richard. 1979. *Philosophy and the Mirror of Nature*. Princeton, NJ: Princeton University Press.

———. 1991. *Objectivity, Relativism, and Truth: Philosophical Papers.* Vol. 1. Cambridge: Cambridge University Press.

———. 1994. "The Unpatriotic Academy." *New York Times,* 13 February.

Rose, Nicholas. 1999. *Governing the Soul: The Shaping of the Private Self.* New York: Free Association Books.

Russell, Bertrand. 1948. *Human Knowledge: Its Scope and Limits.* New York: Simon and Schuster.

Sarbin, Theodore, and James Mancuso. 1980. *Schizophrenia: Medical Diagnosis or Moral Verdict?* New York: Pergamon.

Sartre, Jean-Paul. 1964. *Nausea.* Translated by Lloyd Alexander. New York: New Directions.

Sass, Louis. 1992. *Madness and Modernism: Insanity in the Light of Modern Art, Literature, and Thought.* Cambridge: Harvard University Press.

Sealey, Geraldine. 2001. "Fragile Psyches: Mental Health Counselors Gear Up for Potential Crisis in New York." *ABC News,* 5 November.

Segal, Lynn. 1999. *Why Feminism?* New York: Columbia University Press.

Shipko, Stuart. 2001. "Akathisia and the Use of SSRI's." Personal communication.

Shorter, Edward. 1997. *A History of Psychiatry: From the Era of the Asylum to the Age of Prozac.* New York: Wiley.

Siebert, Al. 1999. "Brain Disease Hypothesis for Schizophrenia Disconfirmed by All Evidence." *Ethical Human Sciences and Services.* 1:179–190.

Simon, Laurence. 1981. "The Therapist–Patient Relationship: A Holistic View." *American Journal of Psychoanalysis* 41:213–222.

———. 1986. *Cognition and Affect: A Developmental Psychology of the Individual.* Buffalo, NY: Prometheus.

———. 1998. *Psychology, Education, Gods, and Humanity.* Westport, CT: Praeger.

———. 2000a. *Psycho"therapy": Theory, Practice, Modern and Postmodern Influences.* Westport, CT: Praeger.

———. 2000b. "Research into the Origins and Characteristics of Unicorns: Mental Illness as the Unicorn." *Ethical Human Sciences and Services* 2:181–192.

Slife, Brent, and Richard Williams. 1997. "Toward a Theoretical Psychology: Should a Subdiscipline Finally Be Recognized." *American Psychologist:* 52:117–129.

Smith, Daniel. 2001. "Shock and Disbelief." *Atlantic Monthly,* February.

Sobel, Dava. 2000. *Galileo's Daughter: A Historical Memoir of Science, Faith, and Love.* New York: Penguin.

Sowell, Thomas. 1987. *A Conflict of Visions: Ideological Origins of Political Struggle.* New York: Quill.

———. 1995. *The Vision of the Annointed: Self Congratulation as a Basis for Social Policy.* New York: Basic Books.

———. 1996. *Migration and Culture: A World View.* New York: Basic Books.

Spence, Donald. 1994. *The Rhetorical Voice of Psychoanalysis: Displacement of Evidence by Thesis.* Cambridge: Harvard University Press.

Stolorow, R., and G. Atwood. 1992. *Contexts of Being: The Intersubjective Foundation of Psychological Life.* Hillsdale, NJ: Analytic Press.

Strenger, Carlo. 1991. *Between Hermeneutics and Science.* New York: International Universities Press.

————. 1998. *Individuality, The Impossible Project: Psychoanalysis and Self-Creation.* New York: International Universities Press.

————. 1999. "Why Constructivism Will Not Go Away: Commentary on Paper by Mauricio Cortina." *Psychoanalytic Dialogues* 9:609–616.

Sullivan, Harry Stack. 1953. *The Interpersonal Theory of Psychiatry.* New York: Norton.

Sulloway, Frank. 1979. *Freud: Biologist of the Mind: Beyond the Psychoanalytic Legacy.* New York: Basic Books.

Sykes, Charles J. 1992. "I Hear America Whining." *New York Times,* 2 November.

Szasz, Thomas. 1970. *The Manufacture of Madness.* New York: Harper Torchbooks.

————. 1974. *The Myth of Mental Illness.* Rev. ed. New York: Harper and Row.

————. 1987. *The Therapeutic State.* Buffalo, NY: Prometheus.

————. 1990. *Anti-Freud: Karl Kraus' Criticism of Psychoanalysis and Psychiatry.* Syracuse, NY: Syracuse University Press.

————. 2001. *Pharmacracy: Medicine and Politics in America.* Westport, CT: Praeger.

Tetlock, Philip. 1992. "An Alternative Metaphor in the Study of Judgment and Choice: People as Politicians." *Theory and Psychology* 1:452–475.

Toulmin, Stephen. 1992. *Cosmopolis: The Hidden Agenda of Modernity.* Chicago: University of Chicago Press.

Tuchman, Barbara. 1980. "The Decline of Quality." *New York Times Magazine,* 2 November.

Valenstein, Eliot. 1998. *Blaming the Brain.* New York: Simon and Schuster.

Vandenberg, Brian. 1993. Developmental Psychology, God, and the Good." *Theory and Psychology* 3:191–205.

Vastag, Brian. 2001. "Pay Attention: Ritalin Acts Much Like Cocaine." *Journal of the American Medical Association* 286: 1156.

Vygotsky, Lev. 1978. *Mind in Society: The Development of Higher Psychological Processes.* Cambridge: Harvard University Press.

Watts, Alan. 1972. *The Book: On the Taboo Against Knowing Who You Are.* New York: Vintage.

Welsome, Eileen. 1999. *The Plutonium Files: America's Secret Experiments in the Cold War.* New York: Delacourte.

Whitaker, Robert. 2002. *Mad in America: Bad Science, Bad Medicine, and the Enduring Mistreatment of the Mentally Ill.* Reading, MA: Perseus.

Whitehouse, Beth. 2001. "A Nation on Edge." *Newsday,* 5 November.

Wilson, James Q. 1993. *The Moral Sense.* New York: Free Press.

Wilson, Duff, and David Heath. 2001. "The Whistleblower: He Saw the Tests as a Violation of 'Trusting, Desperate Human Beings.'" *Seattle Times,* 13 March.

Winnicott, D. W. 1965. *The Maturational Process and the Facilitating Environment.* New York: International Universities Press.

Wright, Robert. 1994. *The Moral Animal: Evolutionary Psychology and Everyday Life.* New York: Pantheon.

Zakanis, K., P. Paulin, K. Hansen, and D. Jolic. 2000. "Searching the Schizophrenic Brain for Temporal Lobe Deficits: A Systematic Review and Meta-analysis." *Psychological Medicine* 30:451–504.

Index

About the Author

LAURENCE SIMON is Professor of Psychology at Kingsborough Community College, City University of New York. He is also the author of *Psycho-"therapy": Theory, Practice, Modern and Postmodern Influences* (Praeger, 2000) and *Psychology, Education, Gods and Humanity* (Praeger, 1998).